Kenneth Macgowan (1888–1963) directed the Greenwich Village Theater and the Actors Theater in New York and for several years was an independent producer on Broadway. He was a theater critic and editor of *Theater Arts* for six years.

William Melnitz is a professor of theater arts at the University of California, Los Angeles.

Gordon Armstrong is an assistant professor in the Department of Theater at State University of New York, Stony Brook.

GOLDEN AGES
OF THE THEATER

A Classic Now Revised and Expanded

Kenneth Macgowan and William Melnitz
with Gordon Armstrong

A SPECTRUM BOOK

PRENTICE-HALL, INC., *Englewood Cliffs, New Jersey 07632*

Library of Congress Cataloging in Publication Data

MACGOWAN, KENNETH, 1888–1963.
    Golden ages of the theater.

    (A Spectrum Book)
    Bibliography: p.
    Includes index.
    I. Theater—History. 2. Drama—History and criti-
cism. I. Melnitz, William W., joint author. II. Arm-
strong, Gordon, joint author.   III. Title.
PN2101.M28 1979   792'.09   78-12148
ISBN 0-13-357863-1
ISBN 0-13-357855-0 pbk.

Frontispiece   Molière as Sganarelle

The actor playing the leading role in his own comedy about 1660. Drawing by Gerda Becker With, after an engraving by Simonin.

Editorial production supervision and interior design by Carol Smith
Cover design by Michael Freeland
Manufacturing buyer: Cathie Lenard

© 1979 by Prentice-Hall, Inc., *Englewood Cliffs, New Jersey 07632*

A SPECTRUM BOOK

10 9 8 7 6 5 4 3 2 1

Printed in the United States of America

PRENTICE-HALL INTERNATIONAL, INC., *London*
PRENTICE-HALL OF AUSTRALIA PTY. LIMITED, *Sydney*
PRENTICE-HALL OF CANADA, LTD., *Toronto*
PRENTICE-HALL OF INDIA PRIVATE LIMITED, *New Delhi*
PRENTICE-HALL OF JAPAN, INC., *Tokyo*
PRENTICE-HALL OF SOUTHEAST ASIA PTE. LTD., *Singapore*
WHITEHALL BOOKS LIMITED, *Wellington, New Zealand*

CONTENTS

PREFACE
page ix

1: THE GREAT GREEKS AND
THE MUCH LESSER LATINS
page 1

2: MEDIEVAL THEATER:
A HOUSE OF MANY MANSIONS
page 28

3: THE RENAISSANCE THEATER
IN ITALY
page 44

4: SPAIN'S GOLDEN AGE
page 72

5: THE THEATER THAT
ELIZABETH I SUSTAINED
page 96

6: THE BAROQUE THEATER
OF FRANCE
page 141

7: THE NINETEENTH CENTURY:
A TIME OF CHANGE IN EUROPE
page 160

8: THE COMING OF REALISM
page 185

9: THE MODERN THEATER FROM STRINDBERG TO BRECHT
page 216

10: THE THEATER OF TODAY
page 239

BIBLIOGRAPHY
page 276

INDEX
page 281

PREFACE

After fifteen printings, a revised and expanded edition of *Golden Ages of the Theater*, which John Gassner called "the very best up-to-date short history of theater available in English" is in order.

Two completely new chapters have been added to the still pertinent basic material. The wealth of publications in the field of medieval theater called for a new discussion on this topic, and the rapid development of theater in this country and abroad over the last twenty years made an updating of the final chapters mandatory. This meant the authors had to thoroughly research most of the new books and articles as well as many significant theatrical productions—including those of the new *avant-garde*, in order to present them accurately. Kenneth Macgowan's list, consisting of letters and criticisms sent to us since the book's appearance in 1959, was most useful.

Again, as in the Preface to the first edition, we want to make it clear that we deal in this volume only with the main currents of almost three thousand years of playgoing, playacting, and play reading. Obviously so brief an outline cannot cover every topic to the satisfaction of even a single reader. We have, therefore, paid special attention to an updated selective bibliography; it lists the titles of other "paperbacks" that are more specialized but, according to our latest checking, as easily accessible.

The many time-charts have been maintained that visualize the life span of the chief playwrights. Readers have often commented on their usefulness; and it is to be hoped that the old, as well as the numerous new, illustrations will be equally appreciated.

The theater in every period has worked within certain conventions, and its audience has readily accepted all of them. We feel that the theater—in both its imaginative and its realistic phases—should not be taken out of its historical setting, but rather that the meaning of the specific form of theater to the audience of its time should be stressed. There is still truth in Hamlet's assertion that players "are the abstract and brief chronicles of the time."

ACKNOWLEDGMENTS

We owe a substantial debt to various works of scholars of the theater, among them those of Professors H. D. F. Kitto on the classic theater, George Kernodle on the medieval theater, José Barcia on the Spanish theater, James Phillips on the Elizabethan theater, and Martin Esslin and George Wellwarth on the contemporary stage.

Our warmest personal thanks go to Michael Hunter, our editor, for suggesting the revised second edition; to Carol Smith, our production editor, for her encouragement and guidance; to Fred Dahl, an untiring copyeditor; and, not least, to Janice Armstrong for patiently reading proof.

1: THE GREAT GREEKS AND THE MUCH LESSER LATINS

When we watch the dances of primitive man in a motion picture and study myths and rituals, we see theater come to life. But we don't see *the* theater. We don't see a functioning playhouse and all it has come to mean in terms of plays as well as players.

When we do find the theater, when at last we discover a complete organism, we run up against a very curious and baffling fact. Though this theater is made by civilized men—*highly* civilized men—though it exists in a time when writing has become an art, this theater has practically no history. Unless time has destroyed some pertinent Greek manuscript, no writer of the fifth century B.C., which was the great period of Athens, seems to have taken the trouble to tell us exactly how its theater looked and how it evolved, or to describe its earlier plays.

THE MYSTERY OF THE CLASSIC THEATER

The Greek drama springs at us full-armed like Athene from the head of Zeus. Suddenly it exists—glorious and complete—in the great tragedies of Aeschylus, Sophocles, and Euripides, which were produced, appropriately enough, in the city over which Pallas Athene watched. Yet we have no record—written or archaeological—of just what the playhouse of the great and classic fifth century looked like. We know that its plays were given in the open air. We know there was a chorus that chanted and danced about an altar. We know that there were only three speaking actors and that they wore masks and "doubled" their roles as required. We know the kind of clothes and shoes they wore. But except for this we have almost no concrete knowledge about the classic Greek theater and how it functioned. There are literally no ruins of fifth-century theaters.

Nevertheless, we have taken it for granted that the chief playing space was circular and that the audience sat in rising rows that curved a little more than half around it. This concept has been based upon the oldest existing playhouse, but this structure at Epidaurus dates from about 365 B.C., a hundred years after the plays of Aeschylus were acted in Athens. Now, however, come hints of a differently shaped theater in archaic Greece and perhaps in Athens. At Knossos and Phaetos on the island of Crete, we can see what archaeologists call "theatral areas," dating from 2,000 to 1,600 B.C. In each a long straight row of steps joins a shorter one at right angles; these faced a paved area used, perhaps, for ritual dances and ceremonies. An Italian archaeologist has found evidence in a few Greek theaters that leads him to believe they were quadrangular instead of semicircular at an early period.

The only important documents we have today are play manuscripts—and only forty-four out of how many lost hundreds? But, of course, if we had to choose between knowing all about the theater of Aeschylus and having the seven manuscripts we now possess out of his ninety plays, we would decide that we are better off as we stand today.

Except for the few manuscripts of plays, what we know about the Greek theater in its great days comes from scenes painted on vases, a few thousand words of literary criticism written by Aristotle more than a hundred years later, and some astute guesses made by modern archaeologists who have dug up and worked over and reconstructed the Hellenistic theaters built one to three centuries after the death of Euripides. Perhaps we ought to add to this list the writings of Vitruvius, a Roman architect in Caesar's times, and of Pollux, a Greek dictionary-maker about two centuries later. But the two books in which they comment all too briefly on stages, scenery, and machines leave us wondering how much of what they describe is classic Greek, how much is imperial Roman, and how much belongs to the Hellenistic period that lay between. Writing within seventy-five years of the death of the last great dramatist, Euripides, Aristotle was so absorbed in the aesthetics of the tragedies that he tells us almost nothing of the theater that gave them birth.

THE CONTRIBUTION OF ATHENS

The Greece that knew neither Alexander the Great nor the Roman conquerors was a curious civilization. Athens invented the word *democracy* but did not live completely by it. The slaves and the peasantry, commerce and gold mines, enabled the free Athenians to live in the mind and the arts. Its philosophers were original and apperceptive, its sculptors and architects superb. To science the Greeks contributed inductive reasoning and the basic concept of Copernicus. Yet they did not apply to useful ends the steam engine that they invented, Anaxagoras thought the sun about as large as the Peloponnesus, and Aristotle believed that bees carried stones as ballast in a high wind. Athens and much of Greece constituted a community that loved talk and thought and writing, as well as art and athletics, and reached at one bound the first pinnacle of dramatic expression. Yet from Plato and Herodotus to Plutarch, no Greek aesthetician or historian except Aristotle bothered to write fully about the supreme accomplishment of their drama—let alone the physical theater—unless, of course, some manuscript has gone the way of the lost plays and the missing passages of Plato and Aristotle.

Structurally the Western playhouse has altered greatly since the days of Aeschylus. Acting is vastly different. The stage has changed beyond recognition. Our plays are not the stories of mythical heroes told in verse and accompanied by a chanting and dancing chorus. Yet we can trace a clear path of evolution from the Greek theater to the theater of today. Even in the technique of playwriting we can often see a kinship. The structure of Sophocles' *Oedipus Rex* is the structure of Shaffer's *Equus*; each play starts just before its great crisis and unfolds, in exposition, the past that conditions and dominates its dramatic development.

THREE KINDS OF PLAY FOR ONE GOD

The Greek theater presented three kinds of plays: tragedies, which dealt with heroic legends and often used gods for convenient endings; satyr plays, which burlesqued such legends and indulged in bawdy mimicry set off by a chorus of satyrs; and comedies, which dealt in a broadly farcical way with current life. All three were performed at fixed ceremonies of a religious and civic nature. All three employed a chorus in interludes between scenes of action and often within those scenes. All three were written in verse. All three used masks. And all three seem related in one way or another to what might be called fertility ideas.

It is quite as easy to believe that the three forms had a common basis as to believe in any of the separate origins that some authorities have proposed. There are those who claim that tragedy grew out of the celebration and worship of Dionysus, who was a nature god of fertility quite as much as the god of wine. There are those who say that Greek tragedy was rooted in ceremonial rites at the graves of culture heroes and demigods. But the fact remains that tragedies, satyr plays, and comedies were produced as part of the regular annual ceremonies in honor of Dionysus, his figure was carried in the preliminary procession, and his altar stood in the center of the playing floor. Furthermore, the story of Dionysus was the story of fertile nature dying each year and being reborn, the story of eternal fecundity, and fecundity was reflected in the phallic symbols worn by the actors in early comedy. Aristotle says that comedy grew out of phallic songs, which were ribald hymns in honor of Phales, a god of fertility and a companion of Dionysus. Bacchus—another name for Dionysus among both the late Greeks and the Romans—had as his companions a troupe of satyrs, half-men/half-animals with the horns, the tail, and the hoofs of goats. And in the satyr plays, these woodland creatures wore the phallus. In the worship of Dionysus, satyrs put on the skins of goats that had been sacrificed to the god. All this emphasis on capricorn as a Dionysiac accessory should prepare you for the discovery that the word *tragedy* comes from the Greek words *tragos*, or goat, and *ode*, or song. At any rate, Greek tragedy, the satyr play, and comedy seem so involved with the attributes of the god of wine and fertility that some see their common origin in the worship of Dionysus.

4

DRAMATIC ORIGINS

Certain authorities are in refreshing agreement with each other and with Aristotle on the theory that tragedy grew out of the dithyramb, or choral hymn, sung to Dionysus. They presume that, originally, the dithyramb told the story of this deity who began as the child of Zeus and a mortal, who taught man to grow the grape and other fruits and foodstuffs, and who was destroyed and reborn into godhead. But by the time tragedy was ready to appear, the legends of Dionysus had been supplanted in the dithyrambs by the adventures of culture heroes. From then on, though Greek tragedy ignored almost completely the personal exploits of its favorite god, plays became the most important and spectacular feature of his worship.

The question of just where and just when someone made over the dithyramb or mimetic hero ritual into the beginnings of a drama is rather uncertain. About 600 B.C. a poet and musician, Arion, from the island of Lesbos, is reputed to have written the first formal lyrics that replaced the improvised words of the dithyramb, but he did this over in the Peloponnesian peninsula at the city of Corinth. Most authorities think that Thespis, who lived in Attica, took the next step by introducing an actor to talk to the chorus, provide narration, and even act out dramatic episodes. One ancient authority puts him second to someone named Epigenes, who lived near Corinth; another makes Thespis sixteenth on the list of originators. Aristotle says that the Dorians of the Peloponnesus claimed the discovery of both comedy and tragedy.

It seems fairly certain, however, that the change from dithyramb to drama came in the middle of the sixth century, and, if the innovator was not Thespis, he did pretty much what Thespis is supposed to have done. Certainly the man who stepped out of the chorus became at that moment the first dramatist as well as the first actor. Tradition says that Thespis also became the first "trouper" when he put his company on a cart and gave performances in other cities. Since he won, in 534 B.C., the first Athenian prize for tragedy, we may take it that he drove his cart to that ever-receptive city and made it his permanent headquarters. Perhaps his wagon had the form of the ship in which Dionysus was supposed to have first visited Attica, and perhaps it became the boat on wheels—

recorded on vase paintings—in which the priest of Dionysus, with his flute-playing satyrs, was driven into the theater at the beginning of the Dionysiac festivals.

For three centuries after the time of Thespis, Athens was the theatrical capital of the Grecian world. For the playwright there was only one theater. It was the theater of Dionysus at the foot of the Acropolis. The three great writers of tragedy, Aeschylus, Sophocles, and Euripides, and their peer in comedy, Aristophanes, were Athenian citizens. So was the lesser man, Menander, who wrote domestic farce and lived almost a hundred years after Aristophanes and two hundred after Thespis. If other playwrights of this era were not born in the shadow of the Parthenon, they came to Athens from the cities and the islands and the colonies that spread Grecian culture from Sicily and Italy to Asia Minor, and they competed for the honor of seeing their plays acted in the city that Milton called "the eye of Greece, the mother of arts and eloquence." The more important plays were first produced there, then repeated in the provinces, and, even after centuries, revived in distant lands. When Rome, triumphant over Carthage, turned to the making of plays as well as of empire, her dramatists did hardly more than translate or adapt the works of Greece.

THE DIONYSIAC FESTIVALS OF ATHENS

The theater was of vital importance to the Athenian because it was the climax of a religious and civic ritual. Playgoing was not an everyday habit; it was confined to certain fixed days out of every year. The festivals dedicated to Dionysus occurred in late January and early February, and in late March through the beginning of April. The first of these, which was called the Lenaea, was the older, and, as time went on, it was mainly reserved for comedies. The second and the far more important festival was the Great, or City, Dionysia. Then it was that tragedy dominated, and Aeschylus and his successors competed for prizes. The splendor and preeminence of the City Dionysia attracted visitors from all over the Grecian world. It was a week of holiday; all trade was suspended, and government offices—even the courts of law—were closed. At first, admission to the theater was free; later, when there was a small charge, tickets were given to those who could not afford to buy them. The state paid the actors, but the cost of the physical production of each play was met by a rich citizen, whom we would now call an "angel," but who was then honored with the title of *choregus*.

The festivities of the City Dionysia lasted five or six days. The first day was given up to a great procession, led by the priest of Dionysus on his ship-like float, and to sports, games, and general merrymaking. On the second and sometimes the third day came dithyrambic contests. The last three days were devoted to the plays that competed for the annual prizes.

On each of these three days during the fifth century a different playwright presented three tragedies and a satyr play. When these plays all dealt with a single myth or a single group of related characters, they were called a *tetralogy*. A good example of the tetralogy is *Oresteia* of Aeschylus, produced in 458 B.C., which included *Agamemnon, The Libation Pourers, The Eumenides*, all three still in existence, and the lost *Proteus*, a satyr play; all dealt with the tragedy of the House of Atreus. When the satyr play was sometimes dropped, the related plays were called a *trilogy*. Each year Aeschylus generally confined his competing tragedies to a single subject, but Sophocles did this seldom, if ever, and Euripides apparently never.

Greek playwrights were enormously prolific. Aeschylus is said to have written ninety plays and to have won thirteen first prizes. Sophocles wrote over a hundred, winning eighteen contests. Euripides is supposed to have written ninety-two, but, perhaps because of his unconventional attitude toward the gods and toward the almost sacred characters that he dealt with, he won only five victories. Of the nearly three hundred plays written by the three dramatists, the manuscripts of all but thirty-three have been lost; we have seven from Aeschylus, eight from Sophocles, and, interestingly enough, eighteen from Euripides.

The competing playwrights were selected by an official called an *archon*. After the three days of competition there was a time for severe criticism and the awarding of the annual prize by a small jury drawn by lot.

Half a century after Athens instituted the first contests in tragedy, the city added a competition for comedies. At first a single day was given up to five comic plays by different playwrights. Later there was a comedy each afternoon, following the day's tragedies.

Besides the two dramatic festivals in Athens there was a third type, the Rural Dionysia, which was held in the provincial towns of Attica in December. Here the prize-winning plays from Athens were presented, and new and untried playwrights had a chance at what we would call a "try-out."

ROME'S DEBASED DRAMA

Rome, too, had its dramatic festivals. They were called *ludi*, or games, because they were devoted at first entirely to sports and amusements, such as boxing and rope dancing. Farcical performances from the provinces crept in, and in 240 B.C. a Latin writer introduced a Greek tragedy in translation. At first the *ludi* were given in April, July, September, and November, but later they appeared on any convenient occasion—a military triumph or the funeral of an important citizen. In the year before the death of Sulla in 78 B.C., *ludi* were given on forty-eight days; Roscius, a very popular actor of that day, is said to have played one hundred and twenty-eight times in twelve months. The fondness of the Romans for the combination of plays, games, and violent spectacle was so great that at times performances were staged at night with the aid of torches. The motive behind the *ludi*—which were always free— was akin to that of the "bread and circuses" with which the ruling class diverted and placated the proletariat.

If the Roman theater ever had the religious and civic significance of the Greek, it rapidly lost this and became merely "show business." The commercial manager appeared. The magistrates whose duty it was to supply games for the multitude turned to professionals for both plays and performances. The actor–manager had his troupe of slaves, freedmen, and foreigners. He bought a play outright from its author or adapter, paid for costumes and properties, and assumed all the risks of production and presentation. If the play proved popular, he was given money in proportion to its success and sometimes a prize of palm leaves or a crown of silver or gold. An inevitable result was the organization of claques to applaud certain actors and shout down others. The games and spectacles that were given in the same theaters as the plays—and often at the same performances—grew bloodier and more violent. The plays themselves became more licentious or were replaced by pantomimes, tableaux, and lewd dances.

PANTOMIMES INSTEAD OF PLAYS

Under the Empire, the most popular dramatic entertainments were pantomimes that used music and dance, costumes and settings to retell Greek myths. In *The Golden Ass*, written about 150 A.D., Apuleius describes one of these shows, which presented the judgment of Paris. In front of the curtain, "by way of prelude a number of beautiful boys and girls were moving with dignity through the graceful mazes of the Greek Pyrrhic dance. . . . Presently the trumpet blew the Retreat . . . and the backdrops were removed [the curtain fell into a slot in the floor] to disclose a far more elaborate performance."

> *The scene was an artificial wooden mountain, supposed to represent Homer's famous Mount Ida, an imposing piece of stage-architecture, quite high, turfed all over and planted with scores of trees. The designer had contrived that a stream should break out at the top of the mountain and tumble down the side. A herd of she-goats were cropping the grass, and a young man strolled about, supposedly in charge of them, dressed in flowing Asiatic robes with a gold tiara on his head. He represented Paris the Phrygian shepherd. Then a handsome boy came forward . . . the God Mercury.*

> *He came dancing towards Paris and after presenting him with a golden apple explained Jupiter's orders in sign language. . . . The next character to appear was Juno, played by a girl with very fine features. . . . Then Minerva came running in. . . . She was followed by another girl of extraordinary beauty . . . Venus—Venus before marriage. To show her perfect figure to fullest advantage she wore nothing at all except a thin gauze apron.*

Juno was accompanied by Castor and Pollux, Minerva by two young men representing Terror and Fear, and Venus by "a whole school of happy little boys crowding around her, so chubby and white-skinned that you might have taken them to be real cupids flown down from heaven. . . . Juno advanced calmly," and Minerva with "quick, excited writhings." To sentimental Lydian airs, "Venus began dancing to the music with slow, lingering steps and gentle swaying of her hips and head. . . . Her eyelids fluttered luxuriously or opened wide to let fly passionate glances, so that at times she seemed dancing with her eyes alone." She promised "with tense gestures . . . that she would marry him [Paris] to the most beautiful woman in the world, her own human counterpart. Young Paris gladly handed her the golden apple in token of her victory. . . ."

> *Then a fountain of wine, mixed with saffron, broke out from a concealed pipe at the mountain top and its many jets sprinkled the pasturing goats with a scented shower, so that their white hair was stained the rich yellow traditionally associated with the flocks that feed on Mount Ida. The scent filled the whole amphitheatre; and then the stage machinery was set in motion, the earth seemed to gape and the mountain disappeared from view.*

THE GREEK CHORUS AND ACTORS

A unique and curious feature of the Greek theater was the chorus that held over from the days of the ancient dithyramb. Thespis is supposed to have had a chorus of fifty. After Aeschylus produced *The Suppliants*, he reduced the chorus to twelve, while Sophocles increased it to fifteen. These men—who often appeared in women's costumes—chanted and moved in rhythmic patterns. They sometimes spoke through their leader or lamented and argued with one another.

When Aeschylus added another actor to the one that Thespis had introduced and thus made dialog possible, the role of the chorus shrank in importance. In Sophocles' plays the chorus still played a part in the plot, but a smaller part, and the choral ode became almost a lyric interlude between dramatic scenes. Euripides reduced still further the significance of the chorus. The comedy of Aristophanes, which was far stricter and more complicated in form, employed a chorus of twenty-four, but split it in two for scenes of disputation.

There is a rather dubious theory that Sophocles introduced a fourth actor in *Oedipus at Colonus*, a play that he wrote when he was about ninety years old. This seems hardly plausible, because a fourth actor was unnecessary. Through the use of masks and by doubling roles (which was the common practice) Aeschylus could have six characters in *Agamemnon*, and Euripides could have eleven in *The Phoenician Women*.

The Greek actor had to be a highly skilled and very versatile artist. (Imagine the difficulty of playing women like Electra!) While most of his speeches were solemnly declaimed, there was often a great deal of violent action and emotional expression, and certain lyrical passages had to be sung to the accompaniment of a flute player. Greek audiences were highly critical as to the enunciation of the actors and the treatment of the text. When, in the fourth century, actors began to take certain liberties with their lines in a theater where a prompter could not be concealed, Lycurgus prepared authentic texts, and saw that the actors followed them religiously. Taking the opposite attitude from the Romans, who looked down upon actors as little better than the "vagabonds and knaves" of Elizabethan times, the Greeks venerated them as servants of Dionysus, exempted them from military duty, and sometimes entrusted them with diplomatic and political missions.

Though the Romans followed the Greek fashion of not permitting actresses in tragedies or classic comedies, they used as many as six actors in one production. In farces and especially in the pantomimes and tableaux that became more and more popular as the Roman stage decayed, women often took leading roles.

MASKS AND COSTUMES

Like the chorus, the mask is another feature of Greek drama that is alien to our ideas of dramatic production and, like the chorus, it was rooted in religious ritual. The mask was used all over the world long before Thespis smeared his face with purslane or white lead and red cinnabar, or wore a false face of linen, and the mask continued to be worn in the New Comedy of the Greek Menander and in the Roman plays of Plautus and Terence after the chorus had disappeared. Sophocles improved on the linen masks of Thespis by making false faces of carved and painted wood. Cork was also used, and in Rome, terra cotta, or baked clay. Masks were worn by the chorus as well as by the actors.

Though the origin of the mask was religious, its use served some very practical purposes. Without differently designed masks it would have been difficult for one actor to play two roles. Further, since the mask fitted over the actor's head like a helmet, it was larger than his natural face; and its features, which were exaggerated and emphasized in shape and color, could be seen more plainly across the vast distances of theaters seating very often as many as fifteen thousand spectators. The wide-open mouth may have served as a sort of megaphone.

A disadvantage of the mask was, of course, the immobility of its expression. The audience had to use its imagination as lines of dialog indicated a change of mood in a character; yet it was possible for the actor who left the stage wearing a happy visage to return with a sorrowful countenance fitted to the calamity that had happened off stage. A Roman writer of the first Christian century describes a mask, one side of which had a cheerful aspect and the other a serious one, enabling the actor to vary the expression of his face by showing one side or the other to the audience.

The mask indicated the age, sex, mood, and even the station of a character. Tragic masks were usually rather serene and beautiful, but the terrifying features of the Furies in *The Eumenides* are said to have created a panic at the premiere of Aeschylus' tragedy. In some of Aristophanes' comedies the chorus wore the masks of birds, bees, or frogs. The realism of the masks of contemporary persons must have been most faithful, for at the performance of *The Clouds*, when a character representing Socrates made his entrance, the philosopher rose from his seat so that the audience might see the resemblance.

Though the tragedies dealt mainly with people of the Homeric times, the costumes worn by actors and chorus were a happy compromise between historical accuracy—which was impossible to them—and the clothes of the day. The *chiton*, or long garment reaching from neck to ankles, had a grave aspect that must have helped the actor to feel and convey the solemn mood of the heroic characters. Yet the *chiton* and the shorter mantle that might be worn over it were vivid in color—a reminder to us that the statues of Phidias and other Greek sculptors were not the cold, white marble that we now associate with classic art, but were gaily painted in realistic colors. Costumes for comedy were in the current style except when gods or mythological figures appeared.

To set the principals off from the chorus and to comport with the oversize masks, the tragic actor wore an exaggerated headdress, the *onkos*, and perhaps a thick-soled shoe, the *cothurnus*, while the chorus wore low shoes. In comedies the contemporary characters had only the usual common footgear. Here we have the origin of the distinction between "sock and buskin"—the ordinary shoe or slipper of comedy and the high-soled boot of tragedy. Nobody knows at just what period these aids to impressive height first appeared. Padding prevented the actors from seeming thin as well as tall.

SCANT INFORMATION FROM VITRUVIUS

Almost all that we have written should have been liberally larded with "supposedly," "it is said," and "probably." When we come to describing the physical theater in which Greek plays were produced, we are on even shakier ground. Only two ancient writers— Vitruvius and Pollux—have tried to describe it in any detail; and Vitruvius wrote his *De Architectura* shortly before the birth of Christ, while Pollux wrote his *Onomastikon*, a kind of encyclopedia, in the second century of our own era. They often failed to indicate clearly whether the theater they wrote about was Roman, Hellenistic, or truly Classic. They were laboring under the gravest disadvantages in trying to study things long dead and gone. There was no printing press to stimulate the writing of descriptive and technical books or to preserve diaries. Many old manuscripts have been lost, and some that Vitruvius refers to as providing certain facts are among these.

In *De Architectura*, Vitruvius has a great deal to say about constructing temples and baths and country houses, about water supply and clocks and sundials, about "stucco on damp places" and catapults and even astronomy. But, so far as theaters are concerned, most of what he writes deals with acoustics—"how to make the voices from the stage rise more clearly and sweetly to the spectators' ears." He gives as much space to "colonnades and passages behind the scenes" as he does to the proportions of the orchestras, to the seating arrangements, and to the height of the stages in Roman and Hellenistic theaters. He devotes only about sixty words to a scene-changing device of revolving prisms that still puzzles us. Since he calls such machines by the Greek name *periaktoi*, we may suppose that they came down from Attic beginnings. He is hardly more voluble—using some eighty words, all told—about what seemed of vast importance to the theater folk of fifteenth-century Italy: the three types of scenery used in his own day for the forms of drama established by the Greeks—tragedy, comedy, and the satyr play. Vitruvius' only direct comment on the classic Athenian theater suggests that a man "who was in control of the stage" for a play by Aeschylus painted scenery in perspective. He writes, with some asperity, about a small contemporary theater in Asia Minor—which some think was not a theater at all but merely an assembly place— whose scenic background, painted in false perspective, was a jumble of mismated architectural forms. Pollux, writing in the days of the Roman Empire, merely lists some of the paraphernalia of the stage, including trapdoors, cranes, cycloramas, and lightning devices.

Aside from the obscurities of Vitruvius and Pollux, we have little other evidence except architectural ruins. We can see Roman auditoriums and pretty good indications of Roman stage walls in theaters from Asia Minor to France and Spain, and the ashes of Vesuvius have preserved, in Pompeii, paintings of Roman stages— and even of actors appearing on them. But the relics and records of Greek and Hellenistic theaters are not nearly so ample. The Hellenistic is, in fact, rather scanty, and the classic Greek almost nonexistent.

THE SHAPE OF THE THEATER

We have reason to believe that in the days long before Thespis, the dithyrambic chorus chanted and danced in the midst of townspeople and peasantry. We know that when the first Theater of Dionysus was created in Athens, the chorus appeared on a flat, circular area seventy-eight feet across; this *orchestra*—"dancing place"—has been found by archaeologists. But the first stone theater on this site, with a sixty-four-foot *orchestra*, was built more than a hundred years later, when the stage had become Hellenistic in form. The present structure dates from the time of Nero.

As to the auditorium, the place where the audience sat, we know nothing about it in the fifth century. We presume that some time before Thespis, it was found convenient to lay out the *orchestra* ring where two hills met and made a natural hollow, partly surrounded by sloping ground. The "theater in the round" was becoming less circular. We do not know when the Greeks began to dig into a hillside to make the auditorium, which seems to have surrounded two-thirds of the *orchestra* in the fifth century. (A hollow is called a *koilon* in Greek and a *cavea* in Latin. The latter became the Roman word for auditorium, while the Greeks dropped *koilon* in favor of *theatron*, or theater, derived from the Greek word meaning "to see.") At first, it is presumed, the spectators stood or sat on the hillside; next they enjoyed wooden benches. At Syracuse in Sicily, seats were carved out of the natural rock as early as the fourth century. When Lycurgus rebuilt the Theater of Dionysus about 333 B.C., he installed stone seats, a fashion that spread rapidly throughout the Hellenistic world. There are remains of glorious auditoriums from that later period—the beautiful, rock-hewn one at Syracuse, the well-preserved ruins at Epidaurus in Greece, and two in Asia Minor, the high sweep of seats looking out and down over a wide valley at Pergamum, and the chaste and almost miniature structure at Priene.

It is only the *orchestra* and the auditorium of the later Greek theater that seem at all definite and clear. Once we try to learn about the stage—even the Hellenistic stage—we are deep in probabilities and suppositions. As a matter of fact, it is dangerous to believe that any one form or any pattern of developing forms could have existed. The theaters we are concerned with—both Greek and Roman—were built over a period of five hundred years. They were built in scores of cities and in many countries and under widely differing political and racial and cultural conditions. Diversity of structure, so far as the stage goes, was inevitable. So let's not look for something we can't find: one type of Classic theater, one Hellenistic type neatly developed from it, and a pure Roman variety. In addition, some authorities like to recognize a mixed type that they call Graeco-Roman, from the interaction of Hellenistic and Roman.

THE "SKENE," OR STAGE BACKGROUND

In the course of time, Western Europe took *theatron*, the word that the Greeks used for the hillside hollow full of seats, turned it into the word "theater," and made it include the whole playhouse. We have done the same kind of trick with another Greek word, *skene*. What we call a scene in a play or a scene on the stage, or even painted scenery, comes from the word for a wooden hut or tent, *skene*. At Athens in 465 B.C., a *skene* was put up at the edge of the *orchestra* opposite the middle of the rows of seats. The common theory is that this was done to provide a dressing room for the actors and the chorus, and it was certainly a very handy place for a quick change of mask and costume when an actor was playing two or three parts. At any rate, the *skene*, or scene building, became a regular feature of all Greek theaters down through the Hellenistic period. We know that it had short wings at each end, that the wall of the *skene* was pierced, sooner or later, with three doors, and that there were side entrances between the wings of the building and the auditorium. But that is all we are sure of. We have no idea as to when the *skene* turned into a two- or three-storied structure.

There is even some confusion about the word *proskenion*—which finally turned into our "proscenium." *Proskenion* meant something in front of the *skene*. Sometimes this is taken to be the wall of the *skene* itself; sometimes, the playing space—or what we would call the stage—between the *skene* and the *orchestra*. Now the roof of the *skene* was certainly used in the fifth century as a place on which a god could appear, or from which he could be lowered in a crane, to resolve the difficulties of the plot. Some students who have tried to reconstruct Hellenistic theaters believe that this roof was converted into a second stage by having another wall at its rear, and some have provided a third story for the gods and the machine.

Of one thing we can be sure: the height of the stage floor at

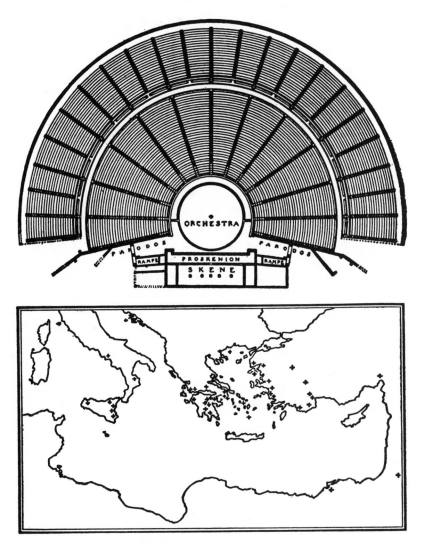

Figure 1.1 The Greek Theater
Above, the Hellenistic playhouse at Epidauris with passageway (called
parados) between stage building and audience area. Below, a map of
Hellenistic theaters. The sites of these theaters—some forty in
number—are known either through ruins or historical allusions. Many
more undoubtedly existed.

various periods. The classic stage was on a level with the *orchestra* or raised by only one or two low steps. The Hellenistic was about twelve feet high and the Roman about five. The Hellenistic was shallow, the Roman deep.

THE ROMAN PLAYHOUSE

We are on fairly solid ground when we come to the Roman theater. The Hellenistic had a full circle of *orchestra* in front of the *skene*. The so-called Graeco-Roman—which spread from one shore of the Mediterranean to the other just before the birth of Christ—thrust the stage of the *skene* over the edge of the *orchestra*. The Romans boldly joined the *skene* building to the auditorium, shrank the *orchestra* to a semicircle, and with their mania for arch-construction, sometimes built the whole theater as a free-standing structure on level ground. Chorus and actors were confined to a low stage, and the diminished *orchestra* became a place where movable seats were placed for Roman "brass" and distinguished visitors. A few steps led up to the stage, which was ornamented richly with columns, panels, and cornices, and which had three doors along the back and one at each side.

The Roman Republic, with a tradition of almost Spartan simplicity, looked askance at the "degeneracy" of Greek art and most things that were Greek, and therefore frowned on the theater as a sybaritic and corrupting institution. The first theater was built of wood in 179 B.C. and soon torn down. In 55 B.C., when the Republic was turning into the Empire, Pompey ventured to build a permanent theater of stone, and got away with it by placing a temple to Venus Victrix above the last row of the auditorium. Thus the tiers of seats became steps leading to the altar, and the whole thing was disguised as a temple. (We are reminded of the famous and distinguished Boston Museum of Victorian times where proper Bostonians could freely go because they paid admission to see a museum of curiosities and got the play free!) Only two other permanent theaters were opened in the city of Rome before the huge Colosseum and its bloody shows dominated Roman entertainment, but scores of Roman theaters were built from England and Spain to Asia Minor. In many, the auditorium was sheltered by awnings, and the stage had a long, narrow roof. Later, at Pompeii and perhaps elsewhere, there were small theaters completely roofed in.

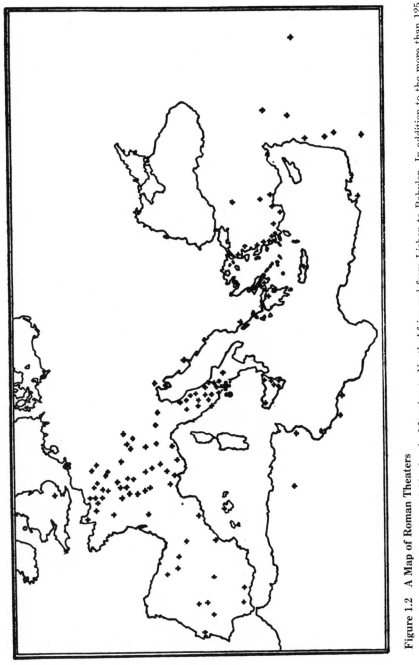

Figure 1.2 A Map of Roman Theaters
These sites stretch from the neighborhood of London to North Africa and from Lisbon to Babylon. In addition to the more than 125 theaters shown here, the Romans erected numerous amphitheaters and coliseums for athletic events and spectacles.

Long before the days of the Roman Empire, Italy had a much simpler and more popular theater. It was a theater of comedy—comedy of the broadest sort. Some of its roots were Greek and some native. At Syracuse shortly before the time of Aristophanes, Greeks were writing farces that had no chorus and dealt at first with mythological figures, and later with everyday episodes such as domestic intrigue and knavery of all sorts. In southern Italy both the plays and the actors of such farces were called *phlyakes*, and today on ancient vases we find scenes that show the players on crude, low, wooden platforms, provided sometimes with a short flight of steps. There is every reason to believe that such stages existed for the rustic *atellanae* farces, which originated much later in the Campania south of Rome and dealt with stock characters of the day. In Rome, where comedy seems to have been better liked than tragedy, there developed the *fabula togata*—the "fable," or comedy, "in native dress." From an Italian wall painting, we know that Egyptian dancers appeared on rough platforms while a member of the company collected coins from the spectators.

SCENERY AND MACHINES

The Greek theater of the fifth century, as well as its Hellenistic descendants, was not so austere as to foreswear spectacle and scenic device. In 458 B.C., Aeschylus' hero Agamemnon entered in a chariot. There was some kind of painted scenery, for Aristotle credits it to Sophocles, and Vitruvius to Aeschylus. In Hellenistic times, scenery may have included ornamented panels set between the columns of the *skene* and the *periaktoi*, or revolving prisms, mentioned by Vitruvius. There is some physical evidence of both. At Priene in Asia Minor there are ridges in the stage columns against which panels, or *pinakes*, must have rested, for there are holes for pegs to keep them in place. In two or three theaters, at the sides of the *skene*, there are stones with sockets in which the center beam of a *periaktos* may have rested. On each of the three sides of these prisms indications of scenes—probably stylized—were painted. Pollux writes of a "lightning machine" that may have consisted of a *periaktos* with zigzags of white painted on black. Nobody knows when the *periaktoi* were first used, but at least two other striking bits of stage machinery were introduced in the fifth century. These were the *eccyclema* and the *mechane*. Though by traditional rule murders could be done only offstage, the resulting carnage could be exhibited to the audience by the *eccyclema*. This was obviously a platform that moved through a doorway, but we don't know whether it revolved on an axis or rolled out on wheels like a modern stage wagon. We know, however, that the term *eccyclema* came from a word meaning "to wheel out," and we have a scene from Aristophanes' comedy *The Archarnians* in which Dicaeopolis knocks on Euripides' door and demands that the dramatist come out. Euripides replies: "But I'm not at leisure." Then shouts Dicaeopolis: "At least be wheeled out!" "Well," replies Euripides, "I'll have myself wheeled out." The *mechane* was some kind of device for making a god appear on an upper stage or in the air or for lowering him to the level of the human beings below—effects that seem to be called for in two of Aeschylus' plays and in many of Euripides'. Pollux describes a crane let down from above to remove a dead body or a living character. In Aristophanes' comedy *The Clouds*, Socrates seems to be suspended in such a machine, for he says, "I tread the air and contemplate the sun."

Scenic devices increase in number as we approach the Roman theater. Pollux lists nineteen—including trapdoors and cycloramas—and almost all may have been used in Hellenistic times. Vitruvius describes three types of stage settings: for tragedy, "with columns, pediments, statues, and other objects suited to kings"; for comedy, "private dwellings with balconies and views representing rows of windows"; and for "satyric scenes," "trees, caverns, mountains, and other rustic objects." Vitruvius' three kinds of sets correspond to the three forms of plays written and produced in the fifth century, but this does not mean that he is describing anything as early as the Hellenistic theater. Roman playhouses sported a curtain that hid the scene until the play began and then sank into a trough.

GREEK THEATER VERSUS GREEK PLAYWRIGHT

The purpose of any theater—its form, its scenic devices, and its actors—is to present the plays popular in its time. The value of any theater lies in its ability to present these plays effectively. Both theater and plays interact upon one another. The theater affects the plays, and the plays—within limits—affect the theater. Let us see how the classic Greek theater influenced the playwright and how the playwright used the peculiar conventions of that theater to achieve dramatic effectiveness.

When the *skene* was no more than a dressing room at one side, the locale of the early plays of Aeschylus was open country. When the scene building with its three doors was introduced, plays could be laid in front of a temple or a palace. Sooner or later the central door was assigned to the hero; a side one was supposed to lead to the room of a secondary character or to guest chambers; and the other was used by a minor person or represented a ruined shrine or a prison. The side entrances between the ends of the auditorium and the *skene* led in one case to the city and in the other case to the harbor or the countryside. The playwrights—who were resourceful directors and often actors—established these conventions to help make clear the action of their plays. They called into being the *eccyclema*, the *mechane*, and probably the painted panels and the *periaktoi* to ease some of the limitations of their stage. Like Shakespeare, they had characters describe things that the audience could not see but had to imagine.

LITERARY LIMITATIONS

The writer of Greek tragedy faced other limitations besides those of the physical theater. These were what we would call "literary limitations." They were conventions of dramatic form carried over from the dithyramb. The most important of these conventions and the one that is hardest for us to understand and accept is the chorus.

To an audience that is used to intimate, personal drama, the chorus may seem an absurd interruption and therefore an impossible limitation on the art of the dramatist. The chorus was neither actor nor bystander. It was, rather, a kind of link with the audience, making the spectator feel a closer participation in the drama. The chorus was an instrument for the expression of complete and ultimate emotion over great or terrible deeds. It translated the feeling of the actor into a different medium. It brought to the audience emotions that the characters in a play sometimes could not completely feel, or emotions that could not be expressed in ordinary words. The chorus turned crude suffering into poetry, even into soothing mystery. The chorus could, and did, "shake lyric splendor over the whole." Greek tragedy lived on two planes, in two worlds. First, the audience was interested in the individual and his personal feelings, then in the chorus and the sublimated emotion. The body departed, but the spirit remained. That was the secret of Greek tragedy.

Though the chorus linked the audience with the drama, it also separated scene from scene. The fact that the choral passages sometimes, but not always, divided the play into five scenes of personal action led the Roman poet Horace to believe that Greek tragedy was written in five acts, and it caused Renaissance critics to assert that all plays must follow this pattern.

Lest you accept the further fallacy that Greek tragedy was bound by what have been called the three unities—the unities of time, place, and action—we must point out that Aristotle found only one unity in the dramas of Aeschylus, Sophocles, and Euripides. This was the unity that all good plays observe: the unity of action. As for time and place, some Greek tragedies had more than one locale, which meant, of course, that they could not observe strict unity of time.

THE FOUR FOUNDERS OF TRAGEDY AND COMEDY

There were writers of tragedy before Aeschylus (he was born about ten years after the first playwriting contest was established in Athens in 534 B.C.), and there were certainly many after Euripides. Yet only a single play in existence, *Rhesus*, is not definitely assigned to one of the three great tragic writers, and some think Euripides wrote this rather inferior script. We have no comedies of the fifth century, except those of Aristophanes, and only one complete play and a few scenes from the New Comedy of Menander. Few of the Greek plays were known to the Western world until 1453, when the Turks captured Constantinople and scholars escaping to Italy brought some play scripts with them. Others were found later among manuscripts in eastern Mediterranean cities. The reason that only certain plays of Aeschylus, Sophocles, Euripides, and Aristophanes and not the works of lesser playwrights were pre-

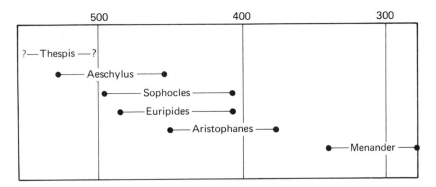

Figure 1.3 The Greek Playwrights

This, like the other time-charts in this book, shows the life spans of the writers, not their periods of playwriting activity. Some dramatists begin their important work while still in their twenties; Shaw was over thirty. Though these charts do not show the exact years of writing activity, they do indicate in a rough way the relationships in time among the various writers.

served to us is, presumably, because they were most often revived and the manuscripts recopied, during the later Hellenistic period.

The three great tragic writers and their plays make a clear and interesting pattern. It is a pattern that follows developments and changes in Greek culture as well as in the theater. Aeschylus, pioneering yet bound by theatrical tradition, depended greatly on the chorus; half of his *Agamemnon* is lyric. His themes were traditional and deeply religious. He stuck close to the old ideas of a world in which Olympian law punished crime and protected the state. His plots were simple and his effects catastrophic. The plays of Sophocles were more intricate in plot, and he was more absorbed in the interplay of characters than in divine justice, though he gave more than lip service to religious tradition. Euripides pioneered in a different way from Aeschylus. He was deeply concerned with character and what were, for his time, unconventional and even impious ideas. In many ways a thoroughly modern man, he might be called the first realist and the first feminist. He forgot the broad issues of morality and religion while he explored what we would call abnormal psychology. If he dealt at all with social ideas, he was likely to write an anti-war play like *The Trojan Women* when his own city was locked in mortal combat with Sparta. Basically, Euripides preferred to probe the inner life of the individual. He changed tragedy from a conflict between man and the divine laws into a conflict in man's own soul between his good and his evil impulses. Though he dealt with mythological characters, he presented them realistically. From at least one manuscript, *Helen*, we know that Euripides attempted, probably for the first time, a kind of play that was neither tragedy nor comedy. He won far fewer prizes than either Aeschylus or Sophocles. In a very real sense he was ahead of his time, for the plays that the Athenians of the fifth century disliked and condemned were vastly popular with their Hellenistic descendants. That is why we have more manuscripts of Euripides' plays than all those of Aeschylus' and Sophocles' put together.

OLD PLOTS BUT NEW CHARACTERS

The plots of practically all Greek dramas were based on myths or legends familiar to their audiences, and many were used again and again. There were a few exceptions: Aeschylus' *The Persians* dealt with a war in which he had fought, and a playwright named Agathon tried unsuccessfully to use new plots about fictional characters. Perhaps because the Greek tragedies used stories hallowed by time, Aristotle wrote: "The plot . . . is the first principle, and, as it were, the soul of tragedy; character holds second place." Actually, so far as the audience was concerned, the very opposite was true. Old plots became exciting again because the dramatists handled the chief characters in fresh ways, giving them new emotional reactions. In *The Greek Way to Western Civilization*, Edith Hamilton has demonstrated this brilliantly by analyzing the completely different ways in which Aeschylus, Sophocles, and Euripides presented Electra.

THE OLD COMEDY AND THE NEW

The comedy of Aristophanes—himself a conservative—lampooned the ways of Athens and its politicians, philosophers, and playwrights. This comic form was far more highly conventionalized than

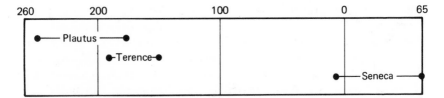

Figure 1.4 The Chief Roman Playwrights

Plautus was dead before Terence began his comedies. Seneca did not write until almost two hundred years later. Rome had no permanent theaters when it had its two outstanding playwrights, and no playwrights except Seneca when it had theaters.

that of tragedy. Yet, within the complex and elaborate pattern, Aristophanes and his fellow playwrights injected scenes that ran from political travesty and comic preachment to bawdy burlesque. *The Frogs* satirized Euripides; *The Clouds*, Socrates.

The contests in comedy began in 486 B.C., not quite fifty years after the first contests in tragedy. In only a little over a century, the Old Comedy of Aristophanes had disappeared, and the New Comedy of Menander had taken its place. Political and aesthetic satire had given way to comic plots from private life. Stock characters like the miserly old man and the scheming slave ruled the stage. They still wore masks, but the chorus was simply a group of caroling citizens who had nothing to do with the plot. Influenced no doubt by the *phlyax*, the New Comedy became, as one authority has put it, the model and the quarry for the Roman comedy of Plautus and Terence. Through antique comedy in Greece and Italy runs a pattern that ends in the *commedia dell'arte* of sixteenth-century Italy.

Roman writers of tragedy simply translated or adapted Greek plays. A few, like Seneca, wrote original scripts, but they were generally content to have them read in private. The theater was too common and degraded an institution for the learned and well-placed.

The development of the Greek and Roman theater and its plays followed a familiar pattern, a pattern in which there is always hope and accomplishment and always disappointment and death. The theater began as a simple thing that imposed rather severe limitations and yet seemed to stimulate the playwrights through those limitations. Still more stimulating—and limiting, too—was the social and political and cultural atmosphere of the fifth century. Tragedy was born in the heroic times when Athens defeated the Persian invaders, and created the nearest approach to democracy that the world had known. Tragedy died in the spiritual confusions and decay that developed out of the Peloponnesian War. When the great playwrights of the fifth century were gone, and no one of equal stature came to take their place, the theater tried to fill the void with physical display and new ingenuities of production. The collapse of the Roman Empire carried down with it a theater that had fallen almost equally into decay. The theater of Dionysus died like its god, slain and torn apart by the enemies of its eternal spirit. It was to be born again, like Dionysus, in the spring of the Renaissance.

2: MEDIEVAL THEATER: A HOUSE OF MANY MANSIONS

The beginnings of a medieval theater can be traced, however obscurely, to many ceremonial occasions—no one of which may be said to be a definitive source. The notion of a linear progression from church drama to mystery plays and the great cycles, and from there to morality plays that form the basis of Renaissance drama, has been rightly pointed out by George Kernodle as erroneous. We have not one but many theaters, all subject to the influences of medieval society itself. Theater was a reflection of disparate elements that composed a complex medieval mind. The varied types of drama that emerged mirrored its values. Ceremonial events—both clerical and secular—created, established, and maintained a cohesive society.

ORIGIN OF MEDIEVAL DRAMA

The early renaissance in the arts, exemplified by Dante Alighieri's *Divine Comedy*, Boccaccio's *Decameron* tales, and the paintings of Giotto di Bondone, did not find expression on medieval stages. A

Roman Catholic church that had condemned the Roman theater—
and rightly—was not about to allow history to repeat itself.
Medieval drama arose not as an expression to create *in vacuo*, but
as a response to ceremonial occasions of the community at large.
Artisans, tradesmen, and citizens from all walks of life worked together to create a ritual theater emblematic of the whole. The
drama that emerged was a public celebration of universal values,
rather than an occasion to proclaim the worth of an individual.

THE ROMAN STAGE—"CHURCH OF THE DEVIL"

The early church fathers had sought for years to abolish the morbid
dramatic spectacles of the Roman amphitheaters, which featured
animal baiting, gladiatorial contests, sea battles, and naked dancing. As early as 200 A.D. Tertullian, a Roman theologian who was
converted to Christianity circa 197, was calling the theater "the
Shrine of Venus" and "the Church of the Devil." In the fifth century
actors were forbidden by church law from practicing their profession, on pain of excommunication. That same century a monk named
Telemachus was stoned to death by a mob of spectators when he
attempted to stop a gladiatorial contest. At the insistence of the
church the Roman emperors finally took decisive action. By 568 A.D.
all spectacles and public entertainments in Rome were outlawed.
Church councils continued their attacks on *histriones*, as the players
were called, but these and other warnings to the faithful in the
succeeding five centuries only curbed, but did not eradicate, a per-
vasive acting tradition.

THE MIMES BECOME JUGGLERS AND JONGLEURS

Wandering minstrels, jugglers, and jongleurs, remnants of an acting tradition that traced its roots back to the Roman "mimes" and
the Greek *phlyakes*, continued to ply their trade through the "Dark
Ages." In the sixth century the Byzantine emperor Justinian the
Great (483–565 A.D.) justified his marriage to Theodora by decreeing
that a noble might wed an actress if she gave up her profession. But
emperor's edicts of this sort were the exception rather than the

rule. Even as late as the thirteenth century a bishop of Lindesfarne advised his monks that it was better to feed paupers at the monastery gates than to admit excommunicated actors within sanctified ground. By all accounts civil authorities and fathers of the early church found theatrical tradition a thorn in their respective sides.

LITURGICAL DRAMA

The Roman Catholic liturgy of the early Middle Ages contained many dramatic elements: during the singing of the mass, bread and wine were consecrated as the body and blood of Jesus Christ, while seven canonical "hours" offered a colorful procession of priests and choirs. Antiphonal singing or chanting, during which one voice or group of voices answered another in an exchange of biblical narratives, had been prominent since Saint Gregory (ca. 540–604 A.D.) had promoted the development of the Gregorian chant or *Plain Song* during the sixth century. The procession for Palm Sunday, which had begun two centuries before Gregory's elevation to the papacy, enacted Christ's last journey from the Mount of Olives to his arrest and crucifixion. A homely touch was added to the Palm Sunday processional of Winchester, England, where the *Regularis Concordia* of 970 A.D. represented the Mount of Olives as a nearby church. Drama did not begin in the medieval church service. It had been there for centuries.

One celebrated elaboration of Christian church rites was documented in France in the ninth century. Amalarius, Bishop of Metz, recommended to his peers that the celebrant of the mass represent, by gestures, the struggles of Jesus Christ. Amalarius' own histrionics so electrified his parishioners that crowds of worshippers came to the church demanding that the bishop repeat the sacred acts.

THE MEDIEVAL CHURCH TROPE

In Gregorian *Plain Song*, the *trope* is a short, distinctive cadence at the close of a melody. In the Western church the trope came to mean a phrase, sentence, or verse introduced by the choir as an embellishment of part of the mass. By the ninth century these tropes had become very elaborate. The original wordless musical sequences of Gregorian chants had been replaced by language, to make them easier to memorize.

The earliest recorded trope came from the Easter service of the Monastery of St. Martial, at Limoges (ca. 923–934 A.D.). Known as the *Quem Queritis* trope from the first two words of the *Interrogatio*, it was probably sung just before the priest approached the altar to celebrate the sacrament of the Lord's Supper.

The Easter trope from the monastery of St. Gall (ca. 950) was the simplest and the most explicit.* In its entirety the trope consisted of four lines in Latin and told the story of the three Marys and their visit to the sepulchre:

QUESTION	*INTERROGATIO*
Whom do you seek in the sepulchre, O followers of Christ?	*Quem Queritis in sepulchro, O Christicolae?*
ANSWER	*RESPONSIO*
Jesus of Nazareth, who was crucified, O Heavenly dwellers.	*Jesum Nazarenum crucifixum, O Caelicola.*
He is not here, He has arisen as He has foretold; go, announce that He has risen from the sepulchre.	*Non est hic, surrexit sicut praedixerat; ite, nuntiate quia surrexit de sepulchro.*
I have arisen.	*Resurrexi.*

The *Regularis Concordia* of Winchester included extensive stage directions for four brethren to act out the trope of Christ rising from the sepulchre, concluding with these instructions:

> *And let them lay the cloth upon the altar. When the antiphon is finished, let the Prior, rejoicing with them at the triumph of our King, in that he rose having conquered death, begin the hymn* Te Deum Laudamus *(We Praise You O God). When this is begun, all the bells peal in unison.*

This simple scene proved so popular with those who saw and heard it that priests added new material: Mary Magdalene met Christ clad

---

*David Bevington, ed., *Medieval Drama* (Boston: Houghton Mifflin Company, 1975), p. 26. Copyright © 1975 by Houghton Mifflin Company. Reprinted by permission.

as a gardener, Peter and John were discovered running toward the sepulchre, and the Marys bought spices from a new character, the Spice Merchant. The latter character's part was built up to the point where he became the comedian of the play in the fourteenth century.

EXPANSION OF LITURGICAL DRAMA

The dramatic elaboration of the Easter trope, the liturgical scene of the resurrection of Christ at Easter, quickly spread to Christmas ceremonials. Once begun, Christmas tropes expanded into liturgical plays much more rapidly than their Easter counterparts. By the end of the eleventh century the broad appeal of these scenes was evidenced by their translation from Latin into the vernacular and from trope into liturgical plays.

As liturgical plays increased in number, other settings besides the sepulchre of Christ invaded the church building. Heaven, Hell, and Limbo, as well as such earthly locales as Herod's Throne, the manger at Bethlehem, Egypt, and Galilee, were indicated by properties and backgrounds.

BEGINNINGS OF A SECULAR DRAMA

The Anglo-Norman play *Jeu d'Adam (Play of Adam)*, the first extant, nonliturgical play on record, was performed on the steps of a French cathedral in the twelfth century. *Adam* told not only the story of Adam and Eve driven from the Garden of Eden, but also the stories of Cain and Abel and of David and the Prophets foretelling the coming of Christ.

The writer of *Adam* dealt most carefully with scenery, properties, and even acting. Anticipating Hamlet's advice to the players, a priest wrote (as translated by Allerdyce Nicoll), among other things:

> *And Adam must be well trained when to reply and to be neither too quick nor too slow in his replies. And not only he, but all*

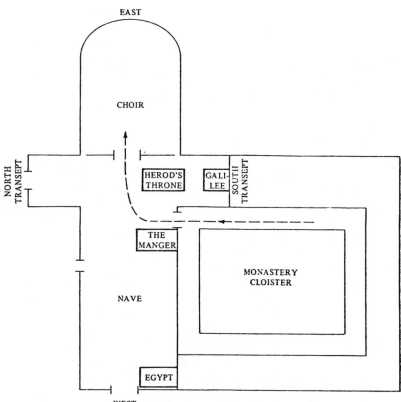

Figure 2.1 Plan of the Church of St. Benoit-sur-Loirs (Fluery) with Arrangement of Mansions

Based on Karl Young, *Ordo Rachelis (University of Wisconsin Studies in Language and Literature,* Number 4, Madison, 1919). See also Arnold Williams, *The Drama of Medieval England* (East Lansing: Michigan State University Press, 1961), p. 35.

the personnages must be trained to speak composedly, and to fit convenient gesture to the matter of their speech . . . .

Adam is the first play we know of that was given out of doors. Part of the setting was obviously the front of a church, for a stage direction instructed God to enter and leave by one of its doors.

THE FESTIVAL OF CORPUS CHRISTI

The relationship of liturgical plays performed within and without the church to the great cycle plays of the later medieval period is no longer as certain as once was thought. For while the feast day of Corpus Christi was created by papal decree, numerous social and economic influences soon moved feast days from clerical to secular control.

The Corpus Christi festival was promulgated for sixty days after Easter, generally falling between May 23 and June 24. However, medieval calendars were inaccurate, and an educated guess would place the date of the festival between June 4 and July 6. In 1264 Pope Urban IV declared the need to celebrate Christ's Last Supper. Since the Easter festival was already crowded, a new date was set—the Thursday after Trinity Sunday. Finally implemented by Pope Clement V in 1311, the Feast of Corpus Christi was celebrated in England from the early part of the fourteenth century until the latter half of the sixteenth century.

CORPUS CHRISTI—A FEAST OF SCHOLARSHIP

Interpretation of the cycle plays performed at the Feast of Corpus Christi has provoked almost as much controversy as the original dating of the festival itself, particularly with regard to the antecedents, the sponsorship, or the means of presentation of the pageants. E. K. Chambers (*English Literature at the Close of the Middle Ages*) and Hardin Craig (*English Religious Drama of the Middle Ages*) suggest that cycle pageants developed directly from church drama, while O. B. Hardison (*Christian Rite and Christian Drama in the Middle Ages*) argues that there was a mingling of forms derived from a vernacular tradition, coupled to the ritual forms of the Catholic church. At the other end of the spectrum, Rosemary Woolf, in *The English Mystery Plays*, stated "the cycles developed from a vernacular tradition that completely separated itself from the church tropes," while V. A. Kolve, in his influential book *A Play Called Corpus Christi*, posited that "the vernacular cycles constitute an entirely new genre, quite separate from any liturgical influence . . . and reflect the doctrinal concerns of the festival of Corpus Christi." And finally, Alan Nelson has argued in *The Medieval English Stage* that fifteenth-century processions "developed out of fourteenth century festival processions," while the doctrinal relationships between the feast of Corpus Christi and the dramatic content of the play were almost entirely incidental. One has the option of adopting several points of view. However, it is most likely that many different ways of staging cycle plays were used, and it is difficult to determine which method was used for which plays.

PROCESSIONS OR PLAY FIRST?

An even larger debate flourishes on the nature of the public performances of the Corpus Christi pageants. Kolve believed the plays were a genuine popular drama, "performed processionally at stations in the towns," while Hardin Craig dated the processions' beginnings much later than the plays'. Alan Nelson, in a recent study, stated that the processions came first, beginning in England about 1318, and only later evolved into a format of processionals, followed by the production of cycle pageants.

Much emphasis has been placed on descriptions of the English pageant wagons, consonant with the theory that they were the center of play production. Historical accounts (such as *The Trial and Flagellation with Other Studies in the Chester Cycle* edited by W. W. Greg) described the wagons as "a theater . . . very large and high, placed upon wheels," and "a high place made like a house with two rooms, being open to the top: . . . in the lower room they apparelled and dressed themselves; and in the upper room they played." But if the pageant consisted of both procession and play productions, given separately, descriptions of the pageant wagons reflect only a portion of the total scenic effect that sustained the festival for two hundred years.

Since the presentation of yearly pageants reflected craft guild rivalries and the prestige of city fathers, the choice of materials to be dramatized depended on the presence of local skilled trades able and willing to sponsor an entry in the festival. Pageant wagons must have appeared in processions much in the manner of modern day "floats" built for a Fourth of July or Rose Bowl Parade. Since dramatic productions are quite incompatible with a moving procession, Alan Nelson has argued convincingly that "the pageants were given at or after the conclusion of the procession, perhaps on special stages constructed for the purpose."

PLAYS IN THE ROUND

Martial Rose ("The Staging of the Hegge Plays" in *Medieval Drama* edited by John Russell Brown) has speculated, in agreement with Nelson's proposition, that cycle plays may have been performed in the round or brought together in a public square after the procession. In this way the pageants could be brought forward or taken away as necessary, or they could be used as medieval "mansions" for a common acting area, or *platea*. This hypothesis for staging pageants in the round has extensive historical support. In Cornwall, England, there are extant ruins of earthworks where mystery plays were given in the center, while an audience sat on a series of raised, circular benches near the edges.

ENGLISH CYCLE PLAYS

Out of hundreds of cycle plays produced in England we have only four complete or nearly complete pageants: the forty-eight plays of York; the forty-three plays of N-towne, sometimes referred to as the *Ludus Coventriae* or Hegge Cycle but probably from Lincolnshire or Norfolk; the thirty-two plays of the Towneley Cycle, performed at Wakefield in Yorkshire; and the twenty-four plays of the Chester Cycle. There are fragments of other cycles extant, including two New Testament plays from Coventry, one from Newcastle-on-Tyne, three from Cornwall, and one from Norwich. Nothing more seems to have survived the English Reformation that followed Henry VIII's break with the Church of Rome in 1534. When Elizabeth I came to Coventry in 1567 she attended four Corpus Christi pageants, but by 1585 all English sentiment for Catholic church pageantry was at an end. An Act of Parliament was passed that year declaring it treasonous for any Roman Catholic priest to set foot on English soil.

CONTINENTAL PASSION PLAYS

The continental passion play was the equivalent of the English cycle play. Staging practices varied almost as much as their counterparts in the English cycles, but the variations were restricted to a fixed stage format. The church was not the only stage for presenting passion plays. Frenchmen sometimes used the ancient amphitheaters like that at Orange; Italians gave some of their *sacre rappresentazioni* in the Roman Coliseum; Spaniards performed in the *corrales*, or courtyard theaters, of their large cities; while trestle stages erected in the market places of Frankfurt-am-Main (1350), Mons (1501), and Lucerne (1583), served as acting areas for the passion plays.

Confusion arose over the names of the various kinds of plays that developed. In France, dramatizations of the New Testament and, later, of the Old Testament, were called *mystères*, or "mystery plays," because they dealt with the mystery of the redemption through the nativity, through the passion, or sacrifice, of Christ, and through the resurrection. Eighteenth-century scholars tried to distinguish between mystery plays and miracle plays, which were religious plays based on the lives and legends of the saints. Both forms were known as *mystères* in France, deriving from the Latin, *mysterium* or *ministerium*, referring to an incident of mystical significance for the Roman Catholic church. The term was occasionally applied, erroneously, to mean the "mystery" of the trade guild that performed the play.

In Italy, similar productions were called *sacre rappresentaziones*; in Spain, *autos sacramentales*; and in Germany, *Geistliche Spiele*. The shorter English dramas that we call "moralities" or "morality plays," based on a conflict of abstract ideas, were called "interludes" in their own day.

COSTLY AND SPECTACULAR PRODUCTIONS

A surprising amount of information remains about marketplace productions. Plans remain for the arrangement of "mansions" for the two-day production at Lucerne in 1583, while Hubert Cailleau's painting of the setting for the 1547 production at Valenciennes, staged in the courtyard of a nobleman's castle, is particularly informative. Typically *mansions* indicated locations in what can be described as a "polyscenic stage of juxtaposition." If characters came out of the mansion of Jerusalem, spectators knew that the scene played on the neutral *platea* took place in Jerusalem. Characters arriving from Nazareth in subsequent plays occupied the same *platea*, which then became a part of Nazareth. Hell at Valenciennes was depicted on the far right (stage left) and slightly lower than the earthly mansions, while Paradise rose demonstrably higher at the far left (stage right). The production of the Passion Play at Valenciennes in 1547 took twenty-five days to perform, with the stage and its mansions changing every day for the benefit of spectators seated on the sides of the platform.

Productions of passion plays were not only long but also costly because of their intricate machinery and special effects. For example, Professor Gustàve Cohen of the Sorbonne and the University of Strasbourg discovered, in 1913, a manuscript of *The Mystery of the Passion* from Mons. Segments of the manuscript, translated by Lee Simonson in *The Stage Is Set*, included the following items:

> *To Master Jehan du Fayt and his assistants, numbering seventeen persons, for having helped in Hell for nine days during the said Mystery at 6s. sols a day to each, 45 l. livres 18s.*

> *To Godefroy du Pont for five and one half days of his time employed by him for the fitting of serpents with pipes for throwing flames, at 8s. a day, 44s.*

> *To Jehan des Quesnes, sabot maker, for one willow stump, for making the moulds for two heads, one of a devil, and another of a dragon, 14s.*

> *To Jehan Foucquart, called Docque Docque, for feeding certain birds of every variety, to be used for the creation, 6s.*

> *For live fishes for the aforesaid creation, 16s.*

> *To Jehan de la Desboubz and Collart Pandoul for having brought various trees for the earthly paradise, 7s.*

> *For apples old and new and also cherries to put on the trees of the Earthly Paradise, 5s.*

Besides mechanical animals, trapdoors, an oven to actually bake bread, soft batons to beat Jesus, a "small boat to put in the water," the script included directions for spectacular deluges of water and great bursts of light and sound, as the "Holy Ghost descends in the form of tongues of fire."

The actors—at first all men and later women and children too—were paid for their work. In England a man received three shillings and four pence "for pleaying God," another man four pence "for hangyng Judas," and another, one shilling for playing Noah. Such pay was often well earned: The man who played the part of Jesus at Metz in 1437 "would have died on the rood-tree [the cross], for he fainted and was like to have died had he not been rescued."

THE FARCE PLAY AND THE MORALITY PLAY

Mimes and small troupes of wandering actors performed entertainments, but no record of any literary drama occurred until Adam de la Halle's *Play of the Greenwood* (ca. 1276–77). The play dealt satirically with local villagers' responses to supernatural visits of fairies and goblins. A pastoral tradition began with *The Play of Robin and Marion* (ca. 1283). Its conventions included pursuing knights and fleeing shepherdesses, rejected suitors, and intermittent dancing and games.

Probably the most popular form of secular drama to emerge from the Middle Ages was the farce play, celebrating man's imperfections rather than his virtues. The subject matter of the farce play, concerned as it was with marital infidelity, hypocrisy, or cheating, mirrored society much more closely than church drama. The popularity of the form was revealed in the thirty editions that the French farce *Pièrre Pathelin* (ca. 1470) went through by the year 1600. Farce even intruded into *The Second Shepherd's Play*, a cycle play that told the story of Mak the sheep stealer, caught on the eve of Christ's nativity. The attempt to hide the lamb in swaddling clothes is foiled when the shepherds come into Mak's hovel to see the newborn "babe." A few years later the first completely secular English farce appeared, with the publication of John Heywood's *Johan Johan* (1533), the story of a cuckolded husband's worries *after* he has driven his wife and her priestly lover from the house.

If the farce play was the most popular form of drama for the medieval mind, the morality play is the most popular form of drama to the modern mind. Since 1765 we have called it a "morality" or a "morality play," but to the fourteenth-century Englishman it was "a moral interlude." The first recorded production was *The Play of the Lord's Prayer*, given at York around 1384. Prospects of secularizing biblical allegories of good and evil made the form particularly attractive to inventive scholars and clerics alike. Abstract personifications of virtues and vices such as mercy, humility, good deeds, lust, gluttony, and covetousness, struggled for the soul of man. Humor was often provided, as in the mysteries, by the devil and his assistants. A fragment of *The Pride of Life* (ca. 1400) is the oldest secular morality we possess. A quarter of a century later a very long (3,649-line) morality play, *The Castle of Perseverance*, detailed the rise, fall, and final judgment of man. But perhaps the most popular morality ever written was *Everyman* (ca. 1500), adapted from a Dutch original. Everyman, having received his death summons, watched as, one by one, Kindred, Goods, Fellowship, Strength, and Beauty departed, until at the end only Good Deeds went with him to the grave. Student productions of morality plays appeared in France as early as 1426, but they were never as popular there as in England.

OTHER FESTIVALS
WITHIN AND WITHOUT THE CHURCH

The brief liturgical plays and the longer religious dramas were performed in the church on special occasions until the Reformation and the Counter Reformation put an end to all religious dramas. There is no evidence to suggest that church drama moved into the marketplace to become the basis of cycle drama. Professor Nelson has argued, to the contrary, that the primary force behind guild pageants was secular rather than religious. And Professor Kernodle noted that the guild drama was produced by a very different class—the merchants—for crowds at the midsummer fairs. But some popular festivals were adopted by the church and became a part of their sanctified rites. Other pagan ceremonies created difficulties for church ecclesiastics.

From the time of Pope Gregory the Great in the seventh century, the Roman Catholic church gained its power either by totally controlling or by tolerating popular ceremonials and festivals. The celebration of the birth date of Jesus Christ was proclaimed on the same day as the popular Mithraic feast, which had spread from Persia to Europe. The Roman Catholic church also incorporated the Teutonic Eostratide, or Easter, with its eggs of fertility, into rejoicings over the resurrection of Christ. But some festivities the church adopted or tolerated made serious trouble. Certain pagan agricultural rites, including the sword dance and the mummer's play, in which one of two contestants was killed and then revived as a symbol of the death of winter and the coming of spring, derived from the pre-Christian rites of Dionysus. Another festival, born within the church, disturbed the higher ecclesiastics. It was the Feast of Fools, which, during the twelfth century, developed into a highly offensive ritual. Young clerics, instead of electing the parish idiot or drunkard to be the King of Fools, nominated him Bishop or even Pope of Fools. Further, they indulged in indecent songs and dances in the church, played dice and cards before the altar, and burlesqued the mass. Finally, in 1210, Pope Innocent III issued a papal decree denouncing these practices.

THE EMERGENCE OF PROFESSIONAL THEATER

Although at the beginning of the thirteenth century the supremacy of the Church of Rome was unchallenged, a secular power was emerging in the principal cities of Europe as schools and universities displaced monasteries as the acknowledged centers of learning. The new humanism that would flourish in the Renaissance already impressed the minds of scholars, while rival popes vied with each other for control of the church. Once the sole repository of intellectual and spiritual knowledge, the Roman Catholic church never fully recovered from the thirty-year papal duality that ended in 1417. Its authority was no longer unassailable.

In the sixteenth century the Reformation forced an irrevocable split in the church, a final fissure in the rock of St. Peter. An indigenous popular theater emerged in Reformation countries, and assailed the old enemy. Excommunications followed. At the Council

of Trent (1545–1563), the Roman Catholic church attempted unsuccessfully to reduce the number of new excommunicants by banning
all religious pageants. In 1547 Catholic Italy banned all religious
plays, as did France the following year. Only Spain, secure in the
grasp of the Spanish Grand Inquisitor, permitted its populace the
diversion of *autos sacramentales*.

The few mysteries that survived were the passion plays in the
villages of the Bavarian and Austrian Alps. And the only notable
one evolved in 1633, when peasants of Oberammergau swore to
enact the story of the crucifixion every ten years if they were spared
from a plague that ravaged the surrounding countryside. The time
of church-supported theater had ended; an era of public theater and
of professional acting troupes had arrived.

RE-ENTER THE PROFESSIONAL PLAYER

The professional actor in England emerged from the medieval morality plays. In 1493 Henry VII employed four or five men as the
Players of the King's Interludes. During the first half of the sixteenth century, nobility as well as royalty maintained companies of
actors. Such a company in 1520 played John Heywood's *The Play
Called the Four P's* at court, a new and very merry interlude of
palmer, pardoner, 'pothecary, and pedler. This variety of humanistic drama joined with the morality play to prepare the way for
Elizabethan dramatists and for the Elizabethan theater in and about
London. The irreconcilable split between popular and neoclassical
theater, which later plagued Italy and France, did not hinder the
development of the "barbarous tongue" of Shakespeare and his contemporaries.

In France *soties*, or short, satiric farces, were first acted
around 1400 by *societes joyeuses*, which consisted of Parisien student groups such as *Les Enfants Sans Souci*. The German equivalent of the *soties*, the Shrovetide plays of the shoemaker–poet Hans
Sachs, were, like his many tragedies and comedies, acted by
amateurs. Professionalism did not invade his native land until the
later sixteenth century.

Neither the Roman Catholic church nor the guilds retained
exclusive control of the production of mysteries in France after the

fourteenth century. Groups of amateur actors called *confrèries pieuses* (pious brotherhoods), shared in the production of many of the mysteries. In 1401 Charles VI gave the exclusive right to produce holy drama in Paris to one of these organizations, the *Confrèrie de la Passion*. They gave their performances in a hall on the second floor of the Hopital de la Trinité, and became thereby the first European company of actors to occupy a more or less permanent, though makeshift, playhouse. In 1548, when they had succeeded in building a new theater in the ruins of the Hotel de Bourgogne, formerly the town house of the Duke of Burgundy, they were forbidden to give mysteries, because earlier productions had indulged in farce and innuendo. After nearly thirty years of producing profane drama with marginal success, they began to lease their playhouse to professional companies in the 1570s. Finally, in 1608, the *Confrèrie de la Passion* became landlords of the *Comédiens Ordinaires du Roi*, the King's Players.

By 1608, the professional companies had replaced all amateur actors of religious plays and strolling mimes. The Renaissance and the Reformation had given drama a new content and a new form. International theater of the church had given way to national theaters that culminated in Spain with Lope de Vega and Calderon, in England with Marlowe and Shakespeare, and later, in France, with Corneille, Racine, and Molière.

Notice should be taken of the curious form of drama developed by the chambers of rhetoric in the low countries of Europe. Holland and Belgium had no theatrical heritage, but they did have a tradition of elite scholasticism. Competitions were organized among debating societies to encourage the art of rhetoric. The format for debate consisted of a question delivered to all societies, to which responses were composed in the form of rhetorical drama. Elaborate preparations surrounded the debates, which sometimes lasted a month. The popularity of the chambers of rhetoric waned in the first part of the seventeenth century, when a professional theater finally captured the public taste.

3: THE RENAISSANCE THEATER IN ITALY

After the death of the classic theater came thousands upon thousands of religious performances in the cathedrals and the marketplaces of the Middle Ages. Oddly enough, while the Renaissance theater tried, in a fit of scholarly devotion, to imitate the classic, it ended up as a new and almost modern theatrical form. The overloads of Italy—temporal and spiritual alike—provided theatrical performances of classic plays and pseudo-classic pageantry in courtyards and great halls. Scholars searched through ancient manuscripts for Latin and Greek dramas, and they acted them as they were—or adapted or translated them for performance. Painters, rediscovering the laws of perspective, read what the Roman architect Vitruvius wrote about the classic theater, and they created scenic miracles in princely palaces. At last, in 1584, a group of scholars and aristocrats opened in the city of Vicenza what was probably the first real playhouse that Italy had seen since the fall of Rome, the first one newly built and designed especially for theatrical production and devoted to nothing else.

In just one way the theater of the Italian Renaissance was like the theater of the Middle Ages. It left us few great plays. And so we may question whether it can be called a true theater. True theater means more than a playhouse and actors and scenery. True theater cannot exist without plays that broaden and deepen human understanding, plays that arouse and quicken the spirit of man. From the time of those great poets and storytellers Dante, Petrarch, and Boccaccio—precursors or begetters of the Renaissance—through the supreme years of the painters Leonardo da Vinci and Michelangelo, and on down to the invention of opera, Italy brought forth no fine, enduring drama. Therefore, in a true sense, the theater was not reborn during the Italian Renaissance in spite of all the lavish and magnificent activities of princes and popes, all the earnest and high-minded efforts of artists and academicians. There was no rebirth of the theater—as we know and revere the theater today—because there was no rebirth of the drama.

Yet, paradoxically enough, the modern playhouse with its canvas scenery and its miraculous machines was actually born in this time when men thought they were rediscovering and reconstructing the truly great theater of the classic world.

THE RENAISSANCE AND THE REVIVAL OF LEARNING

To understand what happened to the theater—and to the drama—you must understand the Renaissance. It was not a simple and compact affair. It was not merely the Revival of Learning in the fifteenth century through the discovery of the classic past. The true Renaissance flowed out of the Middle Ages. Almost a hundred years before scholars awoke fully to the glory that was Greece, there were three great, original, and essentially modern writers, Dante, Petrarch, and Boccaccio. A literary revival came before the Revival of Learning. The writers did not imitate the beauty of the classic style. They created a new beauty in their own terms. Though these men wrote in Italian, they knew the classics. In *The Divine Comedy* Dante chose Virgil as his guide to the other world; Boccaccio understood the significance of Greek literature; and Petrarch studied Greek as well as Latin. The three were portents of the coming age.

Their work formed the broad basis of humanism—the new philosophy of life that denied the ancient dogmas of the church and the state and that exalted man as a creature of reason and free will.

Humanism grew and flowered as the discovery and study of classic literature in the late fifteenth and the early sixteenth centuries dealt the death blow to medieval domination over the minds of man. Conceived in "pagan" times, the great works of Plato, Aristotle, and other Greeks strengthened humanism as they undermined the authority of medieval mysticism. They proved the goodness and greatness of man in the past, and to the man of the present they gave confidence in his own abilities. As the new-found beauties and wisdoms of the ancient world provoked more and more inquiry, they destroyed the barriers to man's criticism of the present. To the Italian, seeing the continuity of human culture in the face of differing creeds and races, Greek civilization spelled out his right to spiritual freedom.

With humanism and learning came a great upsurge in painting, in sculpture, in architecture, and also in a few forms of literature—a swift expansion and perfection of the arts that we commonly think of as defining the Renaissance. Sometimes imitative of classic models and sometimes not, these arts achieved genuine and original creation.

Certain events did a great deal to stimulate and extend this cultural movement that one of its great students, Jakob Burckhardt, has called "the discovery of the world and of man." When the Turks captured Constantinople in 1453, eastern scholars fled to Italy, laden down with Greek manuscripts. When the Turks closed the road to India, Italians, Portuguese, and Spaniards were driven to discover and colonize the New World and eventually to circumnavigate the globe. Just a little earlier, the printing press—a German contribution to the many scientific developments of the Renaissance—gave the men of this age a unique and powerful new medium for the diffusion of their knowledge.

Yet even while churchmen, as well as laymen, lent their energies to classical research and became tolerant of humanism, the influence of the hedonistic and the pagan contributed to the moral decay of popes and princes. In addition, learning and scholarship turned too often into antiquarianism and pedantry. It is an unhappy fact that, though classical study recreated the playhouse, it stifled the play. And there was no great audience in Italy of the kind that we shall find in Spain and England to save the drama from the bookishness of academicians and the shallow ostentation of princes.

LINKS TO THE MEDIEVAL THEATER

The religious drama of the Middle Ages continued in Italy until at least 1454, when Florence saw in a *sacre rappresentazione* biblical scenes reenacted against twenty "mansions," or sets. The artist Uccello, who died in 1475 at the age of ninety-eight, executed on a wall of the ducal palace of Urbino a mural showing what seems to be a multiple setting for a mystery play; it includes three rooms connected by two doors, with a third door leading to a landscape. In 1471 a seventeen-year-old poet named Politian showed the temper of the new age by writing in Latin a mystery play in which the fables of classic mythology replaced the stories of saints and biblical figures that had furnished the plots of medieval drama. His *La Favola di Orfeo*—later produced in splendor by Ercole d'Este, Duke of Ferrara—is a link between the mysteries of the Middle Ages and two new art forms that Renaissance Italy was to develop: These were the pastoral play, which died in the English court masque, and the opera, which lives on today.

THE THEATER OF THE "ENTRIES"

Another link with the past may be seen in the "entries," the spectacular festivities that were staged to welcome royalty to a city. These were expensive but probably effective devices for impressing a conquered province with the power of its alien ruler or for assuring a native prince of the loyalty of his people. You may trace entries back to the processions of conquering generals returning in triumph to ancient Rome. Centuries later, in medieval London, houses were draped with flags, banners, rich tapestries, and glowing silks when kings like Richard I and Henry III celebrated a coronation or a marriage. By 1370, richly decorated floats, artificial arches, towers, and even stages for acted tableaux were added to the festivities, and entries became elaborate dramatic ceremonies. Their popularity was enormous, and by the time of the Renaissance entries were more numerous than monarchs. Between 1443 and 1598 Italy enjoyed twenty-five entries, England and Flanders saw more than fifty, and France a hundred.

Sometimes an alien or a distrusted monarch showed the populace—his audience—a magnificent procession of costumed marchers and richly decorated floats. Far more often, however, a beloved monarch became himself the audience—a peripatetic one—as he passed a mile or more of spectacular displays that had been built and painted by a thousand or more workmen and artists. Among the sights to impress the eye of the sovereign were structures with one or more stages. Sometimes two stages shared a single platform; sometimes one was above the other.

Upon these stages there first appeared dumbshows, or *tableaux vivants*, sometimes with modelled figures, sometimes with living actors. Lettered scrolls presented what we might call "subtitles" to the silent scenes. Later, English playwrights such as Peele, Jonson, and Dekker wrote speeches and poems of welcome, and even little passages of dialog. In medieval times the subjects enacted were religious. Later, mythological figures welcomed the ruler.

Early in the Renaissance some of the entry stages displayed elaborate scenic effects. Clouds rose and descended with their divine freight. Curtains were used before they appeared in the Italian theater. Revolving stages turned the scene from a dead tree and a desolate landscape to a verdant prospect; this was half a century before the Renaissance artists introduced scene-changing devices in their theaters.

Entries often ended with a spectacular performance in the ruler's palace, along with a dance and a banquet. In 1489 such a show occurred in the ducal palace at Milan to celebrate a noble nuptial. For *Il Paradiso*, a flattering mythological episode by an inferior poet, Leonardo da Vinci designed a mountain top the two halves of which split at the front and swung back to reveal a glittering heaven. Such were the spectacular pleasures of the court theater of the Renaissance, with or without the excuse of an entry or a wedding.

LATIN COMEDY
FROM THE MIDDLE AGES

A third root of the Renaissance theater is long; it leads far back into the Dark Ages. Perhaps it is tenuous, yet it seems to account for the extraordinary speed with which the Revival of Learning swept Italy and most of Christendom, and it may explain why certain Roman plays were the first to be produced in the Renaissance and were long the most popular.

The dying Empire of the Caesars left Europe the legacy of an international language. The innumerable dialects of a disjointed continent could serve only the local peasants and craftsmen. Confined to small areas, these crude tongues were too limited in words and sentence structure for the exchange of significant and sophisticated ideas. And so, churchmen and princes, wandering scholars and itinerant merchants, literate men of every part of middle and western Europe read, wrote, and spoke Latin.

It took no Revival of Learning to rediscover Roman comedy. Among the manuscripts slowly gathered together, first on monastery shelves and later in the universities during the Middle Ages, were eight plays by Plautus and six by Terence. Renaissance research added twelve more from Plautus, but scholars had read his *Menaechmi* (*The Brothers*) centuries before Ercole d'Este made it his second production at Ferrara in 1486, as well as Plautus' *Amphitruo*, which was his third.

In medieval days the ribald buffoonery of Plautus doubtless attracted the interest of the kind of young cleric who delighted in the Feast of Fools. The soberer brothers preferred the more refined Terence, and they often adapted his plays for performance in the schools. A German nun named Hroswitha seems to have been equally attracted by the pleasures of playacting and the style of Terence, yet she was fearful that the pagan plots would corrupt the sisterhood. Accordingly, Hroswitha wrote six Latin plays in the Terentian manner, but she used for her characters such figures from Christian history as Abraham, Paphnutius, and Dulcitius. The churchmen of the Renaissance were not so righteously fastidious. Clerics laughed over Plautus's tales of bawdry when they saw them acted. Before Pius II was elevated to the papacy he wrote a witty and indecent comedy modelled on the Roman. Plautus as well as Terence was popular at the Vatican toward the end of the fifteenth century.

THE FIRST THEATER
AND THE FIRST SCENERY?

It is easier to speculate over the medieval rudiments of the Renaissance theater than it is to describe accurately its beginnings in Italy. Who built the first temporary theater and where? When did true scenery first appear? Who was the first producer—a prince of the church or a prince of the state? There are no good answers to any of these questions.

One authority says that "Alberti put a *theatrum* in the palace built in the Vatican for Nicholas V in 1452, but there is no record of its use for dramatic performances at that time." The writer doesn't cite his source for this, or explain that *theatrum* can mean a place for exhibition as well as a permanent playhouse. With no more evidence to go on, a second authority writes that "Alberti designed a theater proper for Pope Nicholas V." A third scholar implies that in 1486 Duke Ercole d'Este had his architect build a theater based on the writings of the Roman architect Vitruvius. A fourth identifies this playhouse with the one that seems to have been built for the poet–playwright Ariosto in 1532 and that burned down the next year, leaving not a trace of plans or sketches. All this confusion comes from the fact that many a nobleman or prelate had a habit of turning a great hall into a temporary showplace by putting a scaffolded stage and sometimes a proscenium frame at one end—while it all came down when the performance was over.

There is also some confusion over when scenery was first used and what it looked like. A Renaissance writer praised Cardinal Riario because he "first equipped a stage for Tragedy beautifully" in an outdoor production, probably between 1484 and 1486, and mentioned that the cardinal "first revealed to our age the appearance of a painted scene." But was this a true setting appropriate to the place and action of the drama? We know that a number of famous artists painted backgrounds that had no relation to the plays performed in palace halls. The elephant and the other figures in Mantegna's panels *The Triumph of Caesar* were no more appropriate than their title to the comedies of Plautus, *The Brothers* and *The Carthagenian*, which were acted in the great hall of the Marquis of Mantua in 1490 and for which the artist especially created these paintings on paper.

From a contemporary account we know that when the remarkable patron of the theater Ercole d'Este produced *Menaechmi* in 1486 it was in a courtyard and upon "a wooden stage with five battlemented houses. There was a window and a door in each. Then a ship came in . . . and crossed the courtyard. It had ten persons in it and was fitted with oars and a sail in a most realistic manner." The next year Ercole provided "a paradise with stars" for Plautus' *Amphitruo*. We have mentioned Leonardo's *Il Paradiso* of 1489. And in 1491 Ercole revived *Menaechmi* indoors and had Nicollo del Cogo paint "a prospect of four castles." Certainly as early as the 1480s scenery was achieving illusion.

ACADEMICIANS AS PRODUCERS

In this same decade the Roman Academy began producing Latin comedies and an occasional tragedy by Seneca. Soon many other academies were set up in many other cities, most of them staging Roman plays or helping their princes to stage them. Within a century, a group of scholars and aristocrats, gathered together under the imposing title of the Olympic Academy, made the first enduring attempt to build a permanent theater on the classic model.

The academies of the Renaissance were extraordinary institutions, curious, powerful, and unique. Taking their title from the *Academia*—a grove near ancient Athens where the philosopher Plato taught—these dedicated bodies of scholars became the heart of humanism, the chief agents of the Revival of Learning. Their passionate zeal infected churchmen and nobles, and their discoveries of classic art, architecture, and literature turned the study of antiquity into a fashionable pursuit. Aided by the printing press, word of what the academies found and learned spread throughout Europe with amazing speed.

Unfortunately, these Italian scholars frowned upon their native tongue as a means of artistic expression. Deserting the language that had served Dante and Petrarch so well, they spoke only Latin in their meetings and wrote their books and dissertations in the same ancient tongue. They even latinized their names; the leader of the Roman Academy, Giulio Pomponio Leto, became Julius Pomponius Laetus. This academic fervor for a dead language has left its mark today on the diplomas that certain universities give to "Jacobus Petrus Miller" and "Guilelmus Henricus McFadden."

Another peculiarity of these scholars was their extraordinary fondness for the drama. Pomponius Laetus launched the Roman Academy into competition with the Duke of Ferrara as the pioneer producer of Roman plays, and other academies followed.

We do not know for certain what kind of setting Cardinal Riario supplied for the performances of the Roman Academy on the Capitoline Hill or in the tomb of Hadrian, called the Castel Sant' Angelo, or within the cardinal's palace. Certainly scenic designers can't have gained much from Vitruvius, the Roman whose scanty contributions to our knowledge of the classic theater we have mentioned. His book on architecture, discovered by the Italians in 1414, and published in the original Latin in 1486, described houses with painted columns and other architectural details, but it told nothing about how they were arranged upon the stage. To solve that problem, the early scene designers seem to have turned back to the multiple stages and arcades used in the entries and provided four or five doorways curtained under arches and separated by ornate columns. Thus each character had a "house" with his name neatly lettered above his door. In an edition of Terence published in 1493 there is a setting of this kind. One of the curtains is drawn aside to show an inner room with a window.

THE FIRST PERMANENT THEATERS IN ITALY

From this simple beginning it took long experiments in the designing of scenery, stage machines, and playhouses to bring forth the first modern type of theater, the Teatro Farnese of Parma, about 1618. After Ariosto's theater of 1532 in Ferrara, about which we know nothing, the next permanent building especially erected for the production of plays was the Teatro Olimpico in Vicenza. A distinguished architect, Andrea Palladio, designed it for the Olympic Academy of that city and began its erection in 1580. It was the first attempt to recreate what the academicians thought was a Roman

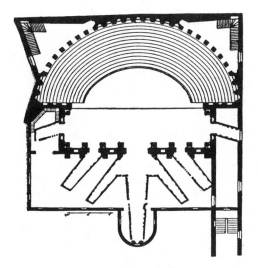

Figure 3.1　An Italian Renaissance Theater
This is a plan of the Teatro Olimpico. (From Moritz, *Das Antike Theater*, and Cheney, *The Theater*.)

theater. The thirteen rows of seats followed the shape of an ellipse instead of a semi-circle, thus providing better sight lines and more intimacy. There was a flat orchestra floor for the chorus and a raised and raked stage backed by a long wall with three doorways, flanked by two shorter ones, each with a single opening. For the central opening, Palladio adopted the triumphal arch that Roman conquerors built to celebrate their return from victorious campaigns. He probably intended either to close the openings with curtains or doors or perhaps to place *periaktoi* behind them. He died, however, in 1580, and the man who took over the completion of the theater, Vicenzo Scamozzi, made a radical change. Behind the five doorways he built short vistas of streets—three from the central arch—all radiating out like the spokes of a wheel. Built of wood and plaster, with three-dimensional ornament, they reproduced in violently forced perspective certain streets in a town of Boeotia in Greece.

The Teatro Olimpico was finished in 1584, and opened the next year with an elaborate production of Sophocles' *Oedipus Rex* in Italian, involving special music and a cast of 108. The opening performance on March 3, 1585, was described by Filippo Pigafetta:

> . . . *The theater can easily accommodate 3,000 spectators. It is*
> *such a charming sight that everybody is usually pleased by it*
> *due to the exquisite beauty of its proportions. The eyes of the*
> *layman receive the overall impression of an incredible loveli-*
> *ness, which arises from the friezes, architraves, cornices, fes-*
> *toons, columns with very beautiful capitals, and bases with*
> *many metropes sculptured in low stucco relief. . . . The stage*
> *perspective is likewise admirable, very well understood and*
> *seen, with its five principal sections, or rather entrances, which*
> *represent the seven streets of Thebes. . . . When the time had*
> *come to lower the curtain, a very sweet smell of perfume made*
> *itself felt to indicate that in the city of Thebes, according to the*
> *ancient legend, incense was burned to placate the wrath of the*
> *gods. Then there was a sound of trumpets and drums, and four*
> *squibs exploded. In a twinkle of an eye the curtain fell before*
> *the stage. . . . Then began the tragedy proper, and not one*
> *point was missed throughout the entire action. The actors are of*
> *the best sort, and they are dressed neatly and lavishly accord-*
> *ing to each one's station. The King had a guard of twenty-four*
> *archers dressed in Turkish fashion, pages, and courtiers. The*
> *Queen was surrounded by matrons, ladies in waiting, and*
> *pages. Her brother, Creon, was likewise accompanied by an*
> *appropriate entourage. The chorus consisted of 15 persons,*
> *seven on each side, and their leader in the center.* *

In the small town of Sabbioneta, Scamozzi tried an even more radical experiment. At the end of the 1580s, Duke Vespasiano Gonzaga of Mantua, who had provided the town of Sabbioneta with a palace, a mint, and a printing plant, all on a small scale, decided to build a tiny theater for the *Academia dei Confidenti*. Because of the smallness of the structure—it seated only two hundred fifty against Olimpico's three thousand—Scamozzi was apparently forced to give up multiple doorways in favor of a single vista that began at the very sides of the stage.

The theater in Sabbioneta may have influenced another architect, Giambattista Aleotti, when he designed the Teatro Farnese in Parma, twenty miles away. The auditorium was highly conven-

*A. M. Nagler, *A Source Book in Theatrical History* (New York: Dover Publications, Inc., 1952), pp. 81–86. Copyright © 1952 by A. M. Nagler. Reprinted by permission of the publisher.

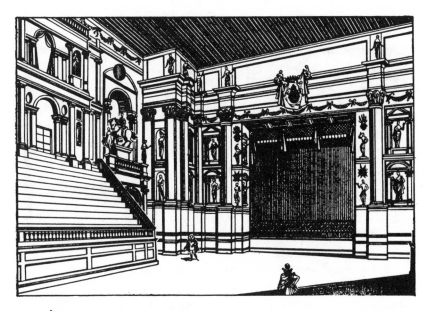

Figure 3.2   The Teatro Farnese
The modern picture-frame opening and curtain was built by the Prince of Parma in 1618 or 1619. The audience occupied the rising horseshoe of seats and the floor (which was sometimes flooded to make a sea for boats) as well. *(Drawing by Gerda Becker With.)*

tional. A horseshoe of raised seats held thirty-five hundred spectators, and between it and the stage was an orchestra floor that was used for spectacle and even flooded for at least one production. The stage, however, was almost modern in design. It had a wide proscenium and a deep stage behind. It is rather surprising that the Teatro Farnese had no curtain when it opened in 1618, for curtains had been often used in court spectacles. Ariosto had employed one in the production of his play *I Suppositi* at the Vatican in 1519. In his poem *Orlando Furioso* he writes of what was to be seen "at the curtain-fall," because, as in ancient Rome, the curtains of the Renaissance usually descended into a trough instead of being raised.

The Teatro Farnese, rebuilt after bomb damage in World War II, and the theaters in Vicenza and Sabbioneta remain as living evidence—along with designs for scenery and contemporary de-

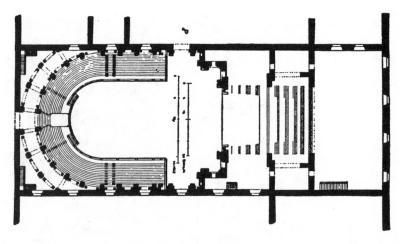

Figure 3.3   The Teatro Farnese in Parma
This theater may be seen in greater detail on the preceding page.

scriptions of theatrical productions—of the energy that artists and academicians, princes and popes, devoted to their attempts to recreate the classic stage. Except on a very few occasions, their enormous and feverish activity brought forth a theatrical art that

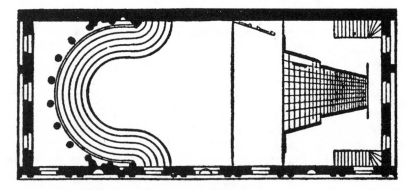

Figure 3.4   The Theater in Sabbioneta
The smallness of the stage seems to have forced the architect to provide only one proscenium. Nearby Parma may have been influenced by this when the Teatro Farnese was build. (Both plans from Moritz, *Das Antike Theater*, and Cheney, *The Theater*.)

was not at all classic. Like other creators of the Italian Renaissance, they tried to emulate the ancients, and they ended by being highly original. The Teatro Olimpico was a plausible imitation of the past; the Teatro Farnese a startling preview of the future.

SCANT GUIDANCE FROM VITRUVIUS

The reason for the failure of the academicians as archaeologists of the theater and for their success as originators of a new visual art lay in what we would now call a lack of source material. Take Vitruvius and his *De Architectura*, which dominated theatrical theory for nearly three centuries. This revered book was almost the only key that the Renaissance had to the classic theater, and, as we have already said, Vitruvius supplied very little useful information. Yet his account of the *periaktoi*, his observations about perspective in the theater, and his description of the three kinds of classic settings were enough to set the greatest of Italian artists—Mantegna, Brunelleschi, Ghirlandajo, Michelangelo, Andrea del Sarto, Raphael, and Leonardo da Vinci—to painting scenery on many occasions. Lesser men like Bramante and Peruzzi (as absorbed as Paolo Uccello in thinking, "Oh, what a delightful thing is this perspective!") became scenic specialists.

SERLIO ON THE CRAFT OF THE SCENE PAINTER

In 1545 one of Peruzzi's pupils, Sebastiano Serlio, an architect as well as a painter, brought together in Book II of his *Architettura* what he believed was the nature of the classic theater, as sifted through Vitruvius, and what he knew were the stage practices of his contemporaries. He was the first to publish drawings of the three types of classic scenery: the tragic set with its lofty palaces, the comic set with its ordinary city houses, and the set for the satyr play with its landscape of trees, hills, and cottages. Far more important, he described how he—and, we may presume, the other designers—built and painted scenery.

Thus we know that the settings of his time combined false perspective with certain three-dimensional elements. The backing was flat, but the wings were bent at an angle like the splayed-out corner of a house, and they sported cornices and other architectural ornaments. "I made all my scenes of laths covered with linen, the cornice bearing out." The retreating sides of his wings were cut and painted in false perspective so that all the horizontal lines slanted backward and downward to the vanishing point of the scene painted on the backing. The wings toward the rear were treated somewhat differently from those farther "downstage." Serlio wrote: "if you make any flat buildings, they must stand somewhat farre inward, that you may not see them on the sides." These "upstage" wings had no raised cornices or other three-dimensional ornaments: "the Painting worke must supplie the place by shadows without any bossing out."

If the tops of the wings and the houses painted on them should slant downward to a distant vanishing point, why shouldn't their bases slant upward? In an effort to make false perspective as complete as possible, Serlio gave his stage what we call a "rake." The first few feet were flat; then the floor rose steadily toward the back. We do not know when raked stages came into general use, but they remained in fashion till late Victorian days. Slanting stage floors are still to be found in some old European theaters, and "upstage" and "downstage" remain part of the common theatrical vocabulary.

Serlio provided a good deal of information on how to imitate thunder and lightning and to move mechanical figures of men, animals, or planets on invisible wires. He explained how to create colored light by placing a bottle of red wine or colored water in front of a torch and how to reflect it upon the stage by means of a "bright Basin" behind the torch.

From 1500 to 1650 Italian scene designers used other scenic patterns besides the angular, two-sided wings and the backdrop. One used prisms, or *periaktoi*, and another employed flat wings and backings composed of two great screens. The prisms may have been used mostly in single pairs on the flat forestage with wings and backdrops on the raked floor behind them. But in 1583 an Italian, da Vignola, printed a stage plan with two *periaktoi* on each side of the stage and a very large prism taking the place of the backdrop. In 1632 the German architect Furtenbach recommended the use of *periaktoi*, and in 1638 the Italian Sabbatini provided detailed plans for their use.

THEATER PRACTICE ACCORDING TO SABBATINI

Sabbatini's book of 1638, *Practica di fabricar scene e machine ne' teatri*, dealt elaborately with scenic perspective and machines for creating stage effects such as descending clouds and rolling waves. Sabbatini also explained various ways of making quick scene changes. The three-sided *periaktoi* could be made even more versatile by fastening extra flats on the sides that had been seen and were now turned away from the audience. Painted cloths could be pulled across the two-sided wings. Sabbatini showed how groups of three or four angular wings could be nested behind one another along each side of the stage, and how the innermost wing in each group could be moved back to cover the front wing of the next group to the rear, thus changing the setting.

It seems likely that *periaktoi*—which presented great difficulties on a raked stage—were much less popular than the bent, or angled, wings and particularly the flat wings, which were introduced as early as 1600 and which continued in almost universal use well into the nineteenth century. To make quick scene changes, three or four of these wings were placed one behind another in groups on each side of the stage; when the downstage ones were withdrawn the corresponding backdrop was "flown" or lowered into the basement; or, if it consisted of a great screen-like structure split in the middle, the two halves were pulled away to reveal a new pair. These flat wings were often set in grooves, which persisted down to 1900 in some small playhouses. At the turn of the century our theaters still used the "sky borders" invented during the Renaissance to complete the setting. Sabbatini and other artists went beyond this, however, when they used curved and slanting sections of sky-painted canvas six feet wide to form a series of arches over the stage.

Elaborate devices for quickly changing scenes bring up a point that has been curiously neglected. Until the last quarter of the nineteenth century, scene changing was done in full view of the audience. It was part of the entertainment. People enjoyed watching one scene magically dissolve into another. The idea persisted in the transformation scenes of extravaganzas and pantomimes not so many decades ago. Then why did the Roman, the Renaissance, and

Figure 3.5 Flat Wings for Walls

In addition to the *periaktoi*, the Italians developed "wings" to represent houses or walls along the sides of the stage. At first they were placed diagonally; soon they were placed parallel to the backing. Flat wings persisted in many places up until the First World War. The example shown here is from the Drottningholm Palace Theater in Sweden; first made in the eighteenth century, these wings were for a time forgotten, but they were discovered in 1922. Typically they ran in grooves, top and bottom. They show the means used for obtaining false perspective. (Drawing by Gerda Becker With.)

the Restoration theaters all have curtains? They were there merely to hide the first setting and to close the play. Until about 1800 in England there was no "act curtain": The audience knew that the act was over when all the players left the stage. And in England until 1881 there was no curtain to hide changes of scene during an act; then Henry Irving introduced the so-called "scene curtain" to hide 135 stagehands, property men, and gas men who were involved with large set-pieces in *The Corsican Brothers*.

Illusion was the aim of the Renaissance designer. Whether or not he used three-dimensional ornament—"bossing out"—or angular wings for the corners of houses, he depended on the wonders of perspective to rival the reality that his audience saw and loved in the murals and canvases of great painters like Michelangelo and da Vinci. And yet, as time passed, no matter how deftly this flat scenery of wings and backdrop was painted in false perspective, it came to seem artificial and "theatrical." For the audiences of the twentieth century, the illusion was gone. Such settings were only for the ballet, and they had to be painted by as great a scenic artist as Leon Bakst of the Ballets Russes.

As a matter of fact, during the Renaissance such scenery was indeed painted by great artists, and it was used, in the main, for something quite as artificial as ballet.

ARTIFICIAL SETTINGS FOR ARTIFICIAL SPECTACLES

As we have told you, the academies and certain princes like Ercole d'Este made a great to-do about reviving Plautus, Terence, and Seneca, while Serlio, Sabbatini, and other designers claimed that they were reproducing the classic stage via Vitruvius. But most of the extraordinary scenes and machines of the Renaissance were not contrived for plays at all—whether Latin, Greek, or Italian. These Gargantuan marvels were lavished on court entertainments dealing with mythological or allegorical subjects and made up of pantomime, dance, song, recitation, and pageantry. Sometimes the occasion was a state wedding or the visit of a foreign prince. Often the spectacular show was interjected between the acts of a Latin play; whether it was a tragedy or a comedy made no difference. These extravagant and amazing interruptions were called *intermezzi* or *intermedii*.

One of the chief creators of such spectacles in the last half of the sixteenth century was Bernardo Buontalenti of Florence, who earned the nickname *delle Girandole* ("of the fireworks") because he turned his hand to pyrotechnic displays quite as readily as to the design of palaces, gardens, fortresses, and military machines. Here is a description of one of his scenic effects:

> *In the third* intermedio *the scene represented a bare landscape as in a severe winter; beds of rivers and torrents, all dry and hard, were to be seen, when suddenly from the west Zephyr was seen to issue forth from a subterranean cave; she held the beautiful Flora by the hand, and sang a most lovely song with her; at the sound of this Spring appeared, with other festive deities, loves, winds, nymphs, and satyrs; and while all these together danced on the stage, the trees were seen to flourish again and renew their leaves.*

Well into the seventeenth century this type of show lingered on as the chief vehicle of display for Renaissance stagecraft. Since it was given by and for the court and not for the public, money was no object. Serlio advised his fellow designers "never to take care what it shall cost." Extravagances reflect favorably on the prince, "for they are things which stately and great persons do, which are enemies of niggardliness." The ruler gave only three or four of these shows a year. For each production, the artist built a new stage in the great hall of the palace—or rebuilt the last one—only to clear it out when the performance was over. Under such conditions there could have been no true playhouse even if the artist–designer had not chosen—as he always did choose—to spill the entertainment off the raised stage and out onto the floor of the hall in a kind of dancing pageant. Here, too, they were following classic tradition. The Greeks danced in the *orchestra*.

"PASTORALS" AND OPERA

The scenic spectacles of the Renaissance found its most legitimate use in two new forms of entertainment. They were forms that came rather late, and they tended to confine the designer to a raised stage and a proscenium arch.

The first was the *pastoral*, a poetic play on a rustic subject. Superficially it may seem an offshoot of the sort of mythological fable that young Politian wrote for Ercole d'Este in 1471, which others imitated. Actually it was a new kind of drama. Instead of following the loose form of the medieval mystery play, the author used a tighter, more dramatic structure. In general, shepherds and shepherdesses, nymphs and fauns, replaced the heroes and heroines of Greek mythology. The scenes became bucolic, and a myrtle grove or an Arcadian landscape with a humble cottage replaced a multiple setting of Olympus, Hades, an Attic palace, and so forth. Sometimes these plays were given in the garden theaters, with backgrounds and wings of clipped hedges, that graced the estates of great nobles in the sixteenth century. Pastorals became enormously popular with the aristocracy and courtiers; their ladies often played the parts of rustics and dryads. Torquato Tasso's *Aminta*, written and produced in 1573, and Battista Guarini's later pastoral *The Faithful Shepherd* were the most successful. Twenty contemporary translations of *Aminta* into French and nine into English testified to the popularity of this early form of the theater of escapism. In the seventeenth century, Inigo Jones, traveler as well as artist, developed from the Italian pastoral the elaborate court masque that Elizabeth I and James I delighted in.

Opera was the second new form of drama to come out of Italy. The earliest pieces seem related to Politian's *Orfeo*, to the pastorals, and even to the *intermezzi*, for all of these used music and song. But authorities claim that the birth of opera was a sheer accident. In 1595 a group of scholars and musicians, the Camerata of Florence, tried to imitate what they thought was Greek tragedy by telling, in *Dafne*, a mythological story in poetic dialog against a musical background. Other experiments followed *Dafne*, and opera became immensely popular with the common people after 1637, when Venice opened the first public theater. By 1700, Venice alone had built eleven more opera houses and produced some three hundred sixty operas, and this mixture of music, drama, and spectacle had spread triumphantly through all Italy to France, Austria, Germany, and England. An Italian enthusiast asserted in 1608 that in opera "the intellect and every noblest sentiment are fascinated at one and the same time by the most delectable arts ever devised by human genius." For over three hundred years opera has remained Italy's favorite form of theater art.

A MAGNIFICENT THEATER BUT NO LASTING PLAYS

Renaissance Italy produced great painting, sculpture, and architecture. It invented opera, and saw Claudio Monteverdi make it a respectable art form through his revolutionary contributions to musical technique. Italians set the shape of the modern theater, and they were its first scenic designers. But, though Dante, Petrarch, and Boccaccio opened the Renaissance with immortal poetry and prose, Italy produced no plays of lasting value. Her playwrights held no more than a guttering candle to the scenic marvels of their stage.

There are a number of possible explanations. No one of them is wholly satisfactory. Added together they may solve this greatest of enigmas in the history of the theater.

Some believed that the Italian Renaissance produced no good plays because the theater placed too much emphasis on scenic display. They can quote from a writer of 1508 who commented upon a play by Ariosto:

> *The subject was a most beautiful one of two youths enamored of two harlots who had been brought to Taranto by a pander. . . . But what was best in all these festivities and representations has been the scenery in which they have been played . . . a view in perspective of a town with houses, churches, belfrys and gardens, such that one could never tire of looking at it, because of the different things that are there all most cleverly designed and executed.*

Not so many years ago critics who were hostile to the so-called "new stagecraft" assailed Adolphe Appia, Gordon Craig, and Max Reinhardt, along with modern devices for changing scenes, as destructive of the growth of true drama. Yet it was in this fifty-year period of scenic rejuvenation that dramatists such as Maeterlinck and Sartre, Shaw and Fry, O'Neill and Miller appeared, while the stage found new and more effective means to keep Shakespeare alive and vibrant.

In the very thing that stimulated and created the Renaissance theater—the rediscovery of the classic stage—lies another and a better reason for the shortcomings of Italian drama. Touched by the academic mania for Latin, many playwrights ignored their mother tongue. Worse still, they imitated the debased Roman drama instead of the Greek. Some turned out adaptations of the dry, rhetorical tragedies of Seneca. More of them imitated the comedies of Plautus and Terence, thus pushing them further into obscenity. Academicians accepted what they thought were the "classic rules" of dramaturgy, added some misinterpretations of their own, and forced them on much of the drama of Italy and France through a good part of the sixteenth century.

Yet the sad state of the Italian playwrights cannot be blamed entirely on idolatry of the classics. Those who wrote in Italian and on Italian subjects were not much better than those who wrote in Latin. Their plays were more popular in appeal, but they were often shallow or vicious. After the pastoral *Aminta*, Tasso turned to the incestuous horrors of *Torrismondo*. Although Ariosto wrote plays of contemporary life he followed the patterns of Roman comedy and never approached the distinction of his own romantic epic *Orlando Furioso*. Machiavelli forgot all the academic rules and wrote sharp, bitter comedies of his times.

It was, perhaps, the social and political atmosphere of the Italian Renaissance that worked most heavily against the creation of a significant and lasting drama. Throughout the Renaissance, Italy was a country of petty states dominated by native autocrats and oligarchies, or ruled over by Spain, France, the Holy Roman Empire, or the Papacy. The closest approach to national peace lasted less than fifty years—from 1447 to 1492—and it was interrupted by intermittent local struggles between some of the city-states; at best, the despots built their power on corruption and cunning instead of open violence. In the fourteenth and the six-

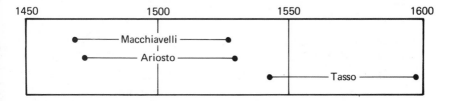

Figure 3.6 Italians of the Renaissance
Machiavelli's playwriting was confined to the last third of his life. Ariosto and Tasso began their work for the theater when they were about thirty.

teenth centuries, the people were held in subjection by mercenary armies and through half of the fifteenth by murder and guile. Against this picture of martial and political violence we must balance the courtly ideal of the perfect prince, exemplified by Ercole d'Este and Francesco Sforza. The prince and his courtiers aspired to the highest ideal of humanism: "the complete man," the embodiment of culture. But this was an idealistic conception that reached the people only through the magnificent palaces and churches and the beautiful paintings and statues that glorified the rulers of Italy and masked their political crimes. Where Italian princes ruled and the arts flourished, cruelty and corruption went hand in hand with culture. And because there was no free nation and there were no free cities, Italy had no staunch and patriotic citizenry. It lacked the sound, vigorous, self-reliant, and ambitious populace that loved and dominated the theater of Madrid and London.

For almost two centuries, the theater and its plays were dedicated to a very limited—and limiting—audience. It was an audience of scholars who were often pedants, churchmen who were sometimes far too worldly, and courtiers who were usually intemperate in all things. The audience broadened somewhat as Italian dialog replaced Latin, but it was never the vigorous and imaginative audience that nourished Lope de Vega in Spain and Shakespeare in England. The fine arts can flourish under princely patronage, for the artist works alone. But the dramatist can live only in the public theater where a play is a product of cooperation between writer, actors, and a vital audience. And when at last Italy built playhouses for the populace, opera took over.

THE PEOPLE'S THEATER

By 1550 scholars, painters, and poets—blessed and be-moneyed by the princes of church and state—had evolved a spectacular stage for an insignificant drama. In the next seventy years Italy built three permanent theaters and accidentally invented opera. All this was the product of amateur effort, amateur in the worst sense as well as the best, and it was limited in vital quality and appeal. This aristocratic theater became professional and found a popular audience— two essential steps in the development of theatrical art—only when

Italy began to spawn opera houses in the last half of the seventeenth century.

But another sort of professional theater was finding its popular audience around 1550. It was a theater of boards and trestles and of an audience that stood in the public square. Its actors passed the hat among the spectators and then delighted the mob with improvised comedy. They had no written plays. But their brains as well as their bodies were so nimble, and their comedic art became so perfect, that they invaded Spain and the Teutonic countries, conquered Paris, and even played in London.

This theater was the *commedia dell'arte*. It got its name only when it was passing out of existence in the eighteenth century. The term *dell'arte* was a critical accolade. Those words signified that there was nothing of the amateur about the comedians and their comedy. Just as today the phrase "the profession" means people who know and practice the special art of acting, *arte*—as the English critic Allardyce Nicoll points out—meant the special art of playing these comedies.

There had been earlier names for this kind of theater, and they had defined its peculiar nature. One was *commedia all'improviso*, which meant that the plays were improvised. The other, *commedia a soggetto*, indicated that the actors improvised their comedies upon a "subject," or plot.

AN ART OF PLOTS AND "BUSINESS"

The *scenarios*, as we now call the plots of the *commedia dell'arte*, were bare outlines of the action. Each was the prompt book of the play and was posted backstage—when there was a stage in the modern sense—so that no actor might miss his cue or play the wrong scene. The head of the troupe went over the scenario with the actors when a new comedy was to be given or an old one revived. He explained the action, the pantomimic "business," and the use of the "props."

Fortunately two Italians wrote about the *commedia dell'arte* in the latter half of the seventeenth century when it was still alive, and we have reports or outlines of some seven hundred scenarios. Almost all are comedies. A few are pastoral in nature, and there are what we now call tragi-comedies. Only a few of the plots written down before 1600 have been preserved in manuscript, but, since most stage material was acted by troupes for generation after generation, many of the earliest scenarios may be among the seven hundred that we now have.

From the seventeenth-century writers we know that not all the performance was improvised. There were written prologs that had little to do with the plot, and there were also set speeches—delivered as soliloquies—with which an actor closed a scene or made an exit. These often ended in rhymed couplets such as we find in Shakespeare, while musical duets, interrupting the action, were written and rehearsed before production.

A writer of 1634 says that "the actors engage in study and load their memories with a great mass of matter, such as stock sentiments, conceits, love speeches, complaints, ejaculations of despair and madness, which they keep ready for all occasions." It is no wild guess that when a company had played an improvised comedy a number of times, most of the dialog had been committed to memory.

A curious feature of the *commedia dell'arte* were the *lazzi*—jokes of one sort or another interjected into the plot. Some of these were verbal.

> *The* lazzo *of Pulcinella's goodness is that he, hearing from the Capitano or another that they wish to kill him, and not being known to them in person, praises himself, saying "Pulcinella is a witty, straightforward, good fellow."*

Most *lazzi* were physical—what we call "stage business." Often they had nothing to do with the action. While two lovers were engaged with their troubles, a comic servant might pretend to catch a fly or eat imaginary cherries from his hat and flip the pits into the hero's face. A special way of tripping up an opponent was considered a *lazzo*. Here, in the words of an Italian comedian, is a specimen that might have come out of an American burlesque show:

> *I find Trivelin stretched on the ground. I think him dead and try to drag him to his feet; then I let my wooden sword fall down. He takes it and hits me on the buttocks . . . I seize and carry him; I lean him against the wings on the righthand side*

*of the stage. I look around at the footlights, and meanwhile he
gets up and leans against the lefthand sidewings. This* lazzo *is
repeated two or three times.*

THE STOCK CHARACTERS

Two things gave the *commedia dell'arte* real distinction and even a
kind of immortality. The first was deft acting; it was praised and
imitated in Spain and France, where its impact was enormous. The
other was the set of characters that the actors slowly created. Many
of their names and figures are familiar today, and some have appeared in England's Christmas pantomimes. In somewhat the same
fashion as the Italians, the comedians of our own radio, television,
and burlesque shows build up individual characters that they play
year in and year out.

Each of the seven men and three women that made up a typical
company played a certain stock figure as long as he was young, or
old, enough. Originally these characters had each been created by
one particular actor. Gradually other actors gave them different
dialects, and changed them in small ways. But certain types were
unchanging, indestructible. The least interesting were the lovers—
the *innamorati*. They looked and dressed like any young people of
the time. Their names were usually the names of the actors and
actresses who played them.

The comic characters were of many kinds. There were almost
always two old men, close relatives of figures in Greek and Roman
farce. One was Pantalone, a money-minded Venetian. He has come
down to us as Shakespeare's "lean and slippered pantaloon" and as
Molière's Harpagon in *The Miser*. The other, Il Dottore, was a
doctor of laws, seldom a physician. Always interfering with other
people's business, he still appears in Rossini's *The Barber of Seville*
and in Mozart's *The Marriage of Figaro*.

A group of *zanni*—from which we get "zanies"—were younger
fun-makers and expert dancers. Arlecchino began as a stupid servant full of pranks. Later he became a smart fellow, and still later
his patched clothes took on the decorative diamond patterns of our
present day Harlequin. Pedrolino, another servant, became the
French Pièrrot, while Pulcinella was metamorphosized into the
humpbacked English Punch. Other comic figures—like cowardly

Brighella, Mezzetino with his red-and-white striped suit, and braggart Il Capitano—are to be found in Callot's engravings and Watteau's oils. In Colombina the Italians gave their heroines a confidante and mischief-maker whom we have turned into Columbine. She was also the progenitor of our musical comedy soubrette.

A most peculiar feature of the *commedia dell'arte* was that all the comedians, and occasionally Colombina, wore masks. Sometimes the masks covered the whole face, sometimes half the face, and sometimes, as in the case of Arlecchino, Pedrolino, and Colombina, just the eyes. Since so many scenes in the *commedia dell'arte* depended on pantomime, it seems strange that the comedians should have sacrificed the mobile expressiveness of their faces. The masks, however, permitted stylized exaggeration of the features appropriate to the characters.

The various companies founded in the sixteenth century rejoiced in interesting names: I Fedeli (The Faithful), I Desiosi (The Desirous), I Confidenti (The Confident), I Accesi (The Inspired), and—the most famous in its time—I Gelosi (The Zealous). Today we have contracts signed by the actors of such companies, contracts that sometimes required periodic attendance at the confessional or that prohibited swearing.

The lesser troupes traveled from town to town in Italy. The more renowned confined themselves to the larger cities. Traveling troupes usually carried their properties and simple stages with a curtain for backdrop. Whenever the strolling players had an opportunity to appear in real theaters, they made the most of scenery, stage machines, and the various special effects that Serlio and Sabbatini have described for us. There were difficulties, of course, when nobles invaded the stage to ogle the actresses, but at least one cardinal provided fines, stripes, or imprisonment for those who sat on the stage, stood in front of the actors, made unseemly noises, or threw "apples, nuts, or garbage at the comedians."

ITALY MAKES THEATER ABROAD

The *commedia dell'arte* was vastly popular with the Italian common people, but it had little effect on the Italian theater. Abroad the story was different. The influence of these comedians can be traced through France, Spain, and England, and, later, Germany. Italian companies won the favor of the French court as well as of the Paris populace. They played with great success in the courtyard theaters of Madrid. They went as far as London to appear before Elizabeth I and James I. They influenced great playwrights abroad if not in their own country. In *All's Well That Ends Well* Shakespeare modeled Captain Parolles on Il Capitano. The plot of *The Comedy of Errors* is as typical of the *commedia dell'arte* as is the charming scene in *The Taming of the Shrew* between fair Bianca and Lucentio disguised as her music teacher. The characters and the stories of the Italians inspired Molière to create *Tartuffe, The Miser, The Imaginary Invalid, George Dandin*, and *The Rogueries of Scapin*. But it was not till almost a hundred years after Molière that Italian playwrights, Goldoni and Gozzi, began to draw upon the rich store of the *commedia dell'arte.*

Through entries, court spectacles, revivals and adaptations of classic plays, *intermezzi*, pastorals, operas, elaborate scenery and stage machines, theaters at Vicenza and Parma, opera houses, and performances of the *commedia dell'arte*, the Italian Renaissance developed and enjoyed more varieties of theatrical activity than any other period in the history of the world—all this in the face of national disunity and internecine strife. But, though Italy created the modern playhouse, it could not create fine and enduring plays. And so this Renaissance was not the rebirth of the true theater.

4: SPAIN'S GOLDEN AGE

IN SPAIN—AT LAST
A FINE PROFESSIONAL THEATER

There was strife in Spain and there were alien conquerors—just as in Italy. But the Moors brought art and science with them in the Dark Ages of the eighth century, and only the ideological conflicts of Christianity, Judaism, and Mohammedanism stopped Spain from becoming a unified and glorious nation. And unity and glory were to come. For, while Italian princes intrigued for power or fought one another with mercenary armies, Spanish kings and the Spanish people drove down and out of Spain the followers of the Muslims who had conquered it seven hundred years before. In this struggle, peasants and townsmen won from their own native rulers a considerable amount of freedom through the abolition of serfdom, the granting of town charters, and the setting up of local and state legislatures called *municipios* and *cortes*. By 1492, the Spanish people were a united nation, vital and burgeoning. Then came imperial expansion and world power—quickening and exhilarating at first, but, as always and everywhere, poisonous and fatal in the end. Resurgent Spain discovered America, and while she was conquering much of the New World, one of her kings—as Charles V of the Holy Roman Empire—ruled the Netherlands, a number of German kingdoms, Burgundy, Sicily, Naples, and Sardinia. He captured Francis I of France, drove the Turks down the Danube, conquered Tunis, and, with a mercenary army, sacked Rome in 1527. The imperial power of Spain in Europe, shaken by the defeat of the Armada in 1588, crumbled away after the loss of the Netherlands in 1609. Yet at home, in the realm of art and literature, a "golden age" persisted for half a century more.

THE GROWTH OF A NATIONAL THEATER

The medieval theater begins in Spain much as in France and England and Germany—largely religious but partly profane. Perhaps it is delayed a bit because of Moorish domination over much of Spain and because of the early antagonism of the Catholic church. But, by the middle of the twelfth century, when half of Spain is freed, we know that someone has written a mystery play about the visit of the Magi to the newborn Jesus. Only 147 lines of dialog are left, but, like contemporary French scripts, they are written in the speech of the people instead of in Latin. In thirteenth-century Spain, just as in France, there are coarse and irreverent comedies. The Spaniards call them *juegos de escarnio*, or plays of mockery, and a king of Leon and Castile forbids the clergy to act in or even see them because they contain "much clowning and lewdness."

With the Renaissance, Spain breaks away to some extent from the Continental pattern. The power of the Catholic religion and the vitality of the Spanish people lie behind this. Sacred dramas continue until 1765—more than two centuries longer than on the rest of the Continent—many of them written by the best and most popular playwrights. The church frowns on humanistic worship of the pagan world, and the popular playwrights waste little time on sterile imitations of classic drama. But, above all, the Spanish audience is eager for romance and comedy and poetic drama, for heroic scenes out of Spanish history and legend, for "cloak and sword" plays laid in its own times, for comic and romantic intrigue, for anything of swift, theatric vitality. A number of secular plays appear before 1500, and within half a century their playwright–producers are creating a new kind of playhouse. Spain matches—and even anticipates—kindred plays and theaters of Elizabethan England.

SPANISH RELIGIOUS DRAMA— "AUTOS SACRAMENTALES"

In Spain the first religious plays, as well as the secular ones, were called *autos*—"actions" or "acts." The earliest sacred dramas seem to have been reenactments of stories from the Bible or the lives of the saints. When the feast of Corpus Christi, celebrating the Blessed Sacrament, became the favorite season for the production of religious plays, their form had changed. Even the first of these *autos sacramentales* differ from the French mystery plays in a number of ways. They seem nearer to the English moralities in dramatic treatment and in methods of production.

The basic material of the *autos sacramentales* could be any sacred subject from the Creation, through the Nativity, to the Day of Judgment. But the playwrights treated these events allegorically instead of literally. They replaced reenactment with a sort of dramatized imagery. A biblical figure became a man of the day. The devil turned into a pirate or a Moor. Abstract qualities or ideas took human form. Again and again we find characters called Death, Virtue, Jealousy, or Pestilence—just as in the English moralities—or even the Days of the Week.

Many elements in the physical production of *autos sacramentales* were common enough in France, but many seem English—or purely Spanish. There were great processions to the church, but these in Spain often involved fantastic figures of giants and monsters moved and animated by men inside. At one time or another the guilds of craftsmen took over from the priests much of the responsibility and all the labor of production. But the city fathers of Spain played a more and more important part; and in the sixteenth and seventeenth centuries they assumed authority and paid the bills, as well as provided us with invaluable records. The *autos sacramentales* were never thrust out of the medieval churches as the French mysteries were; but, after the performance before the high altar, the actors gave the plays, in a more elaborate form, at various spots where the arms of the city had been placed on high. The early *autos* were acted by priests and guildsmen. But, as far back as 1454, town records show that three dancers and jugglers were hired to appear in a religious play. In the next two centuries the best of professional companies were engaged for special productions, and successful dramatists like Gil Vicente, Lope de Vega, and Calderón wrote hundreds of sacred *autos*.

One phase of the Spanish performances was peculiar to this nation that has always loved the dance. This was the introduction of dancing into the very church itself. At first a typical *auto* went somewhat like this: After the parade through the streets, a priest placed the Blessed Sacrament on the altar of the church. Then came the performance for the clergy and the town council. Following the usual religious service, dancers performed where the play had been given before the Blessed Sacrament.

THE SPANISH "CARROS"—
LIKE ENGLISH PAGEANT WAGONS

When the dance was over, another parallel with medieval England appeared. The performers of the *autos* not only presented abstract characters like those of the English morality plays, they rode, like the English actors, on wagons that carried the scenery. The Spanish called their pageant wagons *carros* and their outdoor performance *La Fiesta de los Carros*—the festival of the carts. We should probably call these vehicles "wagons," or even "floats," for they must have been large and heavily built. Two features seem distinctively Spanish. At each stop the wagons were backed up against a platform on which the actors played important scenes. There was another kind of stage, which must have been used only in the parades, called *la roca*. This was a platform carried by twelve men, and on it stood Jesus, Mary, and various evangelists and saints.

Multiple sets appeared as early as 1400 and probably earlier. They grew more and more common in the fifteenth and sixteenth centuries and even continued into the eighteenth. Wagon and platform had often provided three or more settings on the same level, but by 1420 an *auto sacramental* was produced with five "mansions," or settings, built in the French fashion on a single long stage. In 1578 the city of Plasencia erected in the public square a huge platform that included a tank of water sixty feet long and twenty feet wide in which floated a sailing ship. There are records of productions with one setting above another and of a single performance on three levels. Vertical and horizontal stages were very often combined during the fifteenth century. Doubtless the more elaborate multiple settings were confined to the street performances; but there is one mention of a dove descending from on high in the cathedral of Valencia and another of scaffolds erected in two churches. The staging of the *autos* grew simpler when the sacred plays invaded the public playhouses after 1600. Today, however, at Elche and in many other towns, multiple stages are still used for popular religious performances.

A PRODUCTION ON WAGONS IN 1663

In George Ticknor's *History of Spanish Literature*, we have a description of the production in 1663 of an elaborate *auto sacramental* employing wagons, *El divino Orfeo*. The allegorical use of Orpheus and Eurydice springs from the influence of the Italian Renaissance.

> *It opens with the entrance of a huge black car, in the shape of a boat, which is drawn along the street toward the stage where the* auto *is to be acted, and contains the Prince of Darkness, set forth as a pirate, and Envy, as his steersman; both supposed to be thus navigating through a portion of chaos. They hear at a distance sweet music, which proceeds from another car, advancing from the opposite quarter in the form of a celestial globe, covered with the signs of the planets and constellations, and containing Orpheus, who represents allegorically the Creator of all things. This is followed by a third car, setting forth the terrestrial globe, within which are the Seven Days of the Week and Human Nature, all asleep. These cars open, so that the personages they contain can come upon the stage and retire back again, as if behind the scenes, at their pleasure—the machines themselves constituting, in this as in all such representations, an important part of the scenic arrangements of the exhibition. . . .*

DON QUIXOTE MEETS AN "AUTO" ON TOUR

The display of scenery and costumes varied from place to place and from time to time. Through at least four centuries the *autos sacramentales* used cathedrals and great plazas as their playhouses. But before 1580 there must have been humble troupes of strolling players taking crude productions from town to town. In that year Cervantes described one of these traveling companies:

> *Don Quixote was about to make a reply, but was interrupted by the sight of a cart crossing the highway, filled with the most varied and weird assortment of persons and figures that could be imagined. He who drove the mules and served as carter was an ugly demon, and the vehicle was open to the heavens and had neither awning nor framework of branches on which to stretch it. The first figure that Don Quixote beheld was that of Death himself, with a human countenance. Next came an angel with large and painted wings. At one side was an emperor with what appeared to be a gold crown on his head, and at Death's feet was the god Cupid, without a bandage over his eyes, but with his bow, his quiver, and his arrows. There was also a knight in full armor, except that he had no morion, or helmet, but instead wore a hat decked with vari-colored plumes.*

> *Such a sight as this, coming as it did so unexpectedly, somewhat startled Don Quixote and struck fear in Sancho's heart, but the knight was at once cheered by the thought that this must be some new and perilous adventure, and with a mind disposed to confront any danger he stepped in front of the cart and called out in a loud and threatening voice, "O carter, coachman, demon, or whoever you may be! Tell me at once who you are and whither you are bound and who the persons are whom you carry with you in that wagonette, which looks more like Charon's bark than the kind of conveyance in common use."*

> *Stopping the wagon, the demon gave him a most civil reply. "Sir," he said, "we are strolling players of Angulo el Malo's company. [He was a theatrical manager and playwright who was active about 1580.] This morning, which marks the octave of Corpus Christi [the eighth day after the festival], we have performed a theatrical piece in the village which lies beyond*

that hill yonder. It was a play [*Cervantes uses the word* auto]
called The Parliament of Death, *and we have to give it this
afternoon in another village which you can see from here. Since
the distance is so short, and in order to save ourselves the
trouble of undressing and dressing again, we are traveling in
the garments that we wear on the stage. That youth there is
Death, the other is an Angel. That woman, who is the author's
wife, takes the part of a Queen. This one is a Soldier, that one
an Emperor, and I am a Devil."*

COARSE COMEDY MIXED WITH HOLY EDIFICATION

The people of Spain loved the theater in all its forms, and they seem
to have loved all its forms with equal enthusiasm. A public
performance—no matter whether it was sacred or profane—
combined the best features of a vaudeville show and what we used
to call "the legitimate." Singing and dancing, monologs and comic
sketches, even juggling, introduced or interrupted what was supposed to be the main attraction: the play itself. This may not have
been true of all *autos sacramentales* produced in churches, but
when they paraded out into the streets they were certainly just such
a theatrical mishmash.

First there was a repetition of the same fantastic procession
that had borne the actors to the House of God. After a prayer, the
performance began with a prolog that often praised the show itself.
In *El nombre de Jesús*, written by Lope de Vega, an actor and an
actress play a villager and a peasant girl who run into each other
after being separated in the crowd. The girl is so naive and loqua-
cious that it takes only a little prodding to make her chatter on
endlessly about the wonderful procession that she—and all the
crowd, of course—have just seen. Next would come a short farce,
one of the *juegos de escarnio* that the King of Leon and Castille had
condemned in 1252, and then a sacred play. *Entremeses*, which were
the interludes of comedy, dancing, and singing that were given
between the acts of secular plays, seem to have interrupted in the
same way the holy episodes of the *autos sacramentales*.

In 1601 a monk wrote about "*entremeses* treating of robberies
and adulteries, which are ordinarily mingled with the *autos sac-*

ramentales." Ten years later another cleric wrote indignantly about lewd and adulterous scenes acted out in church. The clergy attempted to curb these abuses both in and out of the cathedrals. In 1473 a church council issued a decree against the presentation of monsters, masks, bawdy figures, and "lewd verses, which interfere with the divine offices." There were probably many more decrees, but the ribaldries persisted—in the street shows if not in the churches. The seventeenth and eighteenth centuries saw the attacks increase. Laymen as well as priests inveighed against professional players in *autos*. An anonymous writer objected because an actress played the Mother of God, "and . . . having finished this part, the same actress appears in an *entremes*, representing an innkeeper's wife . . ., simply by putting on a bonnet or tucking up a skirt," and dances while she sings an indecent song. "He who played the part of the Savior in a beard takes it off and comes out and sings and dances 'Here Comes Molly.'" Priests echoed such attacks on the players. It was abominable that "the woman who represents the lewdness of Venus, as well in plays [in the theaters] as in her private life, should represent the purity of the Sovereign Virgin." Such attacks persisted until at last, in 1765, Charles III prohibited by royal decree the performance of all *autos sacramentales*.

"COMEDIAS" AND THE FIRST PLAYWRIGHTS

Charles III also banned another kind of religious play. It was given only in the public playhouses, and it was called a *comedia de santos*. The words *de santos* are obvious enough—"of saints." *Comedia* seems to be clear, yet it isn't. Sometimes it applies to comedy, but just as often to melodrama or tragedy. (The word is also used for theater in a general sense.) Just as in the Middle Ages *auto* originally meant any play, whether religious or not, so in the late Renaissance *comedia* meant any play that was long enough to be given in three acts. For a few years some *comedias* were written in prose. In the "golden age" of Spanish literature—which runs from a little before 1550 to about 1650—all *comedias*, whether saintly or not, were in verse. In the dialog the writer was not restricted to a single type of poetry, as in our own blank verse dramas. Within the same play he would use different kinds of meter and various rhyme schemes, giving each scene the lyric treatment that best suited it.

While Columbus was discovering and exploring the New World, the Spanish dramatist was discovering and exploring this new play form—the *comedia*. Or so a Spaniard wrote a hundred years later. Perhaps it is safer to say that the playwrights of Spain—and Portugal too—slowly developed a new type of native drama between 1500 and 1550.

The first playwright of this era and the founder of the Spanish drama was Juan del Encina. Musician, courtier, and actor too, he wrote chiefly on religious and pastoral subjects, yet he had humor and a real interest in contemporary society. By 1497 he turned out a nativity drama in which the shepherds spoke a local dialect and became the chief figures of the play. This *Égloga de Fileno, Zambardo, y Cardonio* was secular in feeling, and his later work became more and more an expression of his own times.

Most of the successful playwrights who followed Encina dealt mainly with contemporary life, often humorously. Though Bartolomé de Torres Naharro spent much of his life in Italy, he escaped the worship and imitation of classic drama. He wrote a satire on an army of occupation and laid a comedy in the servants' hall of a Roman cardinal. He developed a low comedy character, called a *gracioso*, that was widely used by later playwrights. Perhaps because Torres Naharro was aware of his shortcomings as a playwright, he introduced an *introito*, or prolog, in which he summarized the plot so that the audience would be sure to follow it. Later on the *introito* became a *loa*, often a monolog in praise of the play or of the city in which it was about to be seen. Seeking new matter for these inevitable *loas*, later playwrights fell upon such extraordinary subjects for commendation as the days of the week or even the letter A.

A more skillful dramatist, Juan de la Cueva, turned to national history for many of his subjects, characterized his people with more adroitness, and used popular verse forms brilliantly. Another playwright, Gil Vicente, varied his work with comic scenes of everyday life. The fact that he was a Portuguese who wrote a quarter of his plays in Spanish shows the close ties between the theaters of the two countries.

LOPE DE RUEDA—POPULAR PLAYWRIGHT

Spain's first important dramatists—Encina, Naharro, Cueva, and Vicente—spent much of their time in Italy and wrote primarily for the court and not for the people. Yet their plays had such fresh vitality that they were later acted by professional companies in many cities.

The first playwright who wrote directly for the popular stage was Lope de Rueda. He was the leading figure among the playwrights who were also actor–managers, toured from town to town, and dominated the Spanish stage until 1575. Because Rueda and his fellows supplied their companies with plot and dialog, they were called *autores de comedias*, but when their successors gave up writing and began to hire playwrights as well as actors, the words *autores de comedias* came to mean theatrical managers.

Until 1558, when Rueda left his job as a gold-beater and joined with a bookseller and a few friends in founding a company of strolling players, most secular drama had been performed only at court. Rueda was the founder of the Spanish national theater, both as popular playwright and as popular producer. He too, however, drew inspiration from Italy. The *commedia dell'arte*—as he saw it given by an Italian company that toured Spain—made him an actor. His comedies, six of them in prose and three in verse, followed Italian plots, but their form, their dialog, and their humor were thoroughly Spanish. It was Rueda who invented the *paso* (a comic sketch in prose used as an interlude between the acts) and excelled in this early form of the one-act play. The most famous was *The Olives*, in which a farmer who has just planted an olive shoot quarrels violently with his wife and his daughter over the price they are going to charge for the fruit that won't mature for five years. The idea must have been peculiarly amusing to a people bedeviled as the Spaniards were by rapid inflation.

When Cervantes was eighteen he saw a performance by Rueda's company. Fifty years later he described the stage as made of four benches with planks across them a couple of feet off the ground. The scenic background was an old blanket. Behind it the actors put on their costumes and sang "some old ballad without the accompaniment of a guitar." The costumes and properties of such a troupe, when it was giving a shepherd's play, could go into a single sack "and consisted of four white sheepskins ornamented with gilt leather, four beards and wigs, and four crooks." Recalling the scenic effects and stage machinery of his own day, Cervantes remarked that in a performance like Rueda's, "there were no figures which rose or seemed to rise from the center of the earth . . . nor did clouds with angels or souls descend from the skies." For all that, Rueda "acted with the greatest skill and naturalness that you can imagine."

TOURING COMPANIES—RUEDA'S AND OTHERS

Strolling players like Rueda's company still toured Spain even after permanent theaters had been built in the sixteenth century. In 1603, Agustin de Rojas, who wrote many *loas* as well as *comedias*, set down an amusing catalog of the various kinds of troupes. He divided them into eight species. They increase in size, repertory, and prosperity. "A *bululú*," wrote Rojas, "is a player who travels alone and afoot. He enters a village, goes to the curate, and tells him that he knows a *comedia* and a *loa* or two . . . he mounts upon a chest, and begins to recite, remarking as he goes on: 'Now the lady enters and says so-and-so,' and continues his acting while the curate passes round the hat. . . . A *raque* consists of two men; they enact an *entremes* or portions of an *auto* . . . they wear a beard of sheepskin, play a drum, and charge two *maravedis* . . . they contentedly sleep in their clothes, go barefoot, are always hungry, rid themselves of their fleas amid the grain in summer, and do not feel them in the winter on account of the cold." A *gangarilla* has three or four men, including a boy to play women's roles. They "borrow a woman's skirt and bonnet (which they sometimes forget to return). They play an *auto*, two comic *entremeses*, and charge four *maravedis*." A *cambaleo* has five men and one woman who sings. "They have two *autos*, a *comedia*, and three or four *entremeses*, and a bundle of clothes that a spider could carry." They charge six *maravedis*. And so goes the list, adding players and plays, carts for chests, and donkeys to ride on, until Rojas arrives at the full *compañía*. Here he finds "every kind of grub and trumpery . . . very clever people among them, men much esteemed and persons well-born, and even very respectable women (for where there are many there must be all kinds). They take with them fifty *comedias*, more than 7000 pounds of luggage, sixteen persons who act, thirty who eat, one who takes money at the door (and God knows what he steals)."

PLAYS AT COURT AND IN SCHOOLS

Just as in Italy and England, some plays were written along classic lines and produced in palaces and universities. The first secular play of which we have a manuscript was in the Valencian tongue and staged in a Valencian palace in 1394. Sometimes the plays were in Spanish, sometimes in Latin, and sometimes they mixed the two languages. Translations of Greek tragedies appeared shortly after 1500. Certain universities required the students and faculty to produce two classic plays each year. The Jesuit colleges, as in Italy and France, used the drama for moral edification. But outside the palaces and the schoolrooms, there was no audience for plays patterned after the Greek and the Roman. The people preferred the followers of Encina, who wrote about contemporary life and followed the free form of the *comedia*.

It was at court that the scenic wonders of Italy first found lodging. In 1548, one of Ariosto's comedies was given in the royal palace at Valladolid to celebrate the wedding of a Spanish princess. The scenic display, done in true Italian fashion, so overwhelmed the man who wrote about the performance that he forgot to mention the name of the play. In the same year Philip II saw a comedy in Milan and, when he came to the throne in 1556, he brought an academician from Italy to produce Italian comedies at court. The king had spells of religious fanaticism, and in one of these—when he lay dying in 1598—he suppressed the public theaters. Philip III imported Italian players as well as plays and scenic devices, and his queen, who was very fond of the drama, induced him to install a theater in the *alcázar*, or palace, in Madrid. *Autos sacramentales* were, of course, always welcome at court. Philip III engaged professional players to repeat before his courtiers the religious plays they had given publicly.

Philip IV, the last king of the "golden age," had a passionate love of the theater. During four months of his first year on the throne—he was only sixteen—he had forty-five plays presented at court, and between 1623 and 1654 about three hundred *comedias*. Many of them were "command performances" by professional companies from all over Spain. He hired Italian architects to produce plays and spectacles in his royal gardens, with actors and audience floating on an artificial lake. In one extraordinary production he had the three acts of a *comedia* presented on separate aquatic stages, each by a different company. He spent as much as five hundred thousand *reales* on a single play. (It is hard to translate this amount into today's currency, but Cervantes tells us that a man could live—though probably not luxuriously—on a *real* and a half a day.) In 1632, when Philip IV built the palace called El Buen Retiro (The Good Retreat), he included in one of its halls a remarkable theater. When the scene was an exterior, an opening at the back of the stage turned the gardens of the palace into a far distant backdrop. Three years later he made Calderón, the last great playwright of the "golden age," the director of court performances.

THE "COMMEDIA DELL'ARTE" IN SPAIN

No one knows just when the ubiquitous comedians of the *commedia dell'arte* first reached Spain. As early as 1538 an Italian troupe was popular enough to be invited to appear in a Corpus Christi performance in the southernmost part of the country. This was in Seville, where Lope de Rueda was born and where he then lived. Rueda must have seen later Italian comedians before he left his work bench to become actor and playwright. Between 1538 and 1574, the next recorded date, these alien actors had won sufficient fame to be summoned to court. Alberto Ganassa—who was supposed to have created the character of Harlequin—appeared before Philip II. Shortly afterwards Ganassa and his company played at one of the public theaters that had opened during the past seven or eight years. The troupe gave performances in many other cities, both of their own comedies and of the interludes of *autos sacramentales*. Speaking only Italian, but cannily emphasizing pantomime, they and their successors became so popular that in 1581 a censorious priest inveighed against "these foreigners who carry away many thousands of ducats from Spain every year." The effect of the Italian actors on both playwrights and actors was considerable.

"PATIOS" AND "CORRALES"—
THE FIRST PUBLIC THEATERS

Until 1576 the actors of London put up their stages in innyards. In that year, when the manager of a company of players built the first public theater in England, he is supposed to have followed the pattern of the old innyards. It is important to note that Spain created playhouses rather like those in England, and it created them somewhat earlier.

During the sixteenth century, a good-sized house or inn in southern or eastern Spain was built around a *patio*. Like an English innyard, the *patio* was open to the sky; two or three galleries looked down upon it from all four sides, and there was a covered entryway from the street. By putting a stage platform against the inner end of a patio in an inn, Malaga created a theater as early as 1520. Another appeared at Valencia by 1526, and a third in Seville by 1550.

In northern cities, where *patios* were unknown, the Spaniards made theaters out of courtyards formed by the backs of several houses. These hemmed-in spaces—usually filled with trash and refuse—were called *corrales*. By 1554, Valladolid had turned such a courtyard into a public theater. Barcelona did the same by 1560, Cordoba by 1565. Shortly after 1568 Madrid had five *corrales*. The word *corral* was soon applied to the *patio* playhouse of the south, and it gave way to *teatro* only after 1700 when Spain began to build Italianate opera houses.

In a typical *corral* of the sixteenth century, a broad stage without a front curtain stretched from one side of the courtyard to the other. The rooms and windows of the surrounding houses served as boxes for the more privileged spectators. The management rented the rooms, or the owners paid an annual fee for the exclusive use of these box seats. At the end of the *corral* opposite the stage, set aside for women spectators was a large upper room called— inelegantly—the *cazuela*, or stewpan. There were raised seats along the sides of the *corral* and in front of the stage. The "ground-

Figure 4.1 A Madrid Theater of Shakespeare's Day
Central and northern Spain had no patios, as in the south, but used courtyards—called *corrales*—in the middle of a block of houses. Here the actors set up a rather elaborate stage. This view, made from information available in 1660, probably corresponds rather closely to the Madrid theaters at the end of the sixteenth century. (Drawing by Gerda Becker With, after a sketch by Comba.)

lings" stood in the remaining area. Because they were violently noisy in their applause and disapproval, they were called the "musketeers." (The violence of their disapprobation may be judged from Cervantes' boast in print: "I have written twenty or thirty plays, and they were all received without cucumbers or anything else that can be thrown.")

Because governmental authorities in Spain—as in France and England—made theatrical companies share their incomes with hospitals and charitable bodies, we know that at least six public playhouses were opened in as many Spanish cities between 1520 and 1568. As a matter of fact, the philanthropic institutions—*cofradías*, as they were called—actually controlled many of the theaters. We can't say that they built them, since these amusement places were at first merely *patios* and courtyards turned to a new use. But—and this is most important—these places were to be used for theatrical performances and nothing else, and they were gradually made over into a new and distinctive kind of theater where plays were staged very much as in Shakespeare's Globe. Moreover, whenever Spain built new public theaters, they all followed this same architectural pattern until after 1700.

THEATER MANAGEMENT IN SPAIN

As in London, the spectator paid a certain sum for general admission—unless, as sometimes happened, he could force his way in *gratis*—and, later, another and a larger fee for a seat on the benches or in the rooms above. Admission prices varied from time to time. When the court was in Madrid, they were higher than when the king was away. The theatergoer probably paid as much as he does today. In 1575 general admission was half a *real*, an armchair seat on the lower floor cost one *real* more, and a box seat six *reales*. A theater manager sometimes played the role of ticket speculator, and boosted the price of box seats to as much as thirty-two *reales*. By farming out the sale of the sixteenth-century equivalent of popcorn—fruit, water, and candy—the management added to its income. The playwright sold his work outright. The best got perhaps three hundred *reales* for an *auto* and five hundred fifty *reales* for a *comedia*. He could live a year on the latter fee or buy ten donkeys. A new play was seldom given more than five or six performances in Madrid.

Performances took place in the afternoons. At first the theaters were open only on Sundays and feast days, later on Tuesdays
and Thursdays also and sometimes on other days. But, between the
interruptions of Lent, plagues, royal deaths, the heat of summer,
and the rains of winter, hardly more than two hundred performances could be given each year. Annoyed by the loss of business on
rainy days, the Italian star Ganassa rebuilt Madrid's Corral de la
Pacheca in 1574, adding a roof over the stage and the spectators'
seats, and an awning over the area where the groundlings stood.

The next step in Madrid was the building by the *cofradias* of
two permanent theaters, one in 1579 and one in 1583. In general
they were much like the Corral de la Pacheca; but stairs were built
to reach the galleries and boxes, and dressing rooms were provided
backstage. Gradually the older theaters in Madrid went out of existence. In the next few years playhouses were built in Toledo,
Seville, Valencia, Granada, and Saragossa. The interior of a wooden
structure in Seville—the Coliseo—had forty columns "with marble
bases and capitals." It was rebuilt as a roofed structure in 1632,
"holding between four and five thousand spectators, all of whom [by
some architectural miracle] were equally able to see and hear." We
can find no evidence that prosceniums and front curtains invaded
the *corrales* of the "golden age." It is quite likely, of course, that
they were used in the performances at court, for Philip III and
Philip IV imported Italian architects to stage their shows. The only
evidence, however, is rather late. The first public playhouse
equipped like a modern theater may have been a temporary building
in Madrid where an Italian company gave operas and *comedias* from
about 1708 till 1719. On the same site, in 1738, a large opera house
was completed under the guidance of the Italian diplomat from
Parma, the Marchese di Scotti, and it opened with the opera *Ar-
mida Placita Demetrio*. The stage must surely have had a proscenium, a curtain, and all the other paraphernalia that Italian opera
houses had been employing for a hundred years.

ACTORS, COSTUMES, AND SETTING

In many ways the theaters and the shows of Spain resembled those
of England from 1580 to 1640. In many ways they did not. In London, boys always played women's parts until after the Restoration

in 1660. As we have seen from Rojas' description of the Spanish companies, both boys and women appeared on the rude provincial stages. In Madrid, actresses were not licensed to appear in the public theaters until 1587. This official concession was forced by the competition of the Columbines of the *commedia dell'arte*. Thereafter women players became vastly popular. They invaded court performances, and under Philip IV they were almost worshipped. One of the best, "La Calderona," was the mistress of the king and the mother of his distinguished son, Don Juan of Austria, retiring at last to become the abbess of a convent.

Just as in London—and everywhere else until the end of the eighteenth century—the Spanish player wore on the stage the clothes of his own time. The only exception was when he played a Mohammedan in a historical drama, and even then the costuming could be sloppy. Lope de Vega complained that "the play of today is full of barbarous things: a Turk wearing the neck-gear of a Christian, and a Roman in tight breeches." Actresses wore breeches, too, whenever the playwright could manage it. Costumes grew more and more expensive as the "golden age" advanced. In 1636 an actor paid thirty-six hundred *reales* for a richly embroidered cloak.

If English theaters in the days of Elizabeth and James I followed the pattern now agreed on by most scholars, the *corrales* of Spain seem to have resembled them in their general arrangement, and their stages were used in much the same manner. They had no proscenium or drop-curtain. There were several doors for the actors to make their entrances, as well as a "trap" in the stage. A drapery hid or disclosed an inner stage at the rear. A gallery above provided a balcony or a parapet. There were curtains at the sides as well as the back, and these could be drawn away to reveal an object toward which characters in a play might be walking. There seem to have been crude set-pieces—trees, for instance, painted on pasteboard or linen. But most changes of scene were accomplished, as at the Globe in London, by getting the actors off through one door, leaving the stage bare, and then bringing other actors on through a second door. Descriptive dialog helped out.

In Spain, the elaborate settings of the court performances may have invaded the theaters earlier than in England. In a prolog to a book of *comedias* published in 1622, Lope de Vega attacked scenery and machines through a dialog between a stranger and a character called Theater:

> *Theater:*   Can't you see that I am injured? My arms and legs
>   are broken. I am full of holes made by a thousand
>   trap-doors and nails.
> *Stranger:* Who brought you to this miserable plight?
> *Theater:*   The carpenters—at the orders of the theater mana-
>   gers. . . . The managers depend on machinery, the
>   playwrights on the carpenters, and the spectators on
>   their eyes.

It was this same de Vega who first said: "Give me four trestles, four
boards, two actors, and a passion."

A SHOW OF INFINITE VARIETY

Compared with many performances at court and in the streets,
productions in the earlier theaters must have looked pitifully bare
and simple, but what the audiences listened to was the most complex sort of entertainment ever given in a public playhouse. First
the musicians played. Then came a *loa*. It might be a simple
monolog or, more likely, a skit in verse spoken or sung by two or
more of the cast. After that came the first act, but sometimes there
was a *paso* between the prolog and the play itself, or else a song and
dance. Between the first act and the second and between the second
act and the third, the audience enjoyed another *paso*, or *entremes*.
These entr'act diversions might be supplemented by players who
sang while they danced. And one of these *bailes*—as they called the
dance numbers—ended the performance. The whole entertainment
was probably as long as those interminable bills of our own Victorian stage that often included a tragedy, a short farce or ballet, a
comedy or melodrama, and an epilog—and sometimes an "olio" of
vaudeville turns.

CERVANTES, VEGA, AND CALDERÓN

It may seem extraordinary that the art of playwriting could flourish
under such strange conditions. But the Spanish playwrights were
extraordinary fellows. Most of them lived adventurously, and many

of them transferred to the stage a good deal of the lustiness of their own lives.

Cervantes, the first notable playwright after Rueda, was both a soldier and a member of a holy order—like most of his fellows. He was wounded three times at the naval battle of Lepanto and lost the use of his right hand and arm. He spent five years in an Algerian prison and then fought in the Azores. Poverty dogged his heels and thrust him into jail. He joined the Franciscan order and finished the last half of *Don Quixote* just before he died a poor man. Unfortunately, he gave more of his vitality to that great novel than to the thirty *comedias* and *entremeses* that he claimed he wrote. Compared with the work of Lope de Vega and Calderón, the plays of Cervantes—except perhaps for the *entremeses*—seem dry and formal.

The next important playwright, Lope de Vega, was as ex-

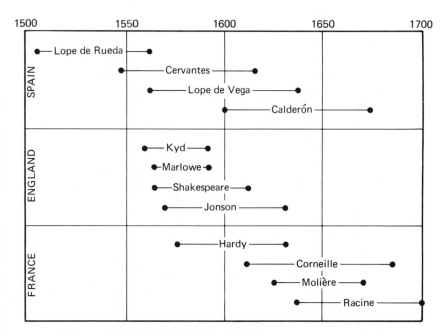

Figure 4.2   The March of National Drama

The four chief dramatists of Spain, England, and France. The Spanish began earlier than the English and continued longer.

traordinary in his plays as in his life, which is saying a good deal. He loved and lost wives, mistresses, and children. He sailed with the Spanish Armada and escaped its fate. For gun wads he once used the same paper on which he had drafted poems to a fickle actress. Scurrilous verses about another lost love and her whole family got him exiled from Madrid on pain of death. Within a few months, he had a son by a devoted wife and another by an even more devoted mistress. When he was almost fifty, he joined a religious brotherhood. He continued to write plays and to have love affairs. But he did his religious devotions, scourged himself till the walls of his cell were spattered with blood, and helped burn a heretic priest at the stake.

Lope de Vega was the great inventor and pioneer of the "golden age" of Spanish drama. He shaped the final form of the *comedia* and gave it distinction. Instead of reworking the plots of others, he gave his rivals fresh stories to steal. One of his lighter plays, *El acero de Madrid* (*Madrid Steel*), supplied Molière with the plot for *The Physician in Spite of Himself.* Sometimes, of course, Vega worked on old romances. He wrote historical pieces, including *The New World Discovered by Columbus.* Vega mixed tragedy with comedy and turned out the first social drama, *Fuente Ovejuna* (*The Sheep Well*). Like another of his plays, *El Alcalde de Zalamea* (*The Mayor of Zalamea*), it dealt sympathetically with the troubles of the lower classes.

Lope de Vega's output of plays was so enormous that Cervantes called him a "prodigy of nature." A year after his death in 1635, a Spanish writer credited him with eighteen hundred *comedias* and over four hundred *autos*, and we have records today of 431 of the secular plays. Lope said in print that "more than a hundred had passed from the Muses to the theater each in twenty-four hours."

In spite of Vega's fecundity, he seems to have maintained a high level of vigorous action and colorful romance, of poetic effectiveness and rhetorical display. Like his audience, he was not interested in deep characterization. Somerset Maugham, in *Don Fernando*, gives us a key to the charm of the poetry that Lope wedded to his drama:

His plays . . . can best be appreciated if you look upon them as

> *operatic "books" in which verse takes the place of music. He will write a bravura passage in which three persons, for instance, embroider upon an idea, each one ending his speech with the same refrain, so that you can almost hear the burst of applause that greets the ingenuity. Sometimes a character will present a theme in four lines and then enlarge upon it in stanzas each of which ends with one of the four lines. It is as much a set aria as "La Donnaé mobile."**

Calderón—last of many notable Spanish playwrights—conquered both court and populace. Knighted by Philip IV after he became director of the court performances, he was later made chaplain of honor to the king. Calderón served in three campaigns, died at eighty-one wealthy and esteemed, and left his fortune to the church for which he had written so many *autos*.

In his two hundred *comedias* and *autos* Calderón borrowed freely from Lope de Vega and other playwrights, a theatrical habit of the Renaissance. The work of a truly religious man, his plays are distinguished by their high spiritual values, their sense of faith, as well as their lofty poetic quality. The modern world still admires Calderón's *La vida es sueño (Life Is a Dream)* and *El gran teatro del mundo (The Great World Theater)*, as well as his own version of Vega's *The Mayor of Zalamea*, in which Calderón incorporated the theme of Vega's *The Sheep Well*. Goethe and Shelley wrote admiringly of Calderón. A number of his plays were translated by the German playwright Grillparzer and by Edward Fitzgerald, who immortalized *The Rubaiyat* of Omar Khayyam. In our own century, Max Reinhardt successfully produced *The Great World Theater* and also *La dama duende* as *Doña Diana*.

The originality of the Spanish drama is proved by its contribution of two great characters to the later theater of other lands. Guillén de Castro wrote a drama about a medieval hero of Spain which Corneille turned into *Le Cid*. Another playwright, Tirso de Molina, created the famous character of Don Juan. Writers in Italy, France, England, and the Netherlands translated or adapted many Spanish *comedias*.

*W. Somerset Maugham, *Don Fernando* (Doubleday & Company, Inc., 1935. Copyright 1935 by W. Somerset Maugham. Reprinted courtesy of Doubleday & Company, Inc.

SPAIN'S INSTINCT FOR DIALOG AND FREE FORM

Two peculiarities about the writers of burgeoning Spain made drama a natural form of expression and enabled it to be a truly popular art: dialog and free form.

Spanish writers seem to have taken naturally to dialog. Even their novels—and Spaniards led in the development of this modern form of long narrative—relied heavily on conversation. *La tragicomedia de Calisto y Melibea* (commonly called *La Celestina* and published in 1499) seems like a long-drawn-out play. The "picaresque" novels of rascally adventure, starting in 1553, exploited dialog, and Don Quixote himself—as you may judge from the scene we have quoted—was fond of talking. Spoken drama was inevitable in Spain.

The Spanish playwright, like the Elizabethan, gained a great deal because he was free from the fetters of classical form. He ignored the unities of time and place, though he generally respected the unity of dramatic action. He never bowed before the idol of the five-act play. For a time he wrote in four acts, but soon he reduced his *comedias* to three. Cervantes claims the credit for this. Vega gives the distinction to his friend Cristobal Virués. In 1553 when Virués was not yet four years old, a playwright named Francisco de Avendaño wrote in three acts.

Our knowledge of the theater of Spain rests on the fortunate fact that its dramatists delighted to write about their craft. Many of these inveighed against the restrictions of the classic form. Tirso de Molina attacked the subject in his play *El vergonzoso en palacio*. Cervantes in the second act of *El rufián dichoso* has a character named Comedy tell Curiosity that she does not respect rules and there lies the only way to progress. Above all, Lope de Vega castigated the classic restrictions. Addressing in verse the learned Academy of Madrid in *The New Art of Writing Plays*, he said:

> *This subject seems easy, and it should be easy for any of you who have written few plays but know all about the art of writing them. I suffer from the disadvantage of having written them without any art. . . . When I have to write a play I lock up the [classical] precepts with six keys, and I banish Terence and*

Plautus from my study. . . . I know that, though they [my plays] might have been better if written in another manner, they would not have found the favor that they have enjoyed.

A FLOURISHING THEATER IN A RUINED NATION

The drama, says Maugham, "at no time and in no country has flourished so luxuriantly as in Spain during the hundred years that ended with Calderón's death." In 1681, when the last of the great playwrights died, Madrid had forty theaters. We know the names of over two thousand actors of the "golden age." Someone has estimated that thirty thousand plays had been written and performed. Most of them must have been pretty poor by any standards, but many were distinguished, and some are now world-famous.

The story of the Spanish theater is all the more amazing because its drama mounted in vitality and importance as Spain sank. Playwriting began with the conquest of the New World. True drama developed, and better and more significant dramatists appeared, even while Spain suffered from poverty and high prices at home and while the wars in the Low Countries drained her dry. Thus, by a strange cultural lag, the stage and the fine arts increased in stature as the nation declined. In a ruined and hungry land—where a gallant gave his beloved presents of food instead of flowers—theaters multiplied and men like Lope de Vega and Calderón won immortality.

5: THE THEATER THAT ELIZABETH I SUSTAINED

Shakespeare called England "Neptune's Park." "Bound in with the triumphant seas," it found protection in "that water-walled bulwark." Many another Briton has hailed the isolation of this island kingdom. As a cold matter of fact, England's isolation has been relative rather than total. It has been merely convenient—in war and in the theater too.

From 1600 to 1900 England spread an empire across the world. Before she took to the seas in global conquests, English bowmen had won the battle of Agincourt, and Henry V, allied with Burgundy, had made himself heir to the French throne in 1420. Through the next hundred years of the Renaissance, English men of letters were visiting Italy, and Italian painters were attending court in London.

No, England was far from isolated. She knew the glories of the ancient world as she knew the glories of Agincourt. And for her scholars a most important part of the Revival of Learning was the revival of the classic drama. Yet England was so much England—so much a people living spiritually in its "other Eden"—that it could bring forth a very different thing, and a much better thing, than fake classicism. This was the unique playhouse of Burbage and the unique drama of Shakespeare.

RENAISSANCE STUDENTS PRODUCE PLAYS

England had heard as much as Spain or France about the concepts of the classic theater that existed in Renaissance Italy. The man who discovered the manuscript of Vitruvius was in England from 1422 to 1424. The man who translated the book into Italian came to London in 1548 to spend eighteen months as ambassador from the republic of Venice. Under Henry VII and Henry VIII, the English Crown employed at least nine Italian painters. Scholars and poets left England at that time to study humanism and the classics in Italy—many of them at the courts of Ferrara and Urbino where the theater flourished. What they learned in Italy brought playwriting and playacting into the universities, the law schools, and even the schools for boys. The imitations of classic drama that they produced were shown at court.

The account books of King's College, Cambridge, show that something theatrical was going on there as early as 1482. There is the same kind of information from Magdalen College, Oxford, two years later. By 1512 the drama was so definitely a part of the curriculum that a certain student was granted a degree provided he wrote a comedy and a hundred songs in praise of the university a year after completing his studies. Cambridge went along with Oxford in believing that acting plays in Latin and Greek was an educational exercise. The 1546 statutes of Queen's College, Cambridge, required the performance of two comedies or tragedies in Greek each year; they set the time of production and provided eight shillings and sixpence for expenses. A few years later Trinity College, Cambridge required at least five plays a year. This attitude and practice continued into the seventeenth century. The young gentlemen who studied law at the Inns of Court in London also took to classic drama; they had long been required to study music and dancing, as well as divinity. As far back as 1526, the records of Gray's Inn list a "goodly disguising plaied." The classic drama also invaded the "grammar schools" of that time. We know that Eton spent

Figure 5.1 Proscenium Doors of the Dorset Garden Theater
The Duke's Theater had two doors on each side of the stage. Most scenes were played on the forestage under the light of the chandeliers. (Drawing by Gerda Becker With, from Cleaver's *The Theater through the Ages*.)

money on two plays in 1525. The choir boys of St. Paul's played Terence's *Phormio* in 1528 for the king and Cardinal Wolsey. There are plentiful records of later performances.

Sometimes Elizabeth I journeyed to the schools and universities to see their productions and visited the Inns of Court. Oftener the students and the young lawyers brought their plays to her palaces.

INTERLUDES BRING COMEDY AND INSTRUCTION

The Revival of Learning brought royal patronage to the interlude and developed a kind of comedy of admonition. At first, one-act pieces (that form a link between the Middle Ages and the Renaissance) were injected as comic relief in an otherwise serious play. Later they became a favorite form of relaxation between the courses of a state dinner. In 1493 Henry VII employed four men as the Players of the King's Interludes. Henry VIII increased the number to eight, while noblemen added similar troupes of players to their households. Instead of embracing the classical side of the Revival of Learning, the writers of interludes turned to humanism and faced the new world rather than the old. Sometimes wisdom overshadowed wit. For instance, *Fulgens and Lucres*, an interlude of 1495 acted between courses at a feast in the great hall of Cardinal Morton, extolled the man who would "eschew idleness," who would devote his time to study, and who would promise his bride neither wealth nor ease, but "moderate riches, and that sufficient for us both."

Our knowledge of English drama in the early Renaissance is hampered by the fact that all but one play were never printed, and all but a few of their manuscripts have disappeared. We know, however, that John Heywood wrote a number of humanistic interludes that avoided allegory. The best liked appears to have been *The Play called the foure P. P.; a newe and a very mery enterlude of a palmer, a pardoner, a potycary, and a pedler*, and it was played at court in 1520. Generally known as *The Four P's*, the comedy had to do with a contest over who could tell the biggest lie, and the winner was the one who said he had never seen a woman out of temper.

Allegory, so popular in the morality plays of the Middle Ages, sometimes added instruction to comedy. Most of the plays were probably written for students to present in their schools or at court. *The Nature of the Four Elements* dramatized new discoveries in science and geography. *Wit and Science*, presented by the boys of St. Paul's in 1530, showed its student–hero courting Lady Science, overcoming the monster Tediousness, and taking part in a burlesque spelling lesson. Interludes, like morality plays, were always in the native tongue.

UNIVERSITY MEN BEGIN TO WRITE PLAYS IN ENGLISH

Even in the schools, England spent less time than Italy or France on exercises in classic dramaturgy. After adapting classic dramas and writing original plays in Greek and Latin, the schoolmasters and students turned to English. They clung to the proper academic form and borrowed a few characters from Terence or Plautus, but their plots and their dialog were original and thoroughly English. *Ralph Roister Doister*, written about 1553 by Nicholas Udall, who had taught at both Eton and Winchester, and *Gammer Gurton's Needle*, produced a little later at Cambridge and credited to "Mr. S. M[aste]r of Art," are the earliest examples of native English comedy. Though the latter is written in rhymed doggerel, we can still produce and enjoy the comedy of the servant who finds an old woman's lost needle only by sitting down in the breeches she had mended with it.

Tragedy had a harder time than comedy in escaping from the bonds of Latin speech and classic themes and form. It is not till about 1560 that we have any record of a full-length tragedy in the English tongue. This play, *Gorboduc, or Ferrex and Porrex*, stuck fast to the rules of classic dramaturgy, but, besides using the language of the day, it substituted for the heroes of Greece and Rome mythical figures out of English history. In spite of its high success in school and court and in spite of the imitations that followed, the play that hid a Latin form in the clothing of English speech never won acclaim with the populace and their professional players. Many academic scholars went right on translating Seneca and writing new plays in Latin until the coming of Shakespeare and his fellows.

Gorboduc is a very dull play in spite of a most violent plot. The younger son of a king kills his brother; his mother kills the son; the people rise in revolt and murder the king and queen; the nobles annihilate the rebels and then quarrel and slay one another over the succession to the crown. The authors—two young lawyers named Thomas Sackville and Thomas Norton—managed to make all this action tedious by talking it to death. They stuck to the classic rule that violence must happen offstage, and they told about it through messengers with speeches running as long as a hundred lines.

Yet this dreary and gruesome contribution to a Christmas feast at one of the Inns of Court gave the Elizabethan stage something more than a tragedy written for the first time in the language of the people. It introduced blank verse to the stage. Hitherto, the poetry of Latin tragedy had been beaten out seven bars to the line—an even more awkward rhythm for dialog than the French alexandrine of six feet. Sackville and Norton had found their meter in the Earl of Surrey's translation of *The Aeneid*, published three years before. They used it stiffly and awkwardly, however, without any of the easy fluency that made blank verse the perfect form for poetic dialog in English. They missed Marlowe's "mighty line" and the lyric freedom of Shakespeare, but, at least, they showed the English playwright the road to dramatic poetry.

The other innovation of Sackville and Norton was a dubious one. They revived the "dumb show" used in the interludes of Renaissance Italy. In *Gorboduc* the action of the dumb show was symbolic: "first the music of hautboys began to play, during which time there came forth from under the stage, as though out of hell, three furies. . . . Hereby was signified the unnatural murders to follow." Subsequent Elizabethan playwrights—with whom the dumb show became unduly popular—showed in pantomime the same action that was later to be played with dialog. By the time of Shakespeare, the dumb show had lost its popularity; he used it only once, in the play-within-the-play of *Hamlet*.

PLAYS ACTED BY CHILDREN FOR COURT AND PUBLIC

The court's own contribution to Elizabethan drama was a curious one. But, then, it was a curious court. The nobles were eager and sensitive, as well as strong-mettled. Elizabeth I may have been a virgin, but she was no prude. You might expect from such folk a fondness for *Gammer Gurton's Needle* or, like Polonius, a "tale of bawdry." And ultimately, they did go for low comedy and high, for blood and thunder, for patriotic histories, and for everything else of vitality that the public theaters came to offer after the opening of Burbage's first playhouse in 1576. But in the earlier years of Elizabeth's reign, her courtiers had to look elsewhere for the refinements of dramatic art. Rather like some *nouveaux riches* of our own time, they were out for culture. Face to face with the ambassadors of France, Spain, and Italy and their households of painters and poets, the English nobles wanted to be taught the refinements of life and literature, knightly chivalry, and courtly love.

The royal troupe of interlude players developed by Henry VIII was pathetically short on refinement and sophistication; so it fell into disfavor in the second year of Elizabeth's reign and never again appeared at court. There were a few refined and refining plays to be seen at the schools for lawyers. In 1566, Gray's Inn produced the second poetic tragedy in English, George Gascoigne's *Jocasta*, and also his comedy in English prose, adapted from Ariosto's *I Suppositi* under the awkward title of *The Supposes*. But, between 1558 and 1584, Elizabeth and her court mainly relied for the finer things of life—in terms of the drama—on a very different and a very curious kind of theater. This was the performance of mature plays by companies of young boys. They were the Children of the Chapel Royal, the Children of Windsor, and the Children of St. Paul's.

For many, many years, these youngsters had been merely choristers, but in the first quarter of the sixteenth century the Children of the Chapel began to act interludes at court. During Elizabeth's reign these boys, who were supposed to be giving all their time to musical studies and the three Rs, took to playacting with a vengeance. Along with the students of Eton and Westminster, the choristers gave far more plays at court than did adult actors. This peculiar mania for juvenile performances spread outside the court. In 1576, Richard Farrant, Master of the Children of Windsor, took over a hall in what had been the Blackfriars Priory and installed a company of boys to give public performances in what was called a "private" theater. Drawn at various times from Windsor, the Chapel, and St. Paul's, the lads gave the professional players serious competition from 1576 to 1584 and for the first fifteen years of the next century. During the latter period, Ben Jonson and other popular dramatists wrote plays for the children to produce.

The children of the Chapel played their part in turning the drama away from the classic form and toward the free-and-easy technique of Shakespeare's day. Richard Edwardes, the Master of the Children in 1564, was a playwright as well as a musician. So it was natural that, after he set the boys to acting other men's plays at court and in the lawyers' inns, he should produce one of his own. In the first of these, *Damon and Pythias*, a child actor spoke a prolog in which Edwardes explained how necessary it was to blend comedy with tragedy. From the classical point of view, this was a heinous offence, but it became the heart of the later Elizabethan drama. The public flocked to *Cambyses*, a play that could be billed as "A lamentable tragedy mixed full of pleasant mirth." In *Hamlet* Shakespeare did not hesitate to place the comic scene of the gravediggers just before Ophelia's funeral. John Lyly, a court playwright who served the children, wrote in stylized and precious prose, but he mixed comedy and tragedy, treated mythological characters romantically, and paid no attention at all to the unities of time and place. By 1588, when his *Endymion* was produced before the queen by the choir boys of St. Paul's, the court was going to the public theaters to see violent plays like Marlowe's *Tamburlaine* and Thomas Kyd's *The Spanish Tragedy*.

PROFESSIONAL PLAYERS AND THEIR EARLY PLAYS

While choir boys and school boys, students at the universities, and lawyers at the Inns of Court were producing plays, the professional actors were far from idle. On village greens and in banquet halls and innyards they were giving shows that may have been crude at times but that were usually popular. Some of the troupes may have danced and juggled better than they acted, but others must have had true skill. There were the players attached to such noble households as those of the Earls of Essex, Leicester, Derby, Worcester, and Warwick, and Lords Effingham, Hunsdon, and Clinton. The names of many of these actors are known, for they went on to play in the London inns and playhouses. Among them is James Burbage, who built the first theater and begat Richard, the best actor in Shakespeare's plays.

We know the titles of only a few of the plays that these companies acted in the provinces, and only a little more about the repertory of the London theaters before 1587. Around the middle of the century, touring troupes were still playing mysteries and moralities and John Heywood's interludes in the villages, the castles, and the city inns. They also gave *Ralph Roister Doister*, *Gammer Gurton's Needle*, and probably *Gorboduc*. Such fare, along with the comedy–drama *Cambyses* and farces padded out with song and dance, served the London playhouses until Christopher Marlowe came down from Cambridge to make English drama eloquent.

Another kind of play made its appearance before Elizabeth I ascended the throne, and it became extremely popular in the 1590s. This was the chronicle play. The first that we know about was *Kynge Johan*, produced in 1538 by its author, John Bale. A Catholic priest who turned Protestant, he wrote for his own touring company a number of pieces that twisted history to serve his new-found convictions. Other men wrote other chronicle plays—changing history to suit the stage and to show rulers less admirable than their Elizabeth. These dramas fed on English patriotism and particularly on the awakened sense of national power that grew out of England's "cold war" with Spain. Victory over the Spanish Armada in 1588 spurred on the playwrights. From the eighties we have about a dozen chronicle plays. In the nineties nearly eighty were produced. It was in those ten years that playwrights of skill and resource came to the London theater. Shakespeare probably began his work with *Henry VI* and *Richard III* between 1590 and 1597.

SUDDENLY—A GREAT THEATER AND GREAT DRAMA

During the last half of Queen Elizabeth's reign some quite extraordinary things happened to the English theater in an extraordinarily short length of time. First of all, in 1576 James Burbage designed and built a new kind of playhouse. In 1587 the first great playwright appeared—Christopher Marlowe with his *Tamburlaine*. Within fifteen years, London saw Shakespeare's *Richard III*, *The Taming of the Shrew, Romeo and Juliet, A Midsummer Night's Dream, Julius Caesar,* and *Hamlet.* Before Elizabeth died, in 1603, the work of ten dramatists of stature had reached the stage. Five more, who were born in her reign, saw their plays done under James I. In a quarter of a century the English drama grew to full maturity.

Court and school contributed to the high distinction of the Elizabethan drama. The queen and her nobles accepted Shakespeare and his fellows with the same enthusiasm as did the common people. The courtiers flocked to the theaters, and Elizabeth, who couldn't go to the public playhouses, saw the plays at court or in the lawyers' inns. The seats of higher learning contributed playwrights. Two-thirds of the dramatists—Shakespeare and Ben Jonson were the outstanding exceptions—had studied at Oxford or Cambridge. Some of the best of them turned actors. Almost all forgot their studies of the classic drama, and they wrote freely and vitally.

MARLOWE LEADS THE WAY

Like many an Elizabethan playwright, Marlowe had a violent life and a short one. Son of a shoemaker yet a master of arts at Cambridge, he died in a tavern brawl before he was thirty. Rash and rebellious, a drunkard and a freethinker, he left us characters and dialog as fiery, intense, and passionate as himself. The few plays that he wrote in his five short years of work may be uneven, but they scale the heights of poetic drama, and they opened the way for Shakespeare. Marlowe made blank verse a new, fluent, and powerful tool for the creation of true poetic tragedy. In a single play, *Doctor Faustus,* he brought splendor to the English stage. Here was lyricism at its peak:

> *Was this the face that launched a thousand ships,*
> *And burnt the topless towers of Ilium?*
> *Sweet Helen, make me immortal with a kiss! . . .*
> *O thou art fairer than the evening air*
> *Clad in the beauty of a thousand stars!*

True to the character of his Faust, the sceptical playwright gave him these magnificent lines as the man faced damnation:

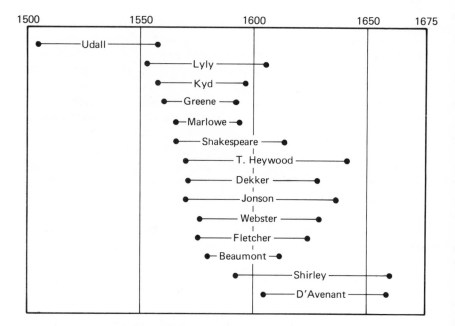

Figure 5.2 From School Comedy to Court Masque

The chief playwrights who lived from the time of Elizabeth I into that of James I died before the closing of the theaters in 1642. The years of the Commonwealth retarded playwriting for a generation.

> *The stars still move, time runs, the clock will strike,*
> *The devil will come, and Faustus must be damn'd.*
> *Oh, I'll leap up to my God!—Who pulls me down?—*
> *See, see, where Christ's blood streams in the firmament!*
> *One drop would save my soul, half a drop: ah, my Christ.*

SEVEN MORE ELIZABETHANS

No university man, Thomas Kyd shared Marlowe's violence as well as "vile heretical conceits denying the divinity of Jesus Christ." For this he was arrested and put to the torture. Released from prison, he was dismissed from the theatrical company of his patron and died in poverty when not yet thirty-six. Before or about the time of

Doctor Faustus, the "sporting Kyd"—as Ben Jonson called him— wrote *The Spanish Tragedy*. It was the first of a long series of "revenge plays" in which ghostly visitations promoted and punished violence. Shakespeare wrote several, including *Richard III*, *Titus Andronicus*, and *Hamlet*. Later came John Marston's *Antonio's Revenge*, George Chapman's *The Revenge of Bussy D'Ambois*, Philip Massinger's *The Roman Actor*, and one that has been revived in the twentieth century, John Webster's *The Duchess of Malfi*. Though *The Spanish Tragedy* was stiffly written, this harrowing play was the most popular and influential tragedy of Elizabethan times. Samuel Pepys, the Restoration diarist, saw it as late as 1668. It was played in Germany and Holland throughout the seventeenth century.

Robert Greene came down from Oxford about 1588, after deserting a wife and "having spent up the marriage-money which I obtained by her." He lived riotously and died at thirty-four after "a surfeit of pickle herringe and Rennish wine." Three times he published pamphlets repenting his sins, and in the last he attacked Shakespeare as "an upstart Crow, beautified with our feathers . . . in his owne conceit the onely Shake-scene in a countrie." Yet he had skill in humor and poetry, his novel *Pandosto* gave Shakespeare the plot for *The Winter's Tale*, and Greene's romantic comedy *The Honorable History of Friar Bacon and Friar Bungay* set a style and was still being played as late as 1630.

An Oxford graduate, George Peele lived till almost forty in spite of being dissolute and improvident. His good humor and his fresh skill in verse made his *The Old Wives' Tale* a success, and he wrote in *Edward I* one of the best of the chronicle plays that competed with those of Shakespeare.

Thomas Dekker and Thomas Heywood—not John, the writer of interludes—lived into their sixties and seventies, but left few more printed plays than the others. They were both victims of collaboration. When Heywood wasn't acting, he had what he called "either an entire hand or at least a main finger" in 220 plays; and Dekker was a "dresser," or play-doctor. Though Dekker was usually poor and spent six years in prison for debt, he had kindliness and charm and "poetry enough for anything"—as may be seen in his *The Shoemaker's Holiday*. Written in 1599, it is still revived occasionally in our universities. Heywood's fame rests—and rather securely—on a single play, *A Woman Killed with Kindness.* Produced in 1603 and dealing with contemporary people, it is the first middle-class tragedy.

BEN JONSON—SHAKESPEARE'S CLOSEST RIVAL

"Rare Ben Jonson"—another exception to the Elizabethan rule that good playwrights die young—all but bridged the time from Shakespeare's beginnings to the closing of the theaters by the Puritans in 1642. He wrote plays for a company of children at Blackfriars and court masques for the scenic specialist Inigo Jones. Between 1605 and 1610 he did his best work for the theater in *Volpone, Bartholomew Fair, Epicoene, or the Silent Woman,* and *The Alchemist.*

Ben Jonson lived a varied life. For a time he was a bricklayer and then a soldier in the Netherlands. He began in the theater as a poorish actor, but he became a good coach, as well as an outstanding dramatist. His career was eventful and his mind disputatious. He killed an actor in a duel, served a short sentence, and was branded on the thumb. He was briefly imprisoned twice more for plays that met with official disfavor. In one case—an affront to the Scots—in which he only figured as a minor collaborator, he "voluntarily imprisoned himself" when he might have escaped. This argues that his attacks on other playwrights were neither malicious nor self-seeking. His attitude toward his friend Shakespeare is typical. After the dramatist's death, Jonson wrote to a Scottish poet that Shakespeare "wanted Arte." When someone said that the author of *Hamlet* had never blotted (erased) a line, Jonson said, "would he had blotted a thousand." Yet he wrote, "[I] lov'd the man, and do honor his memory (on this side of idolatry) as much as any." And in a poem composed for the Shakespeare folio edition of 1623, Jonson said, with rare divination: "He was not of an age, but for all time!"

Through a grant from James I, Jonson became in all but title the poet laureate of England. The honor might have gone equally well to George Chapman. At the end of the sixteenth century he wrote for the public theater and in the next ten years for the children of Blackfriars and St. Paul's—including the horrific revenge play, *Bussy D'Ambois*—but his fame has rested for more than a century on Keat's sonnet celebrating Chapman's translation of Homer.

JACOBEAN COLLABORATORS

The playwrights who wrote after the accession of James I in 1603 were often skillful and polished, but they seldom showed the vitality and imagination of Shakespeare and certain other Elizabethan playwrights. Perhaps the habit of collaboration—supported and enforced by a commercial manager, Philip Henslowe—partly accounts for this. Certainly John Webster wrote without assistance the best poetic tragedy since Shakespeare, *The Duchess of Malfi*, and Philip Massinger was solely responsible for the best comedy, *A New Way to Pay Old Debts*. The most successful collaboration was between Francis Beaumont and John Fletcher with their *Philaster* of 1610 and their *The Maid's Tragedy* of 1611; yet Beaumont wrote a better play, *The Knight of the Burning Pestle*, before he began to collaborate with Fletcher about 1608.

The evils of collaboration go beyond the matter of aesthetics. Because so many men worked together openly or covertly on so many plays, credit for authorship is often confused. Fletcher is an excellent example. Some say he wrote five or six plays by himself; one authority gives him fifty-three. Certain scholars believe he collaborated with Shakespeare on *The Two Noble Kinsmen*, *Henry VIII*, and a lost play called *Cardenio*. Others send Philip Massinger down to Stratford to help out the retired playwright after he had exhausted himself over *The Winter's Tale* and *The Tempest*.

SHAKESPEARE—MAN OF MYSTERY

Shakespeare needed no collaborators. He had genius enough for two. Furthermore, as you will see later, he had the financial security and the aesthetic freedom that came from being a partner, as well as an· actor, in the most successful theater and the most successful company of players in London.

We know very little about the professional careers as well as the personal lives of many Elizabethan playwrights. Some died young. Some had only fleeting popularity. We know a good deal, however, about men of that time who lived as long as Shakespeare—fifty-two years—and had anything remotely approaching his success. Ben Jonson is a case in point. We know much more about his life than we do about Shakespeare's. This is only partly due to Jonson's getting into difficulties with the authorities and his borrowing money from manager Henslowe, who kept careful records. In the main, we know Jonson's life in considerable detail because of comments by his contemporaries and because of the pamphlets he wrote and prefaces he prepared for his published plays. Shakespeare was curiously neglected by his friends and curiously mum on his own part. He put forth no pamphlets, and he wrote no prefaces for the two long poems or the eighteen plays that were published in his lifetime.

The life of the greatest dramatist of the Christian era is one of the most startling and provocative mysteries of literature. We know that he was born in 1564, and we suppose that he had a grammar school education in Stratford-on-Avon. At eighteen he married Anne Hathaway, a woman eight years his senior. His daughter by Anne was born half a year later, and twins arrived in 1585. He seems to have deserted his family at about this time and disappeared. We know nothing more about him until 1592. Then, suddenly, he was prominent enough as an actor for Greene to call him "an upstart Crow" and a "Shake-scene." His first play, *Henry VI*, had reached the stage, for Greene parodied one of its lines—"O Tygers heart, wrappt in a womans hide!"—by writing of Shakespeare's "Tygers hart wrapt in a Players hyde." We can guess that this play and *Titus Andronicus* were acted by Lord Strange's men, just as we can surmise that Shakespeare saw the players of the Earls of Pembroke, Sussex, and Leicester perform in Stratford or that he acted for Strange and for Leicester during the "lost" years. In 1593 he published the poem *Venus and Adonis* and the next year another one, *The Rape of Lucrece*. We know he joined the Lord Chamberlain's company in 1594, for official records show that he was among those paid for acting at court as one of the Chamberlain's "servantes" on December twenty-sixth and twenty-seventh. The next night *The Comedy of Errors* was presented at Gray's Inn.

Between 1594 and 1616 a little more than fifty mentions of the name of Shakespeare occur in print or in written records. No less than twenty-seven have to do with lawsuits or business matters and six with close relatives. In a few cases he is mentioned as an actor in a play. There are three references to his owning a share in the profits of the Globe Theater and of Blackfriars. With one exception critical comments by his contemporaries are, as one authority puts it, "generally brief and either affected or conventional." We have no other facts on his personal life except some allusions to where he lived, two wills in his favor, his own will, and his death and burial.

The few facts that we have on Shakespeare's life and the dates of his plays have been gained by elaborately detailed studies pursued by a large number of scholars during the last two centuries. They have each played the role of a literary Sherlock Holmes.

THE PUBLISHING OF SHAKESPEARE'S PLAYS

No handwriting of Shakespeare's exists except for six signatures. These show four different spellings, and not one includes the "e" in "Shake." His name doesn't appear on the first six of his plays that were printed and published. After 1597, however, eight first editions bear his name. Oddly enough it is spelled either "Shakespeare" or "Shakespeare." Attracted by the martial glamor of a flourished weapon, printers or publishers gave the spelling "Shakespeare" to posterity.

They gave more than the spelling, of course. They preserved thirty-seven of his plays. Very few manuscripts exist of plays acted in London during the time of Elizabeth I, James I, and Charles I, and not too many dramas were printed. Of the 220 collaborations that Thomas Heywood boasted about, only one got into print. About 550 plays were published between 1559 and 1642, but one authority has calculated that almost 1500 were lost in manuscript through carelessness or destroyed in theater fires. The reason that so few plays were published between the accession of Elizabeth I and the closing of the theaters was because the author sold all rights to an acting company, and the acting company sold a manuscript to a publisher only when its need for money was greater than its fear that a rival would pirate a play once it was in print. Authorities believe that some plays were stolen by the publishers through buying "parts" from actors, through paying them to recite the play from memory or through having employees write down the dialog in shorthand. "Copyright" meant no more than that you could produce any play if you had a copy of the manuscript.

Among the eighteen plays published during Shakespeare's lifetime was *Pericles*, which is thought to be a collaboration.

Another appeared in 1622. We should have only about half of his now known plays if two friends and fellow actors, John Heminge and Henry Condell, had not gathered together all existing manuscripts and printed plays and edited them for publication in 1623 as *The Workes of William Shakespeare*. This volume is called the First Folio. It is a "folio" because the standard sheet of printing paper was folded once, producing a page about thirteen and a half by eight and a half inches. The plays first published during Shakespeare's life—and published singly—are called quartos because the paper was folded twice—or quartered—producing a page about eight by six inches. The texts of some of the quartos are close to those in the folios—there were four folios printed between 1623 and 1685—and some of the speeches in the quartos are better. But a number of these first editions are called "bad quartos" and were justly described by Heminge and Condell as "diverse stolne and surreptitious copies, maimed, and deformed by frauds and stealthes of injurious impostores." The thirty-six plays in the First Folio form the Shakespearean Canon, a parallel to the Church Canon of the accepted books of the Bible. The Third Folio added *Pericles* and six certainly spurious plays. *The Two Noble Kinsmen* was never given folio publication, but appeared as a quarto almost twenty years after Shakespeare's death.

SHAKESPEARE'S PROSPERITY

In Shakespeare's time no man could live by playwriting alone. Plays were sold outright for £6 or £8, which meant no more than $180 to $240 in the currency of today. Some playwrights may have received the profits from the second or third performances of their plays, but this can't have amounted to very much. The total income that Shakespeare received from the sale of his plays, spread over a little more than twenty years, was probably only about £300, or less than $10,000 in our money. Because of Burbage's liberality toward his most valuable associates, Shakespeare had, for many years, not only his salary as a player, but also a player's share in the profits, and, after 1599, he had an additional share as one of the ten owners of the Globe.

Shakespeare's financial security saved him from writing innumerable potboilers and collaborating or "dressing" other men's plays. Though many of his fellows wrote far more plays a year, Shakespeare's annual output of almost two plays each season, while he was with Burbage, is an impressive one by modern standards. He was able to do this by a kind of indirect collaboration with the historians, novelists, and playwrights of the past. He took large parts of his plots from older works. All but two of his plays have been traced to sources other than his own fertile mind.

Far more important, Shakespeare's secure position with Burbage's company saved him from the temptation to follow popular trends too closely or to repeat his own successes. He may have written *The Merchant of Venice*—which uses material from two or three earlier works—because of the anti-semitism aroused by the trial and execution of a Jewish physician who was accused of trying to poison Elizabeth. He wrote "revenge plays" in *Richard III* and *Titus Andronicus*, but in between them came *The Comedy of Errors*, adapted from Plautus. *Much Ado About Nothing* and *Henry V* shared the same year. So did *Twelfth Night* and *Hamlet*.

THE ELIZABETHAN PLAYWRIGHTS
IGNORE CLASSIC RULES

The first great step forward for the Elizabethan drama was the designing and building of the unique Theater by James Burbage in 1576 and its companion, The Curtain, by another man the next year. They gave the playwrights a form of stage that suited their current needs and that led their successors to splendid new fecundity. A decade later came the first flowering in Marlowe's *Tamburlaine* and *Doctor Faustus*. Another ten years brought the full fruit of Shakespeare's plays from *Richard III* and *A Midsummer Night's Dream* to *Twelfth Night* and *Hamlet*. No dramatic era ever showed such swift, extraordinary progress.

While Shakespeare was still in Stratford, Elizabethan playwrights had broken with academic tradition. Like Lope de Vega, they had turned their backs on the classic unities and the dictums of Aristotle and Horace. In 1580 Sir Philip Sidney, poet, courtier, and critic, grieved over violations of the classic forms. If he had lived another five years, what would he have said of Shakespeare and his fellows—unless their poetry and power could have overwhelmed him? In Sidney's opinion, tedious *Gorboduc* climbed "to the heights of Seneca his style" and reached "the very end of Poesy." Yet he regretted that it was not "an exact model of all Tragedies. For it is faulty in both Time and Place, the two necessary companions of all corporal actions."

The Elizabethan dramatist not only forgot the unities. Unlike the authors of *Gorboduc*, he showed violent action on the stage, instead of merely talking about it. His violence approached atrocity; in *King Lear* Shakespeare showed the blinding of a man. Like the others, Shakespeare wrote what Sidney had called "neither right tragedy nor right comedy, mingling kings and clowns." Moreover, he mixed poetry and prose, and ignored the rule that verse should be reserved for the nobility and prose for the lowly. In *Twelfth Night* sea captains spoke blank verse, and the Countess Olivia descended to prose. Brutus delivered Caesar's funeral oration without benefit of meter, and Hamlet did likewise in his advice to the players. Half a dozen of Shakespeare's comedies have more lines of prose than of poetry.

FAULTS OF THE TIMES

The Elizabethan playwright was fond of some devices of an older stage that seem absurd or cumbersome today, but Shakespeare used them less—or better—than the other writers. He usually relegated the subplot to his comedies. To introduce a play or to bridge gaps of time, Shakespeare sometimes used speakers by the name of Prolog, Induction, or Chorus, a convention that seems to have come over from an Italian misconception of Greek tragedy. In *Henry V*, Chorus is a long but sturdy bridge of narrative and exhortation leading from one act to another. The speaker called Chorus in *Romeo and Juliet* bunglingly betrays the plot, but in only two places—before the first act and the second. (Modern producers often drop these speeches.) There are only three other Shakespearean Prologs. Shakespeare was chary of another device—the Epilog. He used only eight, none in his tragedies. One other feature of the Elizabethan theater that would seem absurd to present-day audiences was the "jig." A short song and dance probably closed even the performance of Shakespeare's plays—just as it did the shows in Spain. A Continental visitor to London saw a play about Julius Caesar, which may well have been Shakespeare's, and wrote: "At the end of the play two of the actors in men's clothes and 2 in women's clothes performed a dance, as is their custom, wonderfully well together." (Perhaps Shakespeare had objected to a song.)

The weaknesses of Shakespeare—beyond every playwright's normal chance of failure—were the weaknesses of his time and his audience. Elizabethan England loved allegory as much as violence, long-drawn philosophizing as much as soaring poetry. Too often, issues were all black and white, and characters either good or bad. Love at first sight seemed no more implausible than last-minute conversions with the good man turning to evil or the evil man to good. Audiences accepted magical potions as well as disguises that any child would see through. They were content with types instead of characters. It is to the great credit of Shakespeare that he gave us human beings like Hamlet, Henry V, and Catherine of France, Falstaff and Malvolio, Beatrice and Benedick, Richard II and Portia, Marc Antony and Brutus.

Now we must turn from dramatic literature to business, from playwriting to theater building and theater management. But we must consider, first of all, how the pleasure-loving authorities of the court fought for the theaters and their managers against the somewhat puritanical authorities of the City of London.

COURT AGAINST CITY
OVER THE THEATERS

The city fathers began with a legitimate grievance. Whether the plays were given in innyards or in regular theaters, the crowds invited thievery. There were small riots, and the authorities were certain that, in this time of tension between the dominant Protestants and the suppressed Catholics, sedition flourished. Worse still, when the plague threatened London—as it did a good deal of the time—the gathering together of even small crowds helped spread infection. The Puritans had moral objections. A writer called actors "crocodiles which devour the pure chastity both of single and married persons." Their plays teach "all things that appertain to craft, mischief, deceits, and filthiness." "Whosoever shall visit the chapel of Satan, I mean the Theater, shall find there no want of young ruffians." Women cannot come from plays "with safe and chaste minds." Men in the audience "give them pippins, they dally with their garments."

With this, queen and court couldn't agree. They liked plays, and some were patrons of acting companies. So Elizabeth and her Privy Council fought back. In 1574 the queen won the first round by licensing a company called The Earl of Leicester's Men to play "within oure Citie of London" except during common prayer or the plague. The city acquiesced but inveighed against "eavell practizes of incontinencye in great Inns havinge chambers and secrete places adjoyninge to their open stagies and gallyries, inveglynge and alleur of maids." The city set up some rather mild regulations, but the net result was the building of playhouses outside the jurisdiction of the city; at first they were to the north but later south of the Thames in Bankside. For twenty years after Burbage built The Theater, the fight between court and city continued, the queen going so far as to create her own company. The conflict was highlighted by the closing down of the theater–inns at certain times, by new regulations coming from both city and court, and by the shuttering of the outlying theaters during plagues, as well as at least once during normal times by order of the Privy Council.

The grim reality of the plague stands out in a city regulation of 1584 permitting the theaters to reopen only after the number of deaths in London—a city of two hundred thousand—had fallen below fifty a day for twenty straight days. The plague closed the theaters almost all the time between January, 1593, and the spring of the next year. This disaster forced the Strange-Derby company to join the Admiral's Men under Alleyn and Henslowe in a touring venture. After the plague was over, this joint company played a short engagement at Newington Butts and then split up. Alleyn and the Admiral's Men went to Henslowe's house, the Rose. When Derby died, his players found a new patron in Henry Lord Hunsdon, became the Chamberlain's Men, moved to The Theater, and acquired William Shakespeare and Richard Burbage. Without the plague this great company might never have been formed.

CENSORSHIP AND MONOPOLY BEGIN

Regulations set up by the queen's Privy Council brought censorship to the English stage—and also a kind of monopoly.

To overrule the city, a royal patent of 1581 centered all stage authority in the Master of the Revels. This functionary in the office of the Lord Chamberlain had long had the task of providing plays and other amusements for the court. Now he was given national control over "showes, plaies, plaiers and play-makers, together with their playing places, to order and reforme, auctorise and put downe." This meant that all plays had to be approved before production. Censorship was stricter on political matters than on moral. In the light of their day plays were far cleaner than might have been expected. Adultery was a rare theme in comedy. In 1606 "An Acte to Restraine Abuses of Players" was passed to curb blasphemy. One of its results was that the First Folio of 1623 changed a speech of Shakespeare's merry Mistress Page from "what the devil" to "what the dickens."

Monopoly began in 1598 when the Privy Council ordered the companies cut down to two—the Admiral's and the Chamberlain's. Others continued, however, and within four years Worcester's Men were officially licensed. James I took a firmer stand. He closed all but those under the patronage of him and his family. The London stage was to suffer still more from such restrictions in the eighteenth century.

THEATER BUILDERS AND THEATER MANAGERS

After Shakespeare and Marlowe—and far, far ahead of the earls and chamberlains and admirals who lent their patronage to the poor players—we must recognize James Burbage, carpenter–actor, and Philip Henslowe, speculator in almost anything, as the men to whom the Elizabethan drama owes its greatest debt. Close after them come Burbage's two sons (Richard, the actor, and Cuthbert, the business manager) and Henslowe's son-in-law, Edward Alleyn, who shared honors with Richard Burbage as Elizabeth's foremost player.

James Burbage was the pioneer. In 1576, when Shakespeare

was barely twelve, this man built the first public playhouse in England. Not without right, he called it simply The Theater. His example inspired the building of the next theater, a year or so later, close by in Shoreditch, a northeast section of London. This theater—called The Curtain because it was built on a piece of land variously known as Curten Close and Courtein—produced some of the plays of Burbage's actor–dramatist, William Shakespeare, for Burbage once had an agreement to pool the profits of the two houses. In 1599—two years after Burbage's death—the lease expired on the ground where The Theater was built, and Burbage's sons tore down the structure and used the lumber to build the famous Globe in the district called Bankside, south of the Thames. Later, in order to have a second playhouse—this one protected against the rain—Burbage's sons turned into a "private," or roofed, theater a part of Blackfriars priory, which their father had bought shortly before he died.

Henslowe was a businessman. We would call him a speculator. He may have begun as either a dyer's apprentice or a bailiff's assistant, but he became a pawnbroker, a dealer in lime and leather, a buyer and seller of land, and a monopolist of bear-baiting. When he saw that, in ten years, the only two playhouses in London were on their feet as money-making ventures, he went into the theater business. In 1587—twelve years before the Globe was built in Bankside—Henslowe opened the Rose nearby, and in 1600 he put up the Fortune in northern London. When the first Globe burned down in 1613, he promptly turned his Bear Garden, south of the Thames, into the Hope theater. As theater owner, or "housekeeper," he took his share of the profits from the companies that played his houses, but he also had personal and profitable relations with the actors and playwrights. To keep them in line, he became their generous and persistent banker. "Should these fellows come out of my debt," he wrote, "I should have noe rule over them."

Someone else might have built Henslowe's playhouses, but that other person might not have played banker and kept the records from which scholars have learned more about the history of the Elizabethan theater than from any other source. We are deeper in debt to this money-grubber than Ben Jonson ever was. Henslowe wrote in his so-called *Diary* the names and dates of many of the plays in his theaters, as well as the box office receipts and whether the plays were "ne," as he put it, meaning "new." Henslowe's contract for the building of the Fortune—which was modeled on the Globe, though square instead of many-sided—is the only detailed description of an Elizabethan theater.

It would be unfair to add to Henslowe's record of commercial canniness the fact that he got the capital for his speculations by marrying the rich widow of his first employer. The habit of marrying the boss's daughter was a common one in those days. James Burbage secured the money for The Theater from his wife's brother, a wealthy grocer, and the actor Alleyn got himself into partnership with Henslowe by marrying his step-child.

There were other theaters and theater builders. By 1605 London had six public playhouses and a private one, Blackfriars. There was also a stage at Newington Butts, though this may have been merely in an innyard. Another public playhouse, the Hope—as we have already mentioned—was opened in 1613. Three "private theaters" appeared during the reign of James I and Charles I: Whitefriars about 1608, the Phoenix converted from the Cockpit about 1617, and the Salisbury Court in 1629.

WHAT WE KNOW ABOUT THE GLOBE

We know more about the kind of theater that Shakespeare commonly played in than we do about his life. And yet our knowledge of the so-called public playhouse is far from complete. Most scholars believe it took a unique form. This form was approached only by the Spanish *corrales*, which we described earlier, and it was destroyed by the Commonwealth and the Restoration. A few think that it may have been more like the Italian theater or a Dutch variant. This seems a bit far-fetched, for there were no permanent theaters in Italy before 1576, and a German who visited London in 1585 wrote that The Theater and The Curtain were "unusual houses, which are so constructed that they have about three galleries, one above the other."

The only definite evidence that we have on the shape of the Elizabethan theater and stage comes from four sources:

   1. *The great halls and innyards where plays were given before Burbage built the first theater in 1576, and the buildings for bear-baiting and bull-baiting.*

2. *Four sketches ranging in date from about 1596 to 1640.*

3. *The contract for the building of the Fortune.*

4. *Evidence drawn from the stage directions of Elizabethan plays.*

The basic elements of the Elizabethan theater are a stage with a door at each side and a balcony above, to be used by the actors, and a flat floor and galleries at the sides and rear, to hold the audience. Some of these elements were to be found in the so-called great halls of palaces like Hampton Court, of the Inns of Court, and of colleges at Oxford and Cambridge. In the end wall of such a room there was a door at each side leading to the kitchen. These provided entrances for the actors, who played their scenes on the floor or on a low platform between the doors. Above, was the "minstrels' gallery," which served as an upper stage. There were sometimes galleries along the side walls, where some of the audience could sit, and usually a gallery at the back of the hall. The courtyards of the old English inns provided many the same elements. There were two or three galleries on all four sides and doors that could be used by the actors. We presume that a stage was set up at one end and that the players reached the stage by a few steps. The common people could stand in the rest of the innyard, while wealthier spectators could stand or sit on the galleries at the sides and at one end. For certain scenes the actors could use the gallery over the stage.

We know that professional actors gave plays in the great halls from time to time. After the first theaters were built, there are records of frequent performances in the courtyards of the Bell Inn, the Bel Savage, the Cross Keys, and others. Some of these may have been used earlier; others certainly were. In 1557 a play called *A Sackful of News* was suppressed after being given at the Boar's Head. At the Red Lion a play called *Samson* was acted in 1567, and the Bull Inn was used for plays before 1576. There are two reasons why companies still played in innyards after theaters were available. First, there were more troupes than playhouses. Second, the inns—with warm rooms and drink to be had—were more comfortable in the chilly and rainy English winters.

South of the Thames there were buildings that may have suggested to Burbage a way of improving on the innyards. These were structures for bear-baiting and bull-baiting. This popular pastime consisted in watching mastiff dogs attack a tethered animal or one another. Maps of 1560 and earlier show two circular buildings used for these purposes, and each appears to have galleries from which the spectators could watch in safety. The close relation of the baiting places and theaters is obvious, for when Henslowe made the Hope theater out of his Bear Garden, he installed a movable stage and used the building both for plays and for what the Elizabethans called "sport."

DRAWINGS OF ELIZABETHAN PLAYHOUSES

We have not more than four old pictures that purport to show the interior of an Elizabethan theater. Only one of these can be depended upon, and it shows merely a part of the total stage space.

A Dutchman named de Witt visited London about 1596. He was much impressed by the city's "four beautiful theaters," and he described and sketched "the finest and the largest," the Swan. Unfortunately his description is very brief and means little while his sketch was lost and all we have is a copy supposed to have been made by a fellow student. The doors are too close together to fit the stage "business" indicated in most plays. Above them there are boxes for spectators where most authorities think there was an upper stage.

The next sketch is from the title page of a play called *Roxana*, a tragedy in Latin, printed in 1630. It shows curtains and a raised stage, but, again, spectators appear in two boxes where scripts often seem to indicate an upper stage. As *Roxana* was in Latin and first acted at Trinity College, Cambridge, this sketch may show a university production.

The nearest approach to what scholars consider the Elizabethan stage is a drawing reproduced in *Messalina*, a play printed in 1640. Here we have a raised stage with painted curtains behind it. Above is a very shallow stage—hardly more than an unrailed gallery—behind which we see a curtained opening. The drawing isn't wide enough to show entrance doors at the sides. It is more than possible that the artist sketched an actual stage of a theater in London.

Figure 5.3 Contemporary drawings of the Elizabethan Stage

Above at the left is a sketch made from a description by de Witt after he had visited the Swan about 1596. Next to it is a cut from Roxana, published in 1630. At the left is a scene from *Messalina*, printed in 1640.

The last drawing is late. It appeared in 1672 in *The Wits, or Sport upon Sport*, a collection of "drolls," or short comedies acted here and there between 1642 and 1660 while the theaters were banned by the Puritans. The footlights, the candelabra, and the spectators above the stage suggest that this is a joint product of the artist's imagination and a performance in a private hall.

THE CONTRACT FOR THE FORTUNE THEATER

To Henslowe, the careful businessman, we owe the only record of the size, shape, and parts of an Elizabethan theater. When he decided to build the Fortune in 1600, he made—and time has fortunately preserved—a contract with a carpenter to put up a building resembling in all but one detail "the late erected playhouse . . . called the Globe." The difference lay in the fact that the new house was to be square—an idea that Henslowe abandoned when he rebuilt the Fortune after it had been burned to the ground. The contract specified that the building was to be eighty feet "every way" and fifty-five feet within. There were to be three stories with galleries providing "convenient divisions for gentlemen's rooms" and "twopenny rooms"—the first story twelve feet high, the next eleven, and the third nine. The stage was to be forty-three feet wide, and it was to extend halfway across the open yard, making it twenty-seven and a half deep. There was to be a "shadow or cover over the said stage" and a "tiring house," which may have included an inner and an upper stage as well as rooms in which the actors could change their attire. As Henslowe specified "convenient windows" in the tiring house, we may suppose that among these were ones used for balcony scenes, as in *Romeo and Juliet*.

WHAT THE STAGE DIRECTIONS TELL US

Henslowe's contract fails to list many possible features of the stage, falling back on "to be in all other proportions contrived and fashioned like unto the stage of the said playhouse called the Globe." We may presume that there were side entrances even in the early

Theater, or Shakespeare would not have written such a stage direction in *Richard III* as: "Enter on one side, Queen Elizabeth, Duchess of York, and Marquess of Dorset; the other, Anne, Duchess of Gloucester. . . ." In conflicts, opposing forces come in through opposite doors: "Enter on the other side of the field, Richmond, Sir William Brandon, Oxford, and other Officers."

There is no mention of an inner stage in the Fortune contract, but scholars think they have found plenty of evidence even in the early plays: With the curtains closed, the stage could be a street, a country road, a battle scene. When they were open, the inner stage could become a tent, a room in a tavern, a cave, a shop. If the inner stage was occupied by a throne, then that area and the main stage became a palace. In 1953, an English scholar, C. Walter Hodges, attacked the notion of an inner stage, declaring it to be too remote from the spectators. An American scholar, Leslie Hotson, proposed the radical idea that inner below scenes were contained in a special structure built out from the back wall and easily seen by everyone.

Shakespearean authorities believe that there were two other stages on the level of the gallery. These had the "convenient windows" of the Fortune contract, and they were placed above the two side doors to the main stage. In the first balcony scene of *Romeo and Juliet* we read, "Juliet appears above at a window." If this window were merely imagined as part of the gallery, then Romeo would have to speak the lines of his love scene with his back to most of the audience. There are other windows called for in Elizabethan plays, and other balcony scenes with rope ladders for the hero to climb up and come down.

Above the balcony was a still higher stage for the musicians and for scenes far aloft, as, for instance, at a ship's masthead. Thus the Elizabethan theater appears to have had seven useable areas: the main stage, an inner stage on the same level, the gallery, an inner stage on that level, the two windowed stages at the sides, and the high place for the musicians. Naturally, the three levels had to be connected by backstage stairs. There were also stairs to the "cellarage" under the main stage, or platform, and to the "hut."

The hut was the top of the tiring house, and it had room for cannon and other sound machines. From it actors could enter the "shadow," or "heavens"—which was the roof over the stage—and be let down through a trapdoor. Thomas Heywood in *Apology for Ac-*

tors wrote of the heavens "where upon any occasion the gods descended." In *Alphonsus, King of Aragon* a stage direction runs: "After you have sounded thrise, let Venus be let downe from the top of the stage." In *Doctor Faustus*, Marlowe asks for "Musicke while the Throne descends." In the prolog to *Every Man in His Humor*, Ben Jonson, who was not fond of scenic machinery, wrote sarcastically of the kind of play in which a "creaking throne comes down the boys to please."

The main stage seems to have had a number of traps. In the last act of *Hamlet* there must have been a "grave trap." Witches and spirits could rise up through this trap in the main stage, accompanied by smoke. In *The Brazen Age*, Heywood requires openings in both the heavens and the stage: "Jupiter strikes him [Hercules] with a thunderbolt, his body sinks, and from the heavens descends a hand in a cloud, that from the place where Hercules burnt, brings up a starre, and fixeth it in the firmament." Some think the upper stage had a trap, too.

A FLEXIBLE THEATER FOR FREE-RANGING PLAYS

A study of any Elizabethan play shows how flexible the stage had to be to accommodate the many changes of scene—no less than forty-three in *Antony and Cleopatra*. Yet, at the same time, the playwrights had to take more trouble over certain things than the later men who wrote for a stage with a curtain. Unless a death took place on an inner stage—which was impossible to such a violent and corpse-filled scene as the last in *Hamlet*—the author had to devise some reason for carting off the mortal remains. When all the actors left the stage a scene in one locale was over, and a new setting was to be seen or imagined when another group of actors entered. This meant that an actor could not end one scene with an exit and come back at the beginning of the next; someone else had to begin the new scene. Thus, at the end of the first scene in *Hamlet*, Horatio and his friends leave the parapet to tell Hamlet about his father's ghost. The next scene begins with the entrances of the king, the queen, Hamlet, Laertes, and Polonius, and continues for almost 160 lines before Horatio enters to talk with Hamlet. With such dramaturgy and such a stage, free and wide-ranging plays could be acted with great speed and effectiveness. If there were intermissions, there is no textual evidence that these were necessary, except as a relief from the tension of the play or to give the management a chance to sell food and drink to the audience. There are no indications of acts and scenes in almost all of the Shakespearean quartos. Though most of the First Folio plays are so divided, six do not show even act divisions. The Elizabethan playwright did not *think* in five acts, like the classicists of the Renaissance, and his scenes ran along much like those of a motion picture.

Sir Philip Sidney, who must have seen performances at The Theater and The Curtain as well as at court, was much irritated by the way the playwrights threw scene after scene upon the stage:

> *Where you shall have* Asia *of the one side, and* Afric *of the other, and so many under-kingdoms, that the Player, when he cometh in, must ever begin with telling where he is; or else the tale will not be conceived. Now we shall have three Ladies walk to gather flowers, and then we must believe the stage to be a Garden. By and by, we hear news of shipwreck in the same place, and then we are to blame, if we accept it not as a Rock.*

THE AUDIENCE

The audience doesn't seem to have been bothered by all this. It accepted the conventions of the Elizabethan stage just as the Greeks had accepted the conventions of the Greek stage. Shakespeare's audience was a mixed one. In the "gentlemen's rooms" of the gallery, there were lords and ladies just as intelligent as Sidney, just as wise in knowledge of the classic stage. In the "pit"—that flat area between the gallery walls, where the "groundlings" stood almost surrounding the stage—there were tradesmen and apprentices, servants and mechanics, soldiers and sailors. Too often this audience has been pictured as ignorant and rowdy and altogether undesirable. This was certainly the opinion of the puritanical city officials who wrote of "sondrye robberies by pyckinge and Cuttinge of purses." Our unfavorable picture of the audience in the pit is due largely to what the playwrights wrote about them. Hamlet says that the groundlings "for the most part are capable of nothing but inexplicable dumb-shows and noise." Peele disliked writing for the "penny knaves delight." Jonson said that "the beast, the multitude . . . love nothing that is right and proper." The playwrights said almost as much about the actors, but they must have been much more annoyed at the habit of apple eating, nut cracking, and beer drinking that apparently went on throughout the performances. We must remark however, that Nell Gwyn began her career by selling oranges in the Restoration theaters, while English audiences today drink coffee or tea and eat biscuits or ice cream in the intermissions.

James Burbage made no mistake when he kept the "pit" that had been inevitable in the innyards. Thus he insured a much larger audience than could have been seated; some think the Globe held three thousand spectators. It was also an audience that must have grown highly critical when a poor scene made them conscious of tired feet. The high quality of the poetic drama from Marlowe through Shakespeare proves that the Elizabethan audience had sensibility and native intelligence. Few could read, of course, but an audience that couldn't read could have very sharp ears and an eagerness for ideas and emotions that could come only from the stage.

THE "PRIVATE" THEATERS

Beginning in Elizabethan times there was a curious and a vague distinction between the "public" theaters that we have described and the "private" ones. Anyone could buy admission to a private theater, but, because the price of seats ranged from sixpence to two shillings instead of from a penny to a shilling, the audience was a bit more select. In a private theater everyone had a seat. Certain gallants paid an extra twelvepence for stools on the stage until this became such a nuisance that Charles II stopped the practice in his time; it took another century and the authority of a David Garrick to finally do away with it.

Public theaters versus private theaters may seem a distinction without a difference, but it was a very real one. The title page of *The Duchess of Malfi* reads: "As it was Presented privately, at the Black-Friers; and publiquely at the Globe, By the Kings Majesties Servants." In an early and defective edition of *Hamlet*, Gildenstern explains to the prince that the actors have left their theater because

Figure 5.4 Blackfriars Restored

Reconstruction of a "private theater" of Shakespeare's day, by G. Tophan Forrest. Except for the addition of benches in the pit, a roof, and artificial lighting, the structure follows the pattern of the public theaters. (From *The London Times*.)

"the publicke audience that came to them, are turned to private playes, and the humor of children."

The concept of a private theater may go back at least as far as 1574. In that year the London authorities made regulations for the innyard performances but exempted those "withoute publique or common collection of money." They were thinking of the Inns of Court, plays in noblemen's houses, and sporadic appearances of the child actors. Perhaps the term "private theater" arose about 1576—after the opening of The Theater and The Curtain—when Richard Farrant, Master of the Children of Windsor, decided to give performances by his choristers and the Children of the Chapel at Blackfriars. Since this was a rather radical step and since the theater and its actors were still close to the line of vagabondage, Farrant may have thought it wise to announce "private" performances in a "private" theater, though he took money from the public in advance.

The popularity of the child actors and their private theaters was great but intermittent. At various times they had private theaters at Whitefriars, at St. Paul's, and at Porter's Hall, as well as at Blackfriars. James Burbage bought part of Blackfriars in 1596 and made it over into a theater. He died the next year, however, and his sons leased it to the Children of the Chapel. The children fell out of favor with the court, and in 1608 or 1609 Blackfriars became the winter home of the players of the Globe. Like other private theaters, its repertory leaned toward sophisticated comedy.

An outstanding difference between the public and the private theaters was that the latter were roofed and used artificial light. Where public theaters had to open by two in the afternoon, the others could play later and into the evening, as, for instance, when the queen of James I appears to have engaged the Blackfriars and its actors to entertain her and her guests on certain nights in the 1630s.

DID THE ELIZABETHANS USE SCENERY?

There seems to have been a good deal of scenic display in Elizabethan plays done at court or even in the lawyers' inns. Records of the Revels' Office list money spent for a "citie" and a "battlement," for "canvas to cover divers townes and howes and other devisses and clowds," for "the Clowdes and curteynes," for "one great city, one senate house," for "vii Cities, one villadge, one Country howes, one battlement," for "great cloths" and "greate curteynes." Many productions probably showed different "mansions" at

Figure 5.5 Drury Lane in 1808
Built in 1794 and planned "upon a much larger scale than that of any
other theater in Europe," the theater burned down in 1819. A new
Drury Lane was erected on the same site, designed this time to hold
even more spectators—about 3,200. (Drawing by Gerda Becker With,
after an aquatint by Rowlandson and Pugin.)

the same time, after the fashion of the medieval stage, though it
may be argued that the court adopted Serlio's scheme of a single
setting for a street or a woods.

With James I, Italianate scenery and scenic devices definitely
began to invade court performances. Beginning in 1605, they were
employed in the masques staged by Inigo Jones, as we shall see
later. Toward the end of the reign of Charles I, scenery seems to
have spread from court performances to those in the private theaters. In 1636 the queen was so impressed by what she heard about
a production of a play at Oxford that she borrowed the costumes and
scenery for her own players. The university authorities sent the
"Cloathes and Perspectives" and requested that they should not
"come into the hands and use of the common Players"—which

suggests that the private theaters had begun to use such scenery. A writer remarks that a play produced at Blackfriars in 1637 had scenes such as "were only used at Masques." There are two or three other allusions to painted settings at that private theater between 1638 and 1640.

The public theaters, however, used very little in the way of scenery. There were probably some suggestions of settings on an inner stage—hangings or set-pieces for rooms, trees for a wood. Romeo "climbs a wall and leaps down within it." But Henslowe's records list only properties:

> *i rock, i cage, i Hell mouth.*
> *i tomb of Guido, i tomb of Dido, i bedstead.*
> *i wooden hatchet, i leather hatchet*
> *Iris head, & rainbow; i little altar.*
> *i copper target, & xvii foils.*
> *iii timbrels; i dragon in Faustus.*
> *i Pope's miter.*
> *iii Imperial crowns; i plain crown.*

Some believe that, at one time, there may have been lettered signs, or "locality boards," over the side doors of the stage, as there were in the drawings of scenes from Terence. Sidney wrote: "What Child is there, that, coming to a Play, seeing *Thebes* written in great letters upon an old door, doth believe that it is Thebes?"

"GORGIOUS AND SUMPTIOUS APPARELL"

Productions at theaters like the Globe and the Fortune must have been elaborate and impressive in two respects—music and costuming. Henslowe lent money for the purchase of instruments, and stage directions called not only for "flourishes" at the entrance of royalty and generals, but also music to accompany songs, dances, and even whole scenes. As for costumes, in 1577 a clergyman attacked the "gorgious and sumptious apparell" on the stage, a Swiss visitor wrote in 1599 that the players were "very expensively and handsomely dressed," and an Italian—who should have been highly critical—commented on "the sumptuous dresses of the actors."

Most of the costumes must have been of the type then worn in court or in private life, but there were attempts to imitate foreign or class dress. Among other costumes, Henslowe inventoried a Moor's coat, a dress for Neptune, and two Danish suits. A line in a play by Kyd mentions a "Turkish bonnet." Shylock wore a Jewish gabardine. A 1595 sketch of a scene from *Titus Andronicus* shows Turkish trousers on one actor, and an attempt at a Roman cloak. The best of materials had to be used because an actor on the center of the platform was within sixty feet of the most distant spectator, while hundreds stood close to the stage. Though the cost of theater building may seem low to us—Henslowe paid only £520, or not more than $25,000 today, for the first Fortune and about twice as much for the second one built of brick—good cloth was very expensive. Velvet cost a pound a yard, or about $50. There was one way, however, of getting good secondhand clothes. A continental visitor reports that "when distinguished gentlemen or knights die, almost their best clothes are given to their servants, but as it is not fitting that they should wear them they sell them cheaply to the actors."

THE ELIZABETHAN REPERTORY SYSTEM

The playwrights, the public, and the actors had one great advantage in Shakespeare's time that they do not share today in England or the United States. This was the repertory system. There were no long runs. The bill changed nightly, but plays were repeated over and over again at various intervals. For thirty performances in the season of 1593–94 Henslowe lists thirteen plays, most of which were acted twice and some three or four times. A popular play was often given over many years. A play that would have failed if it had been produced for a run could be nursed along through a number of well-spaced performances. The playwright received no royalties, but at least he had the satisfaction of knowing that even his comparative failures drew good houses from time to time.

Because a permanent company was part of the repertory system, the actors improved their technique by constantly working together on a wide variety of plays. The playwright gained from their increased skill. He also profited by being able to develop parts to suit the abilities of the players. Because an actor in such a company was able to play a "fat" part two or three times a week, he was probably willing to give his talents to a smaller part every now and then. Will Kempe, the greatest comic actor in London, who may have acted Falstaff and Bottom, played the tiny role of Peter, the servant of Juliet's nurse.

FROM ROGUES AND VAGABONDS TO THE QUEEN'S MEN

The story of the Elizabethan actors is an interesting one. It is also complex and confusing, and, at times, pretty vague. Quite early, one fact stands out: companies of players had to have the patronage of a nobleman if they wanted to tour in comparative safety. The reasons for this were probably many. At a time when drama was coming to life again through the Revival of Learning, vanity might urge a king or an earl to keep a troupe of actors among his household servants and to let them spread his name across the countryside. The actors profited by reflected glory. They drew larger crowds when they came to a town as the Earl of Leicester's Men than if they were billed as Burbage's Players. Further, they sometimes had a measure of financial support when they wore the livery of a nobleman's servant. Behind all this, however, there must have been a holdover from the feudal way of life which was still of recent memory. At the end of the Middle Ages there was no such thing as a "masterless man," unless he was a fugitive from justice or from his lord. There is a whiff of this in the Tudor Poor Law of 1572 that classed as "rogues and vagabonds" all "Common Players in Enterludes & Minstrals, not belonging to any Baron of this Realme or towards any other honorable Personage of Greater Degree."

Records are scanty, but the Earl of Worcester seems to have had a company of players as early as 1555, the Earl of Warwick and the Earl of Leicester in 1559, and Lord Strange, the future Earl of Derby, in the sixties, and the Baron of Effingham in the seventies. Other noblemen followed the fashion. One authority lists twenty-three companies under noble patronage during the reign of Elizabeth I. Having dropped her own players of interludes in favor of boy actors, she turned back to adults in 1583 and set up the Queen's Men, a brilliant company in their red liveries, who played at court, in London inns, and on tour till about 1590.

THE ACTING COMPANIES

The history of the individual troupes is hard to follow. Companies passed from one nobleman to another. The death of patrons, defection among players, and, worse still, the calamitous plagues that harried England from time to time disrupted old companies and created new ones. Even in London the facts are often dim. Between 1559 and 1586, when there were adult performances at two theaters and no one knows at how many inns, we have records of some dozen companies. In the last fifteen years of Elizabeth's reign most of these disappeared and five new troupes were added. The most successful companies in the 1580s and the early '90s were the Queen's Men, with the famous clown Tarleton, Leicester's Men, with whom Richard Burbage played for a time, and the troupe of Lord Strange, who became the Earl of Derby. Out of these, only Derby's survived long and only under two new names. On Derby's death, they became the Chamberlain's Men, and James I made them the King's Men after his coronation. This troupe, for which Shakespeare wrote and Richard Burbage acted, had only two real rivals. One was the Earl of Worcester's Men, with whom Edward Alleyn had acted before coming to London. The other was made up of the provincial players of the Baron of Effingham, later the Earl of Nottingham. It was called the Admiral's Men because Effingham was Lord High Admiral when he defeated the Spanish Armada. Marlowe wrote—all too briefly—for this company, Alleyn was its star, and Henslowe its landlord and banker. All three companies appeared at court and probably toured from time to time, certainly when plagues swept London.

James I and his family took a hearty interest in the theater. When he was not only heir to the English throne but also king of Scotland, he borrowed Elizabeth's players to help celebrate his marriage by performances in Edinburgh. On his accession, he took over the Chamberlain's company as the King's Men, turned Worcester's into Queen Anne's, and the Admiral's into Prince Henry's. Later, two other of his family maintained troupes. One was his daughter Lady Elizabeth and the other his son Prince Charles, who was to lose his head to the Puritans seven years after they closed down his company.

ECONOMICS IN THE ELIZABETHAN THEATER

The economics of the various acting companies was as complex as their history. Sometimes, but probably not too often, they had a certain amount of support from their noble patrons. Henslowe, however, lent money to the Admiral's company. When companies appeared at court they were paid for "plaieing and other feates of activity." In most cases, troupes were stock companies—in the financial as well as the theatrical sense. Some ten to fifteen players would buy shares at about seventy pounds apiece, a considerable amount in our money. This capital went mainly for plays and costumes. The sharers hired other actors at sixpence a week. The boys who played women's parts were apprenticed to the sharers, who were paid a few shillings a week for the lads' appearances.

Most companies in London rented theaters from their owners on a curious basis. They were entitled to all the penny fees collected at the door. The owners got all the money paid by spectators for moving out of the pit and standing or sitting in the galleries. In many cases, as the popularity of the company increased, the sharers got half of the gallery receipts. The men who collected money at the main door and at the two doors leading to higher-priced seats were called "gatherers." They were ordinarily paid by the actor–sharers, but in Henslowe's theater, that canny man insisted on hiring his own. The money was dropped through a slot in a box—to which we owe our term "box office." The position of the sharers was improved by Cuthbert and Richard Burbage when they decided to build the Globe. We know that they paid half the ground rent and that five of their actors, including Shakespeare, paid the other half. We may presume that the building was financed in the same way and that the five players got half of the theater's "take" as well as their proportion of the acting company's share.

ACTING IN SHAKESPEARE'S DAY

The Elizabethan actor began as rogue and vagabond and ended under the patronage of royalty. When the first companies toured in interludes and rough comedies, six men might have to play twenty-five parts. When the Globe and the Fortune flourished there were well-balanced companies of about twenty skilled and respected players. The livery of earl, queen, or king became them well.

There is a great deal of argument about the style of acting in Shakespeare's day. One group of scholars claims that it was formal and rhetorical; another, that it was natural. Some believe that it varied or developed from one to the other. We know that it must have been spirited and deft, or else the long and intricate speeches that occur so often in so many plays could not have been understood and enjoyed. Gesture and movement must have been important. The actor–playwright Thomas Heywood warned his fellows "not to use any impudent or forced motion in any part of the body, no rough or other violent gesture; nor on the contrary to stand like a stiff starched man."

There are two powerful arguments in favor of the so-called natural acting seen today in performances of Shakespeare at the Old Vic. The first point is the intimacy of the public theaters. The whole of the Globe could be dropped into the auditorium of the average Broadway theater without touching the stage. It was a quarter the size of the opera house type of auditorium where actors like Robert Mantell played Shakespeare around the turn of our century. The actors at the Globe needed to project their voices far less than actors in most of our theaters. The second reason for believing that companies of good and popular actors in Shakespeare's day weren't oratorical and didn't rant rests on what that dramatist had Hamlet say in his advice to the players: "Speak the speech, I pray you, as I pronounce it to you, trippingly on the tongue . . . o'erstep not the modesty of nature; for anything so overdone is from the purpose of playing, whose end, both at the first and now, was and is, to hold, as 'twere, the mirror up to nature."

A very curious feature of Elizabethan acting was the popularity of the boy player. It went further than the productions of the various companies of children. Women's parts on the professional stage were played by boys up to the closing of the theaters in 1642 and even in the early years of the Restoration, when Pepys wrote in his diary: "One Kinaston, a boy, acted the Duke's sister, but made the loveliest lady that ever I saw in my life." Many women went to the public theater—as Shakespeare attests in three epilogs addressed to them—but they were banned from the stage. When two

French companies appeared in London, the first in 1629 and the second a few years later, their actresses were hissed and pelted with rotten apples. The appeal and the skill of the best boy actors may be guessed from the epitaph that Ben Jonson wrote for Salathiel Pavy of Queen Elizabeth's Chapel, when he died at thirteen. Among his lines were these:

> *'Twas a child that so did thrive*
> *In grace and feature,*
> *As heaven and nature seemed to strive*
> *Which owned the creature.*

ACTORS NOW REMEMBERED

By its very nature, acting is the most ephemeral of the theater arts. Until the coming of the phonograph record, film, and finally television, we had no record of an actor's art except portraits, along with the descriptions and opinions of his contemporaries. Shakespeare, Marlowe, Thomas Heywood, Jonson, and Webster were actors, but we really know them only as playwrights. Six other players have lives of their own. Two, Heminge and Condell, immortalized themselves by editing the First Folio of Shakespeare's plays. Richard Tarlton and William Kempe shared in man's love for great clowns and comedians. Tarlton was "the Queen's Majesty's jester, . . . gracious with the Queen, his sovereign, and in the people's general applause." Kempe was, at one time, a member of the English Comedians who toured Holland, Denmark, and Germany, and he wrote a little book about how he danced from London to Norwich. The last pair were the greatest actors of their time, Richard Burbage and Edward Alleyn; but we know more about them for what they did off the boards than on. After their deaths, Ben Jonson celebrated both men in verse. He said of Alleyn, "others speak, but only thou dost act." This supreme adulation did not prevent Jonson from writing of Burbage:

> *He's gone and with him what a world are dead,*
> *Which he revived—to be revivéd soe*
> *No more young Hamlett, ould Heironymoe,*
> *King Lear, the grevéd Moore, and more beside,*
> *That lived in him, have now for ever died.*

Both men, Burbage and Alleyn, live for what they did in theater management. Burbage shared with his best actors the ownership of the Globe and Blackfriars. Alleyn joined with Henslowe in theater-building, bear-baiting, and other speculations, and would have died a millionaire if he hadn't preferred to found and build Dulwich College—where, incidentally, the records of Henslowe were preserved.

THE COURT MASQUES
OF INIGO JONES AND BEN JONSON

The last form of theatrical entertainment that was developed in the time of Elizabeth and perfected under the first two Stuart kings is the *masque*. Its roots are in the court shows of the Italian Renaissance. On Twelfth Night in 1512 young Henry VIII "with xi other wer disguised, after the manner of Italie, called a maske, a thynge not seen afore in Englande." There had been "disguisings" and ballroom pageantry before this, but now for the first time royalty took part in the entertainment. Henry's daughter Elizabeth also enjoyed the masque—a name borrowed from France—and her shows, like her father's, were mainly pantomime. It was James I, abetted by Ben Jonson and Inigo Jones, who turned them into a peculiar sort of lyric entertainment backed up by elaborate scenic display. The Stuarts produced at least a hundred of these expensive spectacles before Cromwell and Parliament curbed their extravagances.

Some of the masques were given at the Inns of Court, but most of them in the royal palaces. Sometimes they celebrated a betrothal, a marriage, an accession to power, or the visit of a foreign prince or minister. Often there was no more excuse than princely display and the adulation of royalty. Courtiers as well as trained singers and dancers took part in them. Prince Henry "walked on" in the silent title role of *The Masque of Oberon*, and Charles I and his queen played parts in some of these spectacles. James I's Queen Anne loved masques even more than the theater, and blacked her face to play one of twelve black women in *The Masque of Blackness*. She induced Ben Jonson, as court poet, to write some thirty masques. And, in order to have a proper stage designer, she brought from her brother's court in Copenhagen the English architect Inigo Jones, who had studied the scenery and machines of Italy.

The scripts that Jonson—and Milton, as well as half a dozen other successful playwrights—wrote were quite short. They make only eight to twelve pages in modern print. Most of the characters were mythological or allegorical—Diana, Boreas, Neptune, Reason, Splendor, Love, and Revel; but Merlin and Arthur got into one of the casts. Lord Bacon—who wrote a masque himself—lists among the choruses and dancers "Satyres, Fooles, Wildemen, Antiques, Ethiopes, Pigmies, and Beastes." Here are a few characteristic titles: *The Masque of Blackness, The Masque of Beauty, The Golden Age Restored,* and *Pleasure Reconciled to Virtue.*

ITALIANATE SCENIC MARVELS IN ENGLAND

The chief distinction of the masque was that it introduced Italianate scenery and stage machines to England—and the proscenium, too, for Jones designed a new frame of symbolic figures and ornament for each of his productions. At first he used the multiple stage with its "mansions," then the single stage set of Serlio. Because he liked startling changes of scene, he leaned more to the revolving prisms called *periaktoi*, together with the bent, or angled, flats, and groups of wings that moved in grooves. Instead of using a front curtain drawn to each side to expose the first scene—which had been done as early as 1565—he introduced a drop curtain painted with designs. At first he let this fall into a slot, *à la* ancient Rome, but later he raised it aloft by a drum and ropes and pulleys. It was never used to hide a change of scene, for Jones delighted in making magical transformations in full view of the audience:

> *The part of the scene which first presented itself was an ugly Hell; which flaming beneath, smoked unto the top of the roof . . . on a sudden was heard a sound of loud music, as if many instruments had made one blast; with which not only the hags themselves, but the hell into which they ran, quite vanished, and the whole face of the scene altered, scare suffering the memory of such a thing; but in the place of it appeared a glorious and magnificent building, figuring the House of*

> *Fame, in the top of which was discovered the twelve Masquers,*
> *sitting upon a throne triumphal, erected in form of a pyramid*
> *and circled with all store of light.*

A courtier who saw *The Masque of Blackness* described one of
the elaborate devices that astounded the audience and at the same
time introduced Queen Anne as part of the show:

> *There was a great engine at the lower end of the room which had*
> *motion, and in it were the images of sea-horses, with other*
> *terrible fishes, which were ridden by the Moors. . . . At the*
> *further end was a great shell in the form of a scallop, wherein*
> *were four seats. On the lowest sat the Queen with my Lady*
> *Bedford.*

The very nature of the masque prevented Ben Jonson from
using his full talent as a dramatist. His poetry was lost and forgotten in the extravagant display of pageantry and spectacle. A man of
his temper was bound to revolt. In 1631 he quarreled with Inigo
Jones. Jonson called him a "maker of properties . . . whirling his
whimsies." He satirized Jones and masques in a play called *The
Tale of a Tub.* In his *expostulation with Inigo Jones*, Jonson wrote:
"Painting and carpentry are the soul of masque."

Painting and carpentry were expensive. Not counting the
elaborate costumes furnished by the nobles who took part, the
production of *The Masque of Oberon* cost almost £1,500—three
times as much as the Fortune theater had cost to build the year
before. In 1618 James I spent £4,000 on a single masque.

Scenic wonders, as we have said, were invading the private
theaters in the late 1630s. But, when Cromwell curbed the court and
closed the playhouses in 1642, the war between scenery and the
Shakespearean stage was ended almost before it had begun. During
the truce of the Commonwealth, a writer of tragedies and masques,
William D'Avenant, pondered the future of scenic display and
brought forth English opera. When the theaters opened again in
1660, the Red Bull playhouse fought, for two or three years, an
unequal battle with the new stages. Perhaps Inigo Jones had
doomed the Globe and the Fortune before the soldiers of the Commonwealth pulled them down.

6: THE
BAROQUE THEATER
OF FRANCE

The theater of France had a strange kind of continuity from the twelfth century to the end of the eighteenth—and, indeed, down to our own time. Well into the Renaissance, the people of the provinces saw medieval mystery plays given in open fields, public squares, Roman amphitheaters, palaces, and even cemeteries. In Paris an amateur company began, in 1402, to produce mysteries in a hall of the Hôpital de la Trinité. It is in the story of this group, the Confrérie de la Passion, that we find a clear thread leading from the medieval drama to the theater of Napoleon's youth.

After a hundred and fifty years of producing mysteries, the Confrérie de la Passion built a playhouse of its own in the ruins of the town house of the Duc de Bourgogne. Forbidden to give religious plays, the brotherhood turned unsuccessfully to farces, comedies, and tragedies. By 1578 they had begun to lease their stage to professional companies of players who were touring France. The Hôtel de Bourgogne continued as an active, producing playhouse

141

until 1783. Thus the stage of France, through a single theater, flows on for 235 years in unbroken continuity from medieval religious drama to what we might almost call the modern stage.

FROM A MEDIEVAL PLAYHOUSE
TO A RETARDED DRAMA

If we put aside—as indeed we must—the converted hall of the Hôpital de la Trinité and the still more makeshift *patios* and *corrales* of Spain and innyards of England, we may say that the Hôtel de Bourgogne, opening about 1550, was the first public playhouse built since the fall of Rome. Yet this does not mean that the theater of France came to its full perfection before the theater of Spain and England. It was not till 1634 that Paris had a second theater for the paying public. Italianate scenery and machines did not appear till 1641. And it was only between 1637 and 1677 that France had notable native playwrights. Contrast this with the swifter progress of Italy, Spain, and England. As early as 1538 Italy was sending abroad companies of exceptionally trained actors. By 1570 Spain could boast numerous popular theaters and a significant drama, and by 1600 London had six playhouses and William Shakespeare.

France had two excuses for being laggard in the theater—just as it was laggard in the fine arts—through the fifteenth and sixteenth centuries.

The first was war—war on its own soil as well as outside its borders. From 1346 to 1450 English armies conquered or harried much of Northern France. For another hundred years France fought intermittently and none too successfully with other European kingdoms and principalities. The disaster of religious civil war crippled France in the last half of the sixteenth century. Unity, power, and a century of prosperity came to France first through Cardinal Richelieu, who made Louis XIII supreme over his nobles as well as his people, and then through Louis XIV, who left France the dominant power in Europe when he died in 1715.

The second hindrance to theatrical progress was monopoly. Through the Middle Ages and the Renaissance, many a monarch and many a municipality liked to give a favorite courtier or a favored group the sole right to make or sell or manage this or that at a nice profit. The theater of France did not escape the blight of such

1402	*Hôpital de la Trinité*	*Confrérie de la Passion*
1548	*Hôtel de Bourgogne*	*Confrérie de la Passion* c. 1600, Troupe Royale (Hardy) 1670, Italian players
1577	*Petit-Bourbon*	Italian players 1645, Torelli productions 1658, Italian players and Molière
1634	*Théâtre du Marais*	Montdory and his company
1641	*Palais-Royal*	*Miramé* (Richelieu) 1660, Molière and Italian players
1660	*Salle des Machines*	Spectacles for Mazarin
1671	*Guénégaud*	Opera 1673, La Grange and Molière's company 1680, Comédie-Française

Figure 6.1   The First Paris Theaters

monopoly. Until 1634 there was, officially, only one public playhouse in Paris because the Confrérie had enjoyed for a hundred years the exclusive privilege of producing plays or licensing their production in the chief city of France. Until Paris began to have other companies in competing playhouses, she had no dramatists of enduring merit.

PLAYS AT FAIRS AND IN TENNIS COURTS

Monopoly is not an easy thing to maintain when you have to deal with people so zealous and unaccountable as actors. The Confrérie found it particularly difficult. The brotherhood had to spend a great deal of time and energy running down, suppressing, or taxing random companies of actors. The great fairs of Saint-Germain in the winter and Saint-Laurent in the summer were particularly troublesome. There touring companies gave fly-by-night performances and often blew town before the Confrérie could prosecute them. Finally, an edict of 1595 legalized plays at the fairs. Then a touring company moved into the Hôtel d'Argent, and others into various tennis courts, all paying the Confrérie a fee for each performance.

The French tennis court made no worse a theater than the hall of an *hôpital*. This place of sport was a long, roofed structure of considerable size. As the popularity of the game slackened somewhat in the fifteen century, many traveling companies used these quarters as temporary theaters all through provincial France. From the Paris fairs, it was only natural that the actors should move over into Paris tennis courts. The first troupe that was set up in legitimate competition with the actors at the Hôtel de Bourgogne used one of these structures for two years while they built a permanent house on the site of another tennis court. This was the Théâtre du Marais, which opened in 1634 under the direction of the fine actor Guillaume Montdory and the powerful patronage of Cardinal Richelieu.

Obviously, there was a political background to the Confrérie's loss of its monopoly. This lay in the tensions and jealousies of Louis XIII and his great prime minister. The king—not content with plays at court—had been supporting at the Hôtel de Bourgogne a company of actors known as the Comédiens Ordinaires du Roi or the Troupe Royale. Richelieu, who was responsible for the growing power of both France and its monarch, liked to irritate his "master" in petty ways. One of these was the backing of Montdory and his Théâtre du Marais. Louis replied by drafting some of Montdory's best players to augment the Troupe Royale.

The next step for Richelieu was to become playwright and producer. He forced five writers—including Pièrre Corneille, who had won fame with comedies and tragedies at the Théâtre du Marais—to collaborate with him on some plays that, not unnaturally, proved rather poor. Richelieu provided the plot, and a different dramatist wrote each of the five acts. In 1641, the year before the cardinal's death, he opened a small but beautiful theater in his palace, later known as the Palais-Royal. There, on a stage equipped with Italianate scenic devices, he produced a spectacle called *Miramé*.

COURT THEATERS TURN PUBLIC

There were court theaters before Richelieu and Louis XIII and after them. Kings and courtiers delighted in balls, ballets, and spectacles, but they also liked actors and opera. As early as 1577, the Gelosi troupe of Italian comedians appeared in what may be called the first court theater of France, in the Salle du Petit-Bourbon. In 1645 Cardinal Mazarin, the Italian-born prime minister of Louis XIV, brought from Venice the greatest scenic magician of his time, Giacomo Torelli, to stage operas at court. For the cardinal, he reproduced a spectacular Italian opera, *La Festa theatrale della finta pazzia*, and for the seven-year-old king he added such engaging furbelows as a ballet of monkeys, flying parrots, and mechanical ostriches. To celebrate the wedding of Louis XIV in 1660, Mazarin built a theater in the Tuileries, one of the royal residences. The name of this theater—the Salle des Machines—indicates the kind of shows he provided.

The attitude of Louis XIV toward his court theaters and the Parisian public was a remarkable one. In his palaces, from the Louvre to Versailles, he provided all manner of performances for his courtiers and their ladies. But—and here he was unique among princes—the king turned over the Petit-Bourbon and the Palais-Royal to acting companies that played month after month to the general public. In addition he gave goodly subsidies to his Italian players to the Troupe Royale, to Molière, and to the company at the Théâtre du Marais.

HARDY—FIRST PROFESSIONAL PLAYWRIGHT OF FRANCE

The drama of France from 1500 to 1700 comes in curious compartments. They seem almost sealed off from one another. First there is the native farce, rooted in the Middle Ages and withering in the Renaissance. Next, scholars and schoolmasters imitate the classic drama of Rome. The first popular playwright, Alexandre Hardy, works in and for the theater, pays scant attention to the classic form, and seems nearest in impulse to Lope de Vega and Shakespeare. Then Corneille and, later, Racine revive the unities of time, place, and action, write mainly on classic themes, and win a popular audience. Sandwiched between these two neo-classicists comes Molière with his comedies of contemporary life. He observes the unities and he writes in verse, yet almost all his characters are of his time, and his dialog is natural as well as witty. In spite of his enormous success with king and commons, the other playwrights do not imitate him.

Lope de Vega of Spain, William Shakespeare of England, Alexandre Hardy of France—in 1600 these were the outstanding playwrights of the three nations. They had turned their backs on the classic drama. They wrote free-ranging plays of many scenes and vivid action. They were popular at the box office. If Hardy had had the genius of the other two, France might have bred a somewhat different drama from that of Corneille and Racine in the seventeenth century.

Hardy worked for the touring company of Valleran-Lecomte but never as an actor. His job was to turn out plays. As the first professional playwright of France, he was prodigious in output. Some say he wrote six hundred pieces; some, twelve hundred. He alone supplied most of the pieces produced by the actors of Valleran-Lecomte after the company invaded Paris by taking over the Hôtel de Bourgogne sometime between 1600 and 1610.

Hardy wrote all manner of plays: tragedies, tragi-comedies, melodramas, and pastorals, everything but comedies. Like any proper classicist, he divided his plays into five acts. In his earlier tragedies he often used the great figures of Greek and Roman times, and he even employed a chorus. But he ignored the unities of time and place, and he showed—often in violent scenes—the episodes that occurred offstage in Greek and Roman plays and that classic playwrights brought to the audience only through narration. The result was a more vigorous drama. Like Lope de Vega and Shakespeare—and Corneille and Racine, too—he wrote in verse, but his dialog, like Molière's, was direct and almost natural. His speeches were never long-winded. His chief contribution to the dramatic form was to invent a new one. It was new at least to France, if not to England and Spain. This was tragi-comedy. According to Aristotle and his garbled echo Horace, tragedy dealt with the kingly and the well-placed; comedy, with lowlier folk. Hardy mixed the two. The ending might be happy or unhappy, but high affairs shared the stage with comic incidents.

CORNEILLE—THE CLASSICIST IN SPITE OF HIMSELF

In Rouen, when Pierre Corneille—greatest poet–dramatist of France—was not yet twenty-four he saw some of Hardy's plays acted by Charles Lenoir and Guillaume Montdory. Affected by the plays and the performers, Corneille turned to the theater, and he became, like Hardy, a successful professional playwright. In 1630 Lenoir and Montdory produced Corneille's first play, *Mélite*, in a converted Paris tennis court. Lenoir and several other actors deserted to the Troupe Royale at the Hôtel de Bourgogne. But the success of *Mélite* and the backing of Richelieu encouraged Montdory to found the Théâtre du Marais in another tennis court. Corneille wrote loyally for Montdory's playhouse, as Hardy did for the Bourgogne some years before.

Corneille was not at first, or by instinct, a classicist. That was to come later. He began by writing five comedies of contemporary life and turned out a tragi-comedy, *Clitandre*, before he wrote his first classic tragedy, *Médée*, in 1635. The Spanish drama attracted him greatly. You can see its influence in his next play, the comedy *L'Illusion comique*. Nine years later he made his finest comedy, *Le Menteur*, out of Alarcón's *La verdad sospechosa*. In between—late in 1636 or early in 1637—he scored an enormous success at the Théâtre du Marais with *Le Cid*. This play, too, had a Spanish original and was free in form and romantic in feeling.

Before the production of this "cloak and sword" drama, Corneille could see no more reason for writing as a neo-classicist than for following the freer form of Hardy. The classic regulations had not yet set their stamp on French drama. But, in spite of the popular success of *Le Cid*—it was acted in London within a year—a storm of fierce criticism descended on Corneille for not having observed the classic rules. Corneille withdrew to Rouen for three years and weighed the virtues of his artistic convictions against the advantages following the rules dear to the potent Richelieu. The result was *Horace*, dedicated to the cardinal, *Cinna*, *Polyeucte*, and *Le Mort de Pompée*. They all followed the regulations. He relapsed with *Le Menteur* but turned again to classic tragedy, and he was elected in 1647 to the sacred French Academy. Definitely he was now not only the leading dramatist of France but also the major classicist of its stage.

Corneille had a long and full career. He outlived his close friend Molière and wrote his last play only three years before Racine, his newly ascendent rival, retired from the theater. Corneille contributed to France a new form of play in his comedies of intrigue. For Louis XIV and Mazarin he wrote the "machine plays" that climaxed the baroque theater and that led the way to French opera. Over and above *Le Cid*, his reputation rests on developing classic tragedy. He did more than anyone else to establish the classic regulations. Yet he did not obey them as closely as his followers. He saw larger values in the theater.

RACINE—HIS WORK AND HIS WAYS

Jean Racine came to the theater at a fortunate moment. When Molière gave this young man his first production in 1664, Corneille had already won popular acceptance for the kind of drama that Racine knew how to write with consummate skill: classic tragedy. Racine's first two produced plays, *La Thébaïde* and *Alexandre le Grand*, had a mild success. *Andromaque* established him as the leading playwright of France. The next year he turned to a satire on lawyers, *Les Plaideurs*, modeled on *The Wasps* of Aristophanes. After that, Racine kept to tragedy. In 1670 he clashed directly and successfully with his only rival. His *Bérénice* was produced a week before Corneille's *Tite et Bérénice* and won greater popular and critical acclaim. A similar conflict occurred seven years later, when Racine's finest tragedy, *Phèdre*, competed not very successfully with a play of the same name by an inferior but popularly sentimental playwright.

Piqued by this, Racine accepted appointment as court historian to Louis XIV, retired from the theater, married a rich wife, and devoted himself to a life of domesticity and devoutness. Just before his death, he returned to the stage most discreetly and privately. Mme. de Maintenon—first the mistress and later the secret wife of Louis XIV—asked Racine to write biblical plays for a kind of finishing school for young ladies in St. Cyr. He agreed on condition that the plays should not be publicly produced. The result was the fine and sensitive dramas *Esther* and *Athalie*.

Racine played a most important part in the great days of the French drama, which began with *Le Cid* in 1641 and ended with *Phèdre* in 1677. Except for his comedy *Les Plaideurs* and two oriental plays of contemporary feeling, all his work was on classical subjects. When he departed from the regulations, it was only in details. He gave more emphasis than Corneille to love and pity. His poetic style was more precise and brilliant. But his range of interest was narrower, and he lacked the originality and the warm imagination of his great rival.

In spite of dubious doings in the world of the theater, Racine maintained the highest principles in his plays. He gave virtue an exalted place and he pointed out in a preface to *Phèdre* that "the slightest evil is severely punished; the very thought of crime is made as horrible as the commission of it. . . . We should like our work to be as solid and full of useful instruction as were those of antiquity." Racine and Corneille accepted the aristocratic world as it was. No hint of social criticism crept into their plays.

MOLIÈRE—FROM AMATEUR TO IMMORTAL

Molière, on the other hand, though he supported the king, and the king supported him, wrote of ignoble aristocrats and ridiculed the falsities of their life. Occasionally his valets showed some discontent with their station. And when Molière defended the salutary purpose of comedy in his preface to *Tartuffe*, he wrote: "I do not see why there should be a privileged class."

The comic genius of Molière ennobled the theater of Paris from 1658 to 1673. For ten years it interrupted and overshadowed the development of classic tragedy. Fresh, tonic, and bracing, his work gave the French stage its true distinction between the rich vitality of Corneille in *Le Cid* and *Le Menteur* and the tragic perfection of Racine in *Andromaque*. Even as he was dying in 1673, Molière wrote and acted *Le Malade imaginaire*. This was, as John Palmer has said, "a supreme gesture of the comic spirit—the play in which the great comedian passed from a counterfeiting of death to death itself." No playwright has made so glorious an exit from the stage.

Molière began as an actor—an amateur actor—in 1644. His group, made up mainly of the younger people of two households, was sometimes referred to as Les Enfants de Famille. The actors seem to have preferred to call their venture the Illustre Théâtre. A group of *commedia dell'arte* performers would have been content to name their troupe "The Illustrious" and use the streets as a playhouse. But Molière and his friends hired a tennis court in 1644. After some disastrous performances there, they tried another site. It all ended in Molière's being clapped in jail for debts to a candle

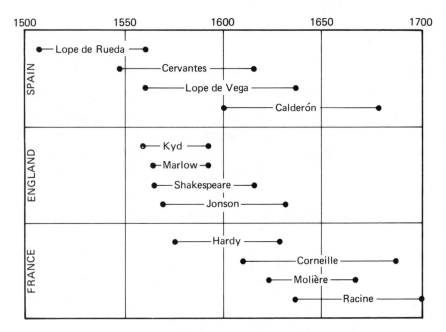

Figure 6.2 French Playwrights and the Spanish

This chart, repeated from our discussion of Spain in the Renaissance, shows how the writers of France came late enough to borrow from Cervantes and Vega as well as Calderón.

merchant, among others. His father, Jean Poquelin, subsequently paid the claims, perhaps out of gratitude for his son's having assumed the name of Molière when he went on the stage. After the unhappy experience of Molière and his friends in Paris, they turned to the provinces and spent thirteen years on tour.

Before the demise of the American touring system, "the road" would often accept what Broadway had rejected. Something like this must have been true in seventeenth-century France. We know all too little about the career of Molière and his fellow actors in the provinces. But we do know that they left Paris late in 1645 and that they didn't return until 1658. We also know that, on leaving, they immediately acquired a patron, the Duc d'Epernon and that in 1653 they were taken under the wing of a new one, the Prince de Conti, who had been a fellow student of Molière's at the Jesuit college.

Like a dozen or more of their competitors, they gave French tragedies, Italian farces, and Spanish plays of intrigue and derring-do. Toward the end, Molière turned playwright and added some Italianate farces and comedies to the repertory. Two of these, *L'Étourdi* and *Le Dépit amoureux*, must have been quite popular, for he revived them later in Paris.

There can be no doubt that the company grew in stature as time went on. New actors joined them, their performances improved in skill, and Molière's plays grew popular. Toward the end, the troupe was hired on a number of occasions to give plays while the *États*, or local legislatures, were in session, and, at least in one case, we know that they were paid rather handsomely. The best evidence of their progress is that when the Prince de Conti turned puritanical and withdrew his patronage, the Duc d'Orléans, brother of the king, presented Molière and his players before Louis XIV and his court in the guard room of the Louvre in Paris.

MOLIÈRE'S MOST DRAMATIC HOUR

It was a critical day for Molière, this twenty-fourth of October, 1658. Now almost thirty-seven—with half of his creative life behind him in the provinces—he was to appear before a twenty-year-old king who was already the arbiter of theatrical art in France. Through Molière's choice of a vehicle for his actors, he doomed the company to failure, but through his resourcefulness and wit he turned the evening into a triumph.

Tragedy had been the chief fare of the Illustre Théâtre. It had figured prominently in the provincial repertory. Molière loved the dark muse with such passion that he did not consider how hopelessly mediocre his troupe would seem in tragedy when compared with the actors of the Hôtel de Bourgogne—who, incidentally, were in the audience at the Louvre. Instead of playing one of his own comedies—which were to make the fame of his company in Paris— he chose Corneille's *Nicomède*. The results were dire. Obviously, "Monsieur" (as the brother of the king was officially termed) had made a grave mistake.

Before the play was over, Molière had sensed defeat and had determined a line of counterattack. When the polite applause ended, he stepped forward and spoke to the king with dignity and grace, with pride as well as a certain pleasant irony. Here is an account of part of his speech as reported by La Grange, an actor who joined Molière the next year:

> *After thanking His Majesty in modest terms for the kindness with which he had overlooked the deficiencies of his company, which had appeared only with the greatest misgivings before so august an assembly, he assured His Majesty that the desire which all had to amuse the greatest King in all the world had caused them to forget that His Majesty had in his service excellent originals of which they were but feeble copies. Since, however, His Majesty had been so good as to suffer their country manners, he begged very humbly to be permitted to present one of the small diversions which had acquired for him a certain reputation and with which he had been accustomed to amuse the provinces.*

The small diversion was *Le Docteur amoureux*. The success of Molière, his acting, and his play was electric. Ignoring the failure of the company in *Nicomède*, Louis XIV let the Troupe de Monsieur share the Salle du Petit-Bourbon with his Italian players.

For the first weeks of Molière's stay at the Petit-Bourbon, that stubborn devotee of the tragic art repeated the same mistake he had made at the Louvre. He played five tragedies by Corneille, and starved at the box office. Then he revived his provincial hits *L'Étourdi* and *Le Dépit amoureux*, and Paris flocked to his theater. From then on, the success of Molière was the success of his own plays. As they grew in number, they grew, too, in quality.

MOLIÈRE AS SOCIAL SATIRIST

Many of the comedies of Molière—the best of them, in fact—brought trials and tribulations as well as success. The first play that he wrote in Paris, *Les Précieuses ridicules* (*The Affected Ladies*), stirred up a hornet's nest among the smart and powerful poseurs of the court. Only the intervention of the king, who happened to be out of Paris at the time of its production, saved this first comedy of manners from suppression.

Figure 6.3   Two French Theaters

Above, the first theater built in Parish, the Bourgogne, as it was in 1645. Below, the open air theater at Versailles built by Louis XIV. Here Molière appeared on the night of his death in 1673 in *La Malade imaginaire*. (Drawings by Gerda Becker With, after engravings by Chauveau, Le Pautre.)

As Molière grew more caustic in his comedies, as he wrote more keenly and discerningly of the foibles of society, of the injustices done women, of the hypocrisy of some members of the clergy, attacks upon him and his plays increased. So, fortunately, did the prosperity of his troupe. In 1662 he was accused of licentiousness and impiety because in *L'École des femmes* (*The School for Wives*) he attacked the right of a guardian to marry off his ward against her will. In his version of the Don Juan story, *Les Festin de Pierre*, he pictured a wicked marquis. Immediately the courtiers accused him of attacking the nobility and of agreeing with the sentiments and behavior of his libertine hero. Again the king supported Molière. To make the royal attitude clear, Louis XIV took over the company from his brother in the summer of 1665, called it the Troupe du Roi, and gave it a subsidy. The greatest of Molière's difficulties arose over *Tartuffe* and lasted from 1664 till 1669. The first three acts of this attack on a religious hypocrite were given as part of a festival at Versailles, *Les Plaisirs de l'isle enchanté*. The onslaughts of many of the clergy and the courtiers became so violent that Louis XIV did not dare license the play for public performance, but he had it read and acted in his palace and other homes of royalty. He secured the endorsement of a legate of the Pope, but others in the Catholic hierarchy denounced Molière as a devil in human form, and the king dared not move till 1667. Even then the troubles of *Tartuffe* were far from over. When it was produced at the Palais-Royal—where Molière had moved from the Petit-Bourbon—the king was out of the city, and the president of the Paris parliament closed the theater. The archbishop of Paris banned the acting, seeing, reading, or hearing of the play, either in public or in private, on pain of excommunication. Louis had to defer another licensing for eighteen months. Then, in 1669, *Tartuffe*—with its name changed to *The Impostor*—became a great and deserved success.

COMEDY-BALLETS TO PLEASE THE KING

The support that the king gave Molière in the battles over these four plays was not due entirely to Louis' good sense. The king valued the plays for what they were—works of comic genius—but he also valued Molière as a man who could write and stage superb entertainments at Versailles and other pleasure places. From 1662 to 1670 he gave a good deal of his time and energy to pleasing *le Grand Monarque* in this fashion. Molière showed great ingenuity in devising spectacular shows and at the same time injecting into them his own plays. He invented for this purpose a form called the comedy-ballet. The first production was actually commissioned by the prime minister Fouquet for his gardens at Vaux-le-Vicomte, but its huge success put ideas into the king's head. Thereafter Molière was to work for only the glory of Louis XIV. The entertainment at Vaux was spectacular in overall effect, for Torelli provided stage machines, the architect Le Brun painted the setting, and Lully composed the music, but the king got quite as much pleasure from the satire around which it all revolved. In *Les Fâcheux* (The Bores) the amorous dalliance of two lovers is interrupted by the advent of one bore after another. Through these *fâcheux*, Molière satirized a dozen facets of society, and the delighted king suggested that the playwright add another bore, the Royal Master of the Hunt. In 1664, Molière wrote a second comedy-ballet, *Le Mariage forcé*, in which the king danced as an Egyptian. The best of half a dozen more was *Le Bourgeois gentilhomme*, produced in 1670.

Having amplified the old equipment of the Palais-Royal, Molière tried his hand, in 1668, at a type of entertainment called the "machine play." Rocks that opened into heavens, flights of demi-gods, palaces that became grottos, living dragons and centaurs—these had entertained Italian princes for more than a century, and Mazarin and Torelli had brought them to Paris twenty years before. In writing and staging *Amphitryon*, Molière showed his usual moderation and good sense. He confined the mechanical contrivances to the prolog, in which Mercury was seated on a cloud and Night appeared in an aerial chariot, and to the last act, in which Mercury flew aloft and disappeared in a cloud.

MOLIÈRE'S ONE TRAGEDY

Molière's love of tragedy made him, in 1660, write one play in that genre. This was *Don Garcie*. It was obviously a failure, and, though he obstinately kept it in his repertory for three years, he never published it, and he finally borrowed some of its best verse for his

Le Misanthrope. The failure of Molière and his company in tragedy
lay in the fact that he disliked the declamatory bombast of the day
and preferred a simpler and more natural kind of diction and performance. For the last production of *Don Garcie* he wrote a little
play, *L'Impromptu de Versailles*, attacking the tragedians of the
Hôtel de Bourgogne. Perhaps if Molière had been an Elizabethan
playwright, his love of both tragedy and comedy, coupled with his
equal facility in poetry and prose, would have made him a rival to
Shakespeare.

A MAN OF MANY PARTS

The bulk of Molière's plays can be divided into three forms: farce,
comedy-ballet, and comedy. But in spirit, content, and style they
often overlap.

From Molière's days in the provinces until two years before his
death, he was the master of the farce of intrigue. Most of these
plays, including *Le médicin malgré lui* (*The Doctor in Spite of Himself*), *L'Avare* (*The Miser*), and *Les Fourberies de Scapin* (*The
Rogueries of Scapin*), were based on Italian or Roman originals, yet
the best of them present human failings or satirize social preten-
sions.

Many of his comedy-ballets are farcical, but many present
some of his finest and purest comedy. *Georges Dandin* and *Le
Bourgeois gentilhomme* included ballets and were produced in court
spectacles. *L'École des maris* (*The School for Husbands*) is a brilliant comedy of manners, like *L'École des femmes* (*The School for
Wives*), which followed in 1662, and *Les Femmes savantes* (*The
Learned Ladies*) of 1672. *Tartuffe* and *Le Misanthrope*, perhaps his
greatest comedies, showed, like so many of his other plays,
Molière's aversion to both bigotry and excess. The last of his social
comedies, *Le Malade imaginaire* (*The Imaginary Invalid*), has
been called "the history of the death of Molière." Touched by family
tragedy and gravely diseased, he wrote gaily of a man who only
imagined himself to be ill. It was a gesture of courageous detach-
ment seldom if ever equalled by any other writer.

Molière died immediately after his last appearance as the imaginary invalid. Partly because he was an actor and had not re-

pented that sin but chiefly because he had been a keen critic of life, he was refused Christian burial until Louis XIV's last intervention for his friend and the true genius of his reign. Molière was buried after sunset, without ceremony, and with only two priests in attendance. There is even doubt as to whether his body was interred in consecrated ground. The grave of the greatest playwright of France is unknown and unmarked.

PLAYHOUSES AND SCENERY

We know very little about the theater buildings of the time. All we can guess about the Hôtel de Bourgogne is based on a fan-shaped drawing made in 1645, a contract for the theater's reconstruction a few years later, and an eighteenth-century plan. The theater hall, located on the second floor, was forty feet wide. The total length was ninety-six feet, which included a stage thirty-three feet deep; later this playing space was deepened by ten feet. The raked stage was six feet high at the front so that those who stood on the floor of the "pit" could see better. Toward the rear the auditorium floor rose in several levels where there were benches. A row of boxes hung out from the side walls and continued along the back. There may have been another row of boxes above and even an open gallery with benches still higher. The stage had no formal proscenium arch until after the remodeling. The Théâtre du Marais is supposed to have been made over in Italian fashion from an old tennis court. We know very little about the Petit-Bourbon except that the stage was shallower than at the Bourgogne. There were two halls in the Palais-Royal that could be used for plays. One seated six hundred and the other three or four thousand. It must have been the latter that Richelieu used for his spectacular *Miramé* in 1641. The stage of the Salle des Machines, which Mazarin built for another Italian designer, was fifty-nine feet high in order to house the machinery for flying backdrops—there were 144 of them, each seventy-five feet wide—and for lifting actors on clouds and chariots. The Guénégaud, an opera house, could hold fifteen hundred people, and the theater erected for the Comédie-Française in 1689 had room for two thousand. Neither played to much more than half capacity.

During the eighteenth century France saw all manner of scenery. In the provinces and at the fairs there was often just a rough curtain behind a stage set on barrels. In the 1640s Richelieu and Mazarin introduced huge Italianate settings painted in false perspective and changing magically before the eyes of the spectators. During the first half of the century, the Hôtel de Bourgogne continued to use the multiple set of the Middle Ages, with as many as five locales visible at the same time. Then when classic tragedy with its unities of time and place became popular, a fourth kind of scenery appeared. This was a single setting, usually the front of a palace. The Italians used a more or less permanent street setting, and most of Molière's comedies were played against a single background.

THE COMÉDIE-FRANÇAISE— LOUIS XIV'S FINAL CONTRIBUTION

The death of Molière altered the fortunes of the four Paris companies. The King, who did not believe that the Troupe du Roi could live without Molière, gave the Palais-Royal to Lully for opera. Molière's actors moved to the Guénégaud. (Just a few years before, in 1671, this house had been built by a nobleman for the Académie Royale des Operas, an institution that ignored Lully.) Through various pressures Louis combined the French-speaking company at the Bourgogne with the actors at the Guénégaud and the Marais. Thus—except for the Italian company that had shared the Bourgogne—Paris in 1680 had only one playhouse, but France had its first—and the world's first—national theater. Gradually it came to be called the Comédie-Française in contradistinction to the Comédie-Italienne. In 1689 it moved into a new playhouse, the first to be built with a horseshoe-shaped auditorium. Today the institution is also known as the Théâtre-Français and in addition—to honor the man who trained so many of its first players—the House of Molière.

This last major gesture of Louis XIV toward the theater was grand, dangerous, and characteristic. It was grand because it created a strong theater supported by the state. It was dangerous because it was a creature of absolutism, a monopoly barring healthful competition. It was characteristic because it expressed the king's love of ordered power as well as his love of the theater. The Comédie-Française has always maintained high standards in its acting and its classic repertory. It has often blocked progress in playwriting and in production.

Throughout the baroque end of the Renaissance, France failed to create the free and imaginative drama of England and Spain. Yet the clarity and logic of the Gallic mind, working through polished poetry, drew from the classic concept of tragedy a notable, if special, form of drama, and the genius of Molière broke the bounds of a rigid verse form and a narrow social environment.

7: THE NINETEENTH CENTURY: A TIME OF CHANGE IN EUROPE

If we look at centuries as periods of social and artistic development—or at least change—we find that they are seldom limited to an even hundred years. This was particularly true of the nineteenth century.

Of all centuries, it was the century of revolution—political revolution and industrial revolution. And these movements appeared before 1800. Political revolution began in 1776 and 1789, and it continued through 1830 and 1848 and 1871, each rebellion breeding reaction as well as progress. Industrial revolution may be said to have started in 1765 when James Watt made a steam engine that could drive machinery, and this revolution ran a steadier course. The outcome of all these upheavals was a slow march toward political and social democracy. There was slower progress in public education, while the population of capitals and manufacturing cities grew enormously.

A CENTURY OF PROGRESS IN THE THEATER

The theater was greatly affected by the peculiar nature of the nineteenth century. There was revolution in playwriting, and there was reaction, too. Creative minds sought fervently for change and betterment. Minds of another sort exploited the new audience of the uncultured who now had money to spend. Playgoers—and theaters—grew in numbers as industrial development swelled the ranks of the middle classes. The vast bulk of these new audiences was under-educated, and they looked to the stage for an escape from the world in which they lived and worked. Between the years of Sheridan and Beaumarchais and the years of Ibsen and Shaw, the state of the theater may seem, on the whole, depressed and depressing. Yet the story of the theater through the full nineteenth century—which we will cover in this essay and the beginning of the next—is a story of definite and important progress. It is progress that can be matched only in the fifth century before Christ and the centuries of the Renaissance.

Playwrights moved from classicism to romanticism and to realism; some few moved toward the poetic, and even toward a hint of the expressionistic. Theaters increased in number, and—more important—they shrank in size. Acting advanced from bravura display of star talents to well-rehearsed ensembles and to a natural style of acting that suited the realistic play. Science provided the stage with gas, limelight, the arc, and the incandescent bulb. Scenery, along with costumes, became historically accurate. The stage gave up wings and backdrops and achieved the realism of the box set. At the same time, theories of more imaginative staging developed.

THE ROMANTIC MOVEMENT IN GERMANY

The romanticism of the early nineteenth century had its roots in Germany and in a new literary movement called *Sturm und Drang*, or Storm and Stress. Taking form in the 1770s, it glorified the individual and exalted emotion as against the rationalism of Voltaire. In the theater its writers abjured the classic rules of French drama, and, though they worshiped Shakespeare, most of them wrote in prose instead of verse. If their dialog had a certain quality of naturalness, the feeling and atmosphere of their dramas breathed romanticism.

In 1773, Johann Wolfgang von Goethe's *Goetz von Berlichingen*—rich in medieval color and romantic in action—helped to break the path for Shakespeare and to establish Storm and Stress as an important movement in the theater. The last important play of this type was Johann Friedrich Schiller's *Die Räuber* (*The Robbers*) of 1781.

GOETHE AS DRAMATIST—AND MORE

As dramatist and director, Johann Wolfgang von Goethe gained in stature from his accomplishments in many other fields. He was, first of all, Germany's greatest poet. He was a leader of thought in the natural sciences, and he studied occult philosophies. He knew much about agriculture, forestry, horticulture, and mining. He drew and painted with skill. Through more than half a century Goethe acted as chief counselor to the Duke of Weimar, and for twenty-six years he was director of the ducal theater.

In spite of Goethe's long experience in the theater, his plays are less actable than any that approach them in thought or poetic expression. He confessed that he had "written in opposition to the stage." As director of a playhouse, he was successful within the limits imposed by a small community. His theories of acting were old-fashioned, but he worked assiduously. All in all, he provided some four thousand different bills, a third of them devoted to opera or operetta. He designed stage settings and theorized on their nature. At the same time he was occupying important posts in the government. From his very considerable labors, he escaped through a two year's sojourn in Italy, a land whose spiritual and physical warmth has always fascinated Teutonic peoples.

During 1786 and 1787, when Goethe was in Italy, a change came over him as a playwright and a philosopher. In the presence of the vast ruins of the Roman world, he turned away from the reality of the emotions, which was the base of Storm and Stress, and began to seek a reality of spirit that, he felt, could be best achieved through a classic and severe approach. *Egmont*, which he finished in Italy, is in prose, and it retains some of the earlier feeling. Then Goethe gave up prose, and rewrote his *Iphigenia* in blank verse. *Faust*—his most renowned play—is a product of both artistic periods. He began to write it in the first days of Storm and Stress, and he finished the second part of this Gargantuan drama only three months before his death in 1832. The tragedy of Gretchen comes out of his youthful impulses; some of Part One and all of Part Two are a product of his new classicism.

SCHILLER—GREATEST OF GERMAN PLAYWRIGHTS

When Goethe brought him to Weimar in 1799, Schiller was already famous as a playwright and within seven years of his death from tuberculosis. In 1781, when Schiller was only twenty-two and a doctor in the army of the Duke of Wuerttemberg, he wrote his first play, *The Robbers*, a drama of fierce resentment. The next year Schiller's own resentment against army life made him go AWOL to Mannheim, where the play had been produced. There Schiller lived under an assumed name and earned his living as court playwright and stage manager. Then followed *Kabale und Liebe*, an attack on the morals of the nobility, and *Don Carlos*, a plea for tolerance. For the next twelve years the stage saw no new plays by Schiller. As a university professor during this period, he gathered material on the Thirty Years' War, material that he was to use in his great trilogy on the warrior Wallenstein. Schiller completed his work in Weimar and wrote four more plays before he died: *Maria Stuart*, *Die Jungfrau von Orleans* (*The Maid of Orleans*), *Die Braut von Messina* (*The Bride of Messina*), and *Wilhelm Tell*, his greatest feat of craftsmanship.

　　Both Schiller and Goethe strove to achieve an ideal beauty, but Schiller was a more powerful dramatist. Most of his plays are less classic in form or feeling than Goethe's, though his *The Bride of Messina* employs lyric choruses and is the nearest approach of his time to ancient tragedy. His plays have the drive and vigor of Storm and Stress, but they move from a glorification of individualism toward something approaching social drama. Goethe's early plays and most of Schiller's anticipated the romantic movement that reached the French stage almost fifty years later.

In Austria and Germany romanticism had two other men of great talent. The Viennese Franz Grillparzer found success in his first play, *Die Ahnfrau* (*The Ancestress*), produced in 1817. He wrote with warmth about Sappho and about Jason and Medea. He turned Calderón's *Life Is a Dream* into *Der Traum ein Leben* (*Dreaming Is Life*), which provided an excellent part for the distinguished German actor Adalbert Matkowsky at the end of the nineteenth century. Grillparzer had a knack for comedy. So had Heinrich von Kleist, who began by writing a "fate drama" at the end of the eighteenth century and who achieved fine humor a little later with *Der Zerbrochene Krug* (*The Broken Pitcher*). It was in his serious plays, however, such as *Penthesilea* and *Die Hermannsschlacht* (*The Battle of Arminius*), that he showed his dramatic power as well as his command of vivid dialog. Bedeviled by graver obsessions than the romanticists' fondness for sleepwalking scenes and savage passions, Kleist has been called the unconscious father of the modern psychological drama. His tragedies went almost unnoticed until the Duke of Saxe-Meiningen revived a number of them seventy years after Kleist had committed suicide in 1811.

HUGO AND "HERNANI"

There has been a great deal too much ado over Victor Hugo's battle for romanticism in the 1820s. As we have pointed out, medieval and renaissance melodramas had flooded the French stage for more than two decades. The fact that the audience on the opening night of Hugo's *Hernani* in 1830 rioted for and against the play has made most critics think of it as the first romantic drama of nineteenth-century France. Actually, it was merely the first success by a really distinguished writer. There would probably have been no ruction if Hugo had not attacked the classical unities in his preface to *Cromwell*—fifty years after Lessing—and if *Hernani* had not been produced in the one remaining home of classical tradition, the Comédie-Française. Like Hugo, the elder Dumas is better known for his novels, particularly *The Three Musketeers*, than for his best play *La Tour de Nesle*.

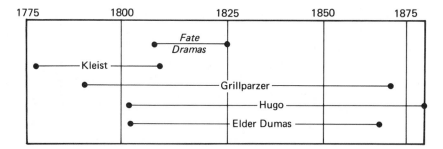

Figure 7.1 The Romantic Movement

The impulse came from the Storm and Stress movement of 1771 to 1781; the climax was French. This chart leaves out the inferior and more popular writers of romantic melodramas—Kotzebue, Pixerécourt, Knowles.

Alfred de Musset, a far finer and more sensitive playwright than Hugo or Dumas or any other Frenchman who had written since Molière, was a romantic, but not in the current fashion. He glorified his passionate affair with the feminist authoress George Sand in *One Does Not Trifle with Love*, but he also wrote with humor. His first group of one-act plays, *Comedies and Proverbs*, have something of the flavor of Molière. He turned his back on the stage after the failure of his first drama, *La Nuit Venitienne* in 1830 and wrote only for publication. In the poetic mood of two of his plays, *Fantasio* and *Lorenzaccio*—set in no definite time or place—de Musset is close to the *symbolisme* of Maeterlinck and later French writers.

ENGLISH ACTOR–MANAGERS OF MERIT

All was not dark on the English stage in the first half of the nineteenth century. There were good actors besides Mrs. Siddons and John Philip Kemble, who had ornamented the eighteenth. Another brother, Charles, and his daughter Fanny played with distinction. The greatest actor was the tempestuous Edmund Kean; Coleridge called his romantic performances "like reading Shakespeare by flashes of lightning." There were two subtle comedians: Charles Mathews, who in his *At Homes* played all the characters in short satiric pieces, and his son Charles James, who acted with and married that remarkable actress–manageress Mme. Vestris. William Charles Macready, the only rival of Edmund Kean, was scholarly and idealistic as well as hot-tempered. He hated his profession, but he acted Shakespeare's plays almost as they had been written, and he produced poetic tragedies by Byron, Browning, and Bulwer-Lytton. Samuel Phelps, like Macready, preferred Shakespeare to his adaptors. At the Sadler's Wells Theater he produced all but seven of the poet's plays between 1844 and 1862.

HISTORICAL ACCURACY IN COSTUMES

The first half of the nineteenth century saw some important developments in costuming, scenic design, and devices for changing sets.

It took the European theater about seventy-five years to accept completely the obvious idea—carried out by Macklin in 1773—that the costumes of a historical play should agree with the times and people it presented. Twentieth-century producers have done *Hamlet* and other old plays in modern dress and in modern scenery as daring experiments. "Modern dress," along with conventional scenery, was the general custom until the second half of the eighteenth century. And it was only between 1810 and 1850 that historical accuracy gradually became established.

Attempts at accuracy of costuming came first. In the 1750s, Diderot praised Mlle. Clairon for discarding her hoop skirts in a Chinese role. A few reforms followed, yet in her *Memoirs*, written twenty-five years later, she was urging actresses to give up massive and monstrous hairdos and adopt "the costume of the role one is playing." Only Talma and the French Revolution could put Clairon's ideas into more general practice in Paris. The German Heinrich Gottfried Koch used medieval costumes in *Goetz von Berlichingen* as early as 1774. And six years later Goethe played Orestes in a kind of classic garb.

The major credit for establishing true historical accuracy in London must go to a remarkable man of French descent, J. R. Planché. He wrote innumerable burlettas and extravaganzas, and he was an accomplished musician. But it was through his scholarly interest in the past that he contributed most notably to the artistic progress of the London stage. In 1823 he persuaded Charles Kemble to mount *King John* in really authentic costumes—"the precise habiliments of the period," as the playbill proclaimed. Planché's *History of British Costume* made a theatrical stir in 1834, and to this we may credit in part the excellence of Macready's costuming. (Macready also sought for accuracy of setting; while Kemble's *Coriolanus* had shown a Rome of imperial marble, Macready's reconstructed the ruder republican city of five centuries before.) Planché's greatest contribution, however, lay in the part he played in the launching of Mme. Lucia Vestris as an actress–manageress who was to establish the vogue of naturally acted comedy and the realistic box-set on the London stage.

MME. VESTRIS—PIONEER

Before the extraordinary Mme. Vestris opened her own theater in 1831, she had sung in opera, played Shakespeare and Sheridan, and made a name for herself as the most celebrated player of "breeches parts" since Nell Gwynn and Peg Woffington. The charm of her singing and dancing were excelled only by the naturalness and vivacity of her acting. But the most remarkable thing about the young woman was her refurbishing and management of the Olympic Theater. She turned a rather disreputable playhouse into the only theater except the King's—which was devoted to opera—where the smarter and more intelligent public of London felt at home. A critic saluted her "little back drawing-room of a theater. . . . Hail, thou sublimation of little laughs! thou bit of the millinery part of heaven!"

Mme. Vestris and Planché brought a curious sort of comedic realism to the Olympic's productions. This lay partly in the fact that the director took advantage of the intimacy of the little house to give the acting a quiet naturalness. A distinguished critic wrote that the players seemed "oblivious of the footlights." Instead of the absurdly stylized costumes always worn by such characters as the serving maid and the young-man-about-town—hitherto as fixed as the wardrobe and masks of the *commedia dell'arte*—Mme. Vestris introduced varied and appropriate costumes of the day. Furniture took on a natural appearance. There were antiques where needed, and all modern pieces where appropriate. Hitherto, the only chairs on the London stage were those that actually had to be sat upon because of the action of the play. Others were painted on the wings or the backdrops; this was going on in other cities as late as 1868, if we credit a sketch for *Faust* at the Hanover Court Theater. In addition to dressing her rooms with as many pieces of furniture as such rooms would normally have, Mme. Vestris played a most important part in introducing the modern type of box-set in London.

THE BOX-SET ARRIVES

No one knows just when wings parallel to the footlights were first replaced by continuous walls for the right and left sides of rooms. Eighteenth-century plans show wings so hinged that they could be aligned from the proscenium to the backing. At the Court Theater of Mannheim, Germany, in 1804, a stage designer joined pairs of wings with flats that contained practicable doors or windows. About that time the French stage must have had something like the walls of a box-set; for in 1811 Goethe inveighed in his autobiography against the French stage for "shutting up the sides of the stage and forming rooms with real walls." There is good evidence that Mme. Vestris used a box-set in November, 1832, for a critic wrote that the stage's "more perfect enclosure gives the appearance of a private chamber, infinitely better than the old contrivance of wings." In 1834, when Drury Lane produced a new play by Planché, a reviewer reported that the "stage was entirely enclosed" and even suggested that there was a ceiling instead of a row of hanging "borders."

The box-set won complete success when Mme. Vestris put on Dion Boucicault's comedy *London Assurance* at Covent Garden in 1841. Critics wrote of the realism of its rooms with their heavy moldings, real doors with doorknobs, ample and correct furniture. For many years, however, scholars gave credit for this reform to the playwright and director Tom Robertson, whose comedies were presented with great success by the actors and managers Squire Bancroft and his wife, Marie Wilton, between 1865 and 1870. Bancroft not only claimed that the settings had "for the first time, ceilings." He said that they had door "locks and similar matter never before seen upon the stage."

HISTORICALLY ACCURATE SCENERY

Settings as well as costumes began to be genuinely accurate around 1810, when Josef Schreyvogel became director of the Burgtheater in Vienna. Count Brühl, in charge of the Royal Theater in Berlin, followed Schreyvogel's example in 1817 with *Henry IV*. Shortly after the middle of the century, two actor–managers in London at last succeeded in bringing historical accuracy to the plays of Shakespeare.

Charles Kean was a far less talented actor than his father Edmund. He made up for this through his ability as a director. His actors were always well cast and well rehearsed. He achieved more of an ensemble than anyone since Mme. Vestris. With the zeal of an antiquarian, he saw to it that his scenery fitted the period of the play. He did the same with the costumes, except for an occasional lapse such as when his wife in *The Winter's Tale* wore a correct Greek dress over a crinoline. Perhaps Kean's most noted revivals were *King John*, *Macbeth*, *Richard II*, and *Henry VIII*. While he made lavish spectacles of the last two plays, he gave *Macbeth* the rude atmosphere of its time and place.

Charles Fechter may have been born in London, but his parents were French and he spent more than half his life in Paris. Before he was thirty, he had created the role of the lover in *La Dame aux camélias* (*Camille*), and, for a time, he was codirector of the Théâtre de l'Odéon, the second state playhouse of France. After playing briefly in Germany and eight years in London, he came to America to work only half a dozen years before he died. His French accent did not prevent the success of his *Hamlet* at the Princess's Theater, London, in 1861. Perhaps it gave an added novelty to a picturesque and highly accented interpretation that was called "revolutionary" and also "gentlemanly melodrama." Like Laurence Olivier on the screen, Fechter played Hamlet in a blond wig. Fechter's massive settings and his medieval costumes outdistanced those of Charles Kean in authenticity and effectiveness. At the Lyceum, he depressed and subdued the footlights. He used ceiling pieces instead of borders, and he originated or developed a new method of scene changing.

SETS UP FROM THE BASEMENT

Before the box-set developed, changes of scene were made quickly before the eyes of the audience by the use of shutters or wings and drops. Curtains to mark the ends of acts probably did not appear in England until about 1800, and there were no scene curtains until 1881 in a production by Irving. We have explained some of the ways of changing scenes that developed in the Renaissance. Backings could be raised or slid aside like shutters. For the sides of the set, *periaktoi* could be turned or wings "nested"; on the Continent, "chariots" in the basement carried the wings in and out through slots in the stage floor, but England preferred to slide them in grooves.

In 1863, Fechter tore out the grooves in the Lyceum. Some accounts say that he installed the Continental "chariot and pole" system; others say that he divided the stage into a jigsaw puzzle of sections that could be lowered for scene changes. During the last quarter of the nineteenth century in a number of European and American playhouses, the entire stage was divided into traps through which sections of settings could be raised from the basement. In some cases—and perhaps in the theater of Fechter—there were long narrow openings called "cuts" which ran along each side of the stage from the front to the rear; perhaps through them the side walls of a box-set could be brought up to the stage level and joined by a backing. Thus science developed more—and not the last—of those stage machines that have been called the largest and most elaborate tools ever employed in art.

GASLIGHT DIMS THE AUDITORIUM

Historical accuracy and box-sets, ceiling pieces and "cuts," were not the only changes in physical production during the first three quarters of the nineteenth century. Another was the introduction of gaslight on the London stage in 1817. In one way, this was a dubious improvement. The number of theater fires increased greatly. Nearly four hundred theaters burned down in America and Europe between 1800 and the coming of electricity. Gas had two great advantages, however, over candles and lamplight. Conveyed by flexible rubber tubing—literally miles of it—from a central source to footlights, borders, and house lights, the flow of gas could be controlled and the lights dimmed in any part of the theater. After about 1860, lights could be completely extinguished, and then relit by electric sparks. For the first time the auditorium could be darkened and all light concentrated upon the stage—a reform advocated by an Italian in 1598 but not generally practiced until Henry Irving's productions in the last quarter of the century. The brilliance of gas made it possible to do away with borders and all but the first row of border lights and to use ceiling pieces.

Oil lamps and even candles continued in use for a number of generations in smaller theaters, while two other forms of very brilliant illumination appeared between 1800 and 1850. About the same time as gas came *limelight*. It was an intense, white light produced by heating a piece of limestone with a very hot combination of gases. Used with a curved mirror, it became a spotlight of great brilliance. Somewhat the same effect was produced by the *arclight*, first introduced at the Paris Opera House in 1846. Made by an electric current heating two rods of carbon to incandescence, this early form of the arc suffered from flicker and noisiness.

VICTORIAN PLAYWRIGHTS

Too much credit went to Robertson and Bancroft as pioneers of the realistic box-set, but they deserve our full respect for writing and producing in the 1860s a series of plays of contemporary life that were far more credible than anything turned out by earlier Englishmen. Well directed by Robertson in settings that seemed almost as real as the rooms from which the audience had come, his plays—most with monosyllabic titles, *Society* (of 1865), *Ours*, *Caste*, *Play*, and *School*—were dubbed "cup and saucer dramas" by the hostile, but they won success for him as well as the Bancrofts.

Robertson might have found a rival in Dion Boucicault.

Boucicault was not yet twenty when he wrote the very successful *London Assurance*, and for fifty years he was a famous playwright, actor, manager, director, and technician. How much of the wit and polish of *London Assurance* was contributed by Mme. Vestris, Mathews, and others, we shall never learn, but we do know that his enormous output—listed at anywhere from one hundred forty to four hundred pieces—included very few original plays and nothing of the quality of *London Assurance*. As a man of business, Boucicault can hardly be blamed for adapting novels and French plays. Managers paid as much for these as for original work, and they were far easier to write. Before he left for the United States in 1852, he had little to his credit except adaptations like *The Corsican Brothers*, written while he was literary adviser to Charles Kean. His work in America culminated in his only fresh contribution to the drama, *The Colleen Bawn*, the first of a series of plays about Irish life, in which he proved a particularly brilliant actor. Except for these plays and his first comedy, he contributed little through his writings.

From Robertson in the sixties to Pinero and Jones in the eighties, English playwrights showed so little talent that Matthew Arnold was justified in saying in 1879: "In England we have no modern drama at all."

NATURALISM VERSUS REALISM

Before we return to the Continent and the progress in playwriting through about three quarters of the nineteenth century, we must pause for some definitions. These will carry us beyond the "romanticism" of Victor Hugo, Goethe, and Schiller and beyond the classicism of Corneille and Racine. (The comedies of Molière and Sheridan are a law unto themselves.) We must try to define "naturalism" and "realism," and to distinguish between them. We must also set apart the "well-made play" of Scribe and Sardou from the "well-made play" of Ibsen and his followers.

Realism should be simple enough. A realistic play is written in colloquial prose. It may be laid in the time of Hannibal, like Sherwood's *The Road to Rome*, but its characters speak naturally, and their psychology is the psychology of men and women as we understand them today. In the realistic play, things seem to happen to people on the stage as naturally, plausibly, and inevitably as they might in real life. Realism has two difficult tasks. One is to reach an elevation of spirit and expression, and the other is to achieve an exciting dramatic effect without violating a feeling of naturalness.

Yes, realism should be easy enough to recognize and define, if the problem were not complicated by another name for a play that is neither romantic nor classic. Obviously, the essence of realism is that its plays must seem natural; but the word *naturalism* was invented over a hundred years ago to apply to a very special kind of naturalness. From 1868 onward, the great Émile Zola applied the term to his novels and the novels of Edmond and Jules de Goncourt. Zola also applied it—hopefully—to the drama. His naturalism was a product of the scientific theories of heredity and evolution that we associate with Charles Darwin and his *On the Origin of Species*, but that Zola adopted from French writers as well. On a philosophical plane, this meant that all men were controlled by the so-called laws of heredity and by the influence of environment, with environment itself a product of heredity. Thus, deprived of free will, most men were doomed to misery. Along with this pessimistic view of society—heightened by the vice and squalor of so much of Paris under the Second Empire of Louis Napoleon—went a theory of writing. To Zola, writing a play or writing a novel was simply a business of observing and recording facts. Imagination and invention were unnecessary. A play was a scientific document, "a slice of life." People and their actions were to be reported as truth, not organized as art. Zola and his followers could not recognize that, in terms of the theater, this was a sheer impossibility. Besides observation, there has to be selectivity and organization, imagination and inventiveness. Otherwise there can be no satisfactory impact on the audience in the theater.

Oddly enough, the plays of Zola and the Goncourt brothers, though they were theatrical failures, were never truly naturalistic. Yet the work of the three men—mainly through their novels and Zola's polemics—had a considerable effect on the French drama. Unfortunately, so far as definitions go, the school of Zola sowed confusion. Today critics and laymen are all too apt to use "naturalism" and "realism" as if they were interchangeable terms for the same real, or natural, quality in most modern plays.

THE "WELL-MADE PLAY"

The expression "well-made play" involves less confusion than naturalism. When Bernard Shaw was a critic in the 1890s, he used those words as a term of opprobrium for the plays of Scribe and Sardou. Shaw was curiously mistaken. Those French plays lacked practically all values except those of theatrical effect, and they were not nearly so well-made as Ibsen's were to be. The shoddy carpentry of Scribe and Sardou provided no more than a false façade. Ibsen built his characters, plots, and themes into a solid structure. He was the master architect of the truly well-made play.

Eugène Scribe—the man who invented the term *pièce bien faite* for the well-made play—turned out more than four hundred pieces of ingenuity. They ranged from a musical sketch of 1816, through comedies, farces, librettos, and melodramas, to one celebrated tragedy. (This tragedy, *Adrienne Lecouvreur*, the story of a long-dead star, Scribe wrote in 1849 with the aid of a minor playwright.) The same ingenuity in comedy, melodrama, and tragedy—and the same lack of substance—appeared in Victorien Sardou, the man who followed Scribe as the most popular playwright of the second half of the century. From the success of *Les Pattes de mouche* (*A Scrap of Paper*) in 1860, he went triumphantly onward through his frisky farce *Divorçons!* (*Let's Get Divorced!*), the historical comedy *Madame Sans-Gêne*, and *Fédora*, *La Tosca*, and other tragedies for Sarah Bernhardt in the eighties, to *Robespierre* for Henry Irving in 1902. Together, Scribe and Sardou worked for more than eighty years at the profitable trade of theatrical carpentry.

REALISM IN GERMANY AND RUSSIA

Before 1850, there was more realism to be found outside France than within it. Germany and Russia made notable contributions.

In the first half of the thirties, Georg Büchner, a young German, turned away from revolutionary propaganda and spent his last three years—he died at twenty-four—in writing plays. His *Leonce and Lena* is a whimsical satire on the aristocracy. *Danton's Death*, produced successfully in 1916 by Max Reinhardt, is a strong, tersely written tragedy, free of the cheap romantic taint of his time. In *Woyzeck*, an almost psychotic tragedy, we find a hint of the expressionism that we will discuss later. In this play—perhaps because Büchner left it in an unfinished and chaotic state—realism comes close to the ideal of naturalism as well as expressionism.

Also in Germany, Friedrich Hebbel turned away momentarily from historical plays in verse and wrote the first realistic tragedy that anticipated the social pessimism of the coming naturalists. This was his *Maria Magdalena* of 1844. The outstanding German playwright between Schiller and Hauptmann, Hebbel won distinction with dramas on biblical subjects, such as *Judith* and *Herodes und Mariamne*, as well as with his *Die Nibelungen*, but he may be remembered longest as the pioneer of realistic tragedy.

Despotism and censorship turned a number of Russian playwrights toward satire and comedy, where realism unites with the fantastic and the grotesque. In this field lie Alexander Griboyedov's *Woe from Wit*, written in the twenties, and Nikolai Gogol's *The Inspector General* and *The Gamblers*, from the thirties and forties. In 1846 Alexander Ostrovsky began the writing of his many realistic comedies of middle-class life, including *Enough Stupidity in Every Wise Man* and *The Bankrupt*. Ten years before his tragedy *The Thunderstorm* appeared in 1859 or 1860, Turgeniev had written his fine comedy–drama *A Month in the Country*. These last two plays are true pieces of realism, but they are not well-made plays in the Ibsen sense. They are written in the vein and pattern of a later Russian, Anton Chekhov.

BALZAC, DUMAS, AND AUGIER

Honoré de Balzac might have been the first great realist among French playwrights. Indeed, Zola called him the first naturalist. But Balzac was too wrapped up in his long series of novels, *La Comédie Humaine*, to write many plays or to give them the care they deserved. The best that can be said for his play of 1848, *La Marâtre (The Stepmother)*, is that it may have given Turgeniev the stimulus to write *A Month in the Country*. By the time Balzac's *Mercadet, le faiseur (Mercadet, the Jobber)* appeared in 1851, the younger Dumas was turning his novel *La Dame aux camélias* into a

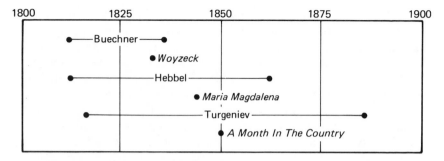

Figure 7.2 Forerunners of Realism

Here in three playwrights and three plays we have the first examples of
the realistic—almost the naturalistic—approach to the drama. This was
well ahead of Zola and Ibsen.

tragedy to which we have given the illogical title of *Camille*. Émile
Augier was trying to use verse in plays with middle-class characters
before he turned to realism.

Dumas *fils*—as the French call him to distinguish him from his
great father—and Augier wrote for the stage through some thirty-
five years. They competed in realistic observation and sometimes
even in their themes. Two years after Dumas' romantic eulogy of a
reformed "daughter of joy" in *Camille*, Augier replied with a por-
trait of an unscrupulous courtesan in *Le Mariage d'Olympe* (*The
Marriage of Olympia*). By this time, Dumas had joined Augier as a
writer of "thesis plays" designed to attack or correct social abuses.
In the same year as Augier's exposure of sexual depravity, Dumas
attacked the Bohemian society in which his father had moved, fastening on it the title of his play, *Le Demi-monde*. From his own
experience as a child born out of wedlock, he drew the materials for
Le Fils naturel (*The Illegitimate Son*). The evils that Dumas and
Augier exposed went beyond the sexual. Between them, they dealt
with the cupidity of the self-made man, anti-clericalism, religious
bigotry, the unscrupulous press, and corruption in politics. Augier's
best work was his comedy of 1854, *Le Gendre de M. Poirier* (*The
Son-in-Law of M. Poirier*), a satire on the relations between an
ambitious middle-class father and the lazy aristocrat who has married his daughter.

Augier and Dumas *fils* turned their backs on the dying drama of romanticism. They despised the trivialities of Scribe and the speciousness of Sardou, and they earnestly exposed the ills of middle- and upper-class society. Their plays competed successfully with the "boulevard" (read "broadway" or "West End") farces of men like Eugène Labiche and the collaborators Meilhac and Halévy. Yet Augier and Dumas never brought to their plays complete reality and never achieved the penetrating power of Ibsen and the dramatists that followed him.

NATURALISM BECOMES REALISM IN FRANCE

Before Ibsen took to realism, there were Frenchmen who tried to give drama the sense of contemporary truth that had been lacking. The Goncourts turned from their naturalistic novels in 1865 to write a play called *Henriette Maréchal*. This mingling of naturalism and realism, and of the morbid and poetic, failed at the Comédie-Française. Five years later, from another and far less noted writer, came a drama of solid power. A one-act play, *La Révolte*, anticipated by ten years the theme and the technical approach of Ibsen's *A Doll's House*, but its author, Count Villiers de L'Isle-Adam, never tried to follow his own lead.

In 1873 Zola followed his polemics for naturalism by dramatizing his novel *Thérèse Raquin*. This was a failure in spite—or perhaps because—of its sensational story of a wife and her lover who murder her husband and, haunted by the eyes of the dumb and paralyzed mother of the dead man, commit suicide. Zola's purpose, as he put it, was to seek "the beast" in this woman and her lover, "to see nothing but the beast, to throw them into a violent drama, and note scrupulously the sensations and acts of these creatures." His only success on the stage came when other writers dramatized his novel *L'Assommoir*.

Other French novelists tried to conquer the stage and failed. Alphonse Daudet wrote only one play of significance, *L'Arlésienne* (*The Woman of Arles*); produced in 1872, it won success later but only as the libretto for Bizet's opera. Gustave Flaubert, author of the novel *Madame Bovary*, had no better luck with his play *Le Candidat*.

The one outstanding dramatist of this period, Henri Becque,

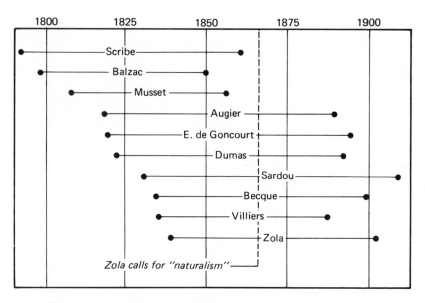

Figure 7.3   French Realism before Antoine

With the exceptions of the meretricious Scribe and Sardou, this chart shows writers who contributed to the growth of the serious realistic play before Antoine opened his Théâtre-libre in 1887. Zola's battle for what he called "naturalism" began in the middle sixties, as the dotted line indicates. Ibsen's consummate realism, which began to develop only in the late seventies, had little effect in Franch before Antoine produced *Ghosts* in 1890.

began writing as early as 1867 but had no financial success until the nineties. He wrote his bitter masterpiece *Les Corbeaux* (*The Vultures*) in 1877, but it was not produced for five years and then had only three performances. In 1885, his brilliant and ironic comedy *La Parisienne* (*The Woman of Paris*) won respect, but, like *Les Corbeaux*, it had to wait another decade to win a place in the national repertory of France.

AUSTRIA'S PLAYWRIGHTS

Except for Hebbel with his realistic *Maria Magdalena* and his historical dramas, Germany had no playwrights of note between the 1830s and the 1890s. Austria did a little better through three actors who turned writers. Before Ferdinand Raimund killed himself in 1836, he wrote folk comedies and allegorical fairy tales. His rival and successor, Johann Nestroy, turned out dialect farces and witty parodies. In the seventies and the eighties, Ludwig Anzengruber wrote folk plays on serious themes. One attacked conservatism in the church, another exposed the depravity of the middle-class. He wrote a rustic farce based on *Romeo and Juliet*, which he called *The Double Suicide*.

ACTORS WITHOUT AN ENSEMBLE

Until the triumph of realism in the last decade of the nineteenth century, acting was essentially and almost everywhere a bravura display of individual talent. Today we still clap a player when he has made an exit after a particularly fine effort, but audiences used to interrupt an actor to applaud the delivery of an emotional speech. Like an operatic aria, the scene was sometimes repeated if the applause was loud enough. Consequently, there was a lack of ensemble in most theaters and of both an inner and an outer resemblance to life. This was changed, in varying degrees, by three men. The work of Richard Wagner, the creator of "music drama," lies outside our field, but his idea of fusing all the factors of production into an expressive whole (*Gesamtkunstwerk*) had its effect on the theater. The Duke of Saxe-Meiningen and his court company demonstrated the virtues of ensemble to all Europe. André Antoine's amateurs at the Théâtre-libre in Paris found world-wide imitators of its realistic treatment of realistic plays.

The stars were many and bright in the theatrical firmament of the nineteenth century. In Paris there were, first, the powerful Frédérick-Lemaître and the eternal Pierrot called Deburau. In the forties and fifties, the actress Rachel reestablished the classic tragedies of Corneille and Racine, toured the world from Russia to the United States, and died at thirty-eight. In the last half of the century came the great comedienne Gabrielle Réjane, the equally great tragedienne Sarah Bernhardt, the elder Coquelin, who played both comedy and tragedy, the fiery Mounet-Sully, and Lucien Guitry, who left his talent as an actor and much more than his talent as a playwright to his son Sacha Guitry. Italian, Czech, and Polish stars found the same international audience as Réjane and Bernhardt. Adelaide Ristori rivaled Rachel when the Italian played in Paris, and, like Tommaso Salvini, she toured and costarred abroad. Fanny Janauschek began in her native Bohemia, then toured Europe, and spent the latter part of her life mainly on the American stage.

ENSEMBLE FIRST IN VIENNA

During a good part of the nineteenth century, the Vienna Burgtheater—then the greatest playhouse of the German-speaking world—rose to distinction through its directors Schreyvogel and Laube and their productions, rather than through its stars. Here there was a considerable measure of ensemble. Visiting stars from Germany—Ludwig Devrient in the early part of the century and, later, Ernst von Possart, Rudolph Schildkraut, and Friedrich Haase—fitted as readily into the company as did permanent members like Adolph Sonnenthal and Friedrich Mitterwurzer, while Poland contributed Modjeska. The example of the Burgtheater did not spread to all the companies of the German court and the municipal theaters. The self-display of stars and a sloppiness in production called for a reform. It came from the tiny duchy of Saxe-Meiningen.

THE MEININGEN PLAYERS

The "Theater Duke," as the duchy's ruler was called through most of his life, saw the work of Charles Kean in London and, surely, the Burgtheater. When, in 1866, he assumed the direction of what we call the Meiningen players he went beyond the historical accuracy and ensemble of both. His company was not a distinguished one. The actors we know best were Joseph Kainz and Albert Bassermann; but they joined the ensemble late, and they won their fame still later in other institutions.

A gifted artist and scene designer, the Duke recognized the value of various playing levels on the stage. He saw to it that his settings, costumes, and properties were illusive as well as accurate. His great distinction, however, lay in long and careful rehearsals. In this, he anticipated Stanislavsky and the Moscow Art Theater. His

Figure 7.4 Two Examples of Nineteenth Century Stage Design

Above, a design by the Duke of Meiningen: a scene from Ibsen's *The Pretenders*. Below, the Duke's sketch and plan for a box-set production of the banquet scene from *Macbeth*. (From Grube, *Geschichte der Meininger*.)

chief players acted small parts as well as big ones. In plays that called for mob scenes he paid equal attention to the supernumeraries. Like Kean, he divided his mobs into small groups, each headed by a competent actor. The Duke's repertory consisted mainly of Shakespeare and Schiller, but he resurrected Kleist and Grillparzer, revived Lessing and Molière, and made the first Continental production of Ibsen's *Ghosts*. The tremendous effect that the Meiningen ensemble had on the European theater from Moscow to London came through the tours from 1874 to 1890 that took the Duke's players to thirty-eight cities in forty-one plays. Stanislavsky acknowledged how much their example influenced his work. Henry Irving was obviously very greatly affected. Before he saw the Meiningen company in London in 1881, he had already proved himself a distinguished actor in *Hamlet*—which he played two hundred times in London in 1874–75 and one hundred eight times in 1878–79—as well as in claptrap like *The Bells*. When, in 1895, he became the first actor to be knighted by a British monarch, no one could say how far this distinction was due to his employment of noted historians, painters, and musicians, to his personal genius and the high quality of his company, which included the brilliant Ellen Terry from 1878 to 1902, or to Irving's intelligent and effective use of the Duke of Meiningen's methods.

STAGES FOR SHAKESPEARE IN GERMANY

If the productions of the Duke of Meiningen had a serious fault, it lay in too lengthy intermissions while settings were being changed, which happened often in the plays of Shakespeare, Schiller, and Kleist. The old wing sets, with or without grooves, had made scene shifting easy. But the Duke liked to vary the level of different parts of the stage, to use large set pieces such as rocks, and even to build box-sets. If he had not been so "modern," he might have turned back profitably to three or four early attempts to create a stage almost as well suited to Shakespeare's plays as the poet's own Globe.

There were Germans who did this. Shortly after 1800, the architect Karl Friederich Schinkel put permanent and molded columns and dark draperies in the place of wings, depending on his backdrop for changes of scene. In the twenties and thirties, a poet and playwright named Ludwig Tieck saw the proscenium doors and the forestages then used in Covent Garden and Drury Lane, and he read a builder's contract for an Elizabethan theater. With the aid of an architect named Gottfried Semper, he reconstructed—on paper only—the old Fortune playhouse. Unfortunately, when Tieck staged *A Midsummer Night's Dream* in 1843, he complicated his set with many stairs and platforms. Three years earlier, Karl Immermann, a director at Düsseldorf, built on his stage a structure that included many of the elements of the Elizabethan playhouse. His failure to find a profitable audience for a theater without the support of duke or king unfortunately obscured the value of his Shakespearean stage. At about the time when the Duke of Meiningen was ending his tours, experiments began at the Munich Court Theater that led to an effective solution early in the twentieth century. This scheme used portals and an inner proscenium within the ordinary picture frame opening.

WILLIAM POEL'S ELIZABETHAN REVIVALS

The first English attempt to play Shakespeare without awkward changes of sets came in 1844, when the elder Ben Webster produced *The Taming of the Shrew* against various curtains between two screens. Not until the last two decades of the century were there any other attempts in England to give Shakespeare's plays in full and with their scenes in the proper order. The most notable pioneer was William Poel. He began in 1881 by staging the First Quarto of *Hamlet* with only curtains for a background. In 1893, when he produced *Measure for Measure* in a London theater, he came as close as he could to an Elizabethan stage within a conventional one. He built an inner proscenium and a raised gallery in the back that could be hidden by transverse curtains for changes of set or properties. This production led to the formation of the Elizabethan Stage Society in 1895. During the next ten years—once in Gray's Inn and usually in other halls such as Shakespeare might have used—Poel gave a few performances of some twenty tragedies and comedies by Shakespeare and his contemporaries, as well as later works by Molière, Calderón, Schiller, and others. Poel's costumes and music were almost always good, and Shaw once said that these performances of Shakespeare were the only ones by which he "had been really moved." Poel made a notable success with the revival, after four hundred years, of the medieval morality play *Everyman* with Edith Wynne Matthison in the title role. Miss Matthison and other players repeated the old drama in Great Britain and America.

REALISM WAITING FOR ITS THEATER

Except for the production of Shakespeare in England, we are ending the story of the nineteenth-century theater of Europe roughly in the middle eighties. By 1885, the stage had learned how to give romantic and historical drama in accurate and often over-elaborate productions. In the face of a general emphasis on stars and star parts, the directors of the Vienna Burgtheater and the Duke of Meiningen had established the value of a rounded ensemble. In the repertories of the state-endowed theaters of Germany and France their directors were presenting a library of new and standard plays in opposition to the growth of long runs. But there was not yet a truly realistic theater with an appropriate technique of acting.

8: THE COMING OF REALISM

There were realistic playwrights before there was a realistic theater, before there was acting that could give the plays their full life, and before there was an audience ready to receive them. The first experimenters, from the Goncourts and Zola to Ibsen and Strindberg, were few, and they faced bitter discouragement. Only the most stubborn and courageous of new playwrights were likely to embrace realism without the encouragement of a director who wanted to produce their plays and knew how to do it properly. The writers needed an interested audience that wanted to see such plays. It might be a small audience, but it had to be a sympathetic one.

ANTOINE'S THÉÂTRE-LIBRE— SHOWCASE FOR REALISM

André Antoine supplied all this through the Théâtre-libre. His Free Theater was a unique venture. It set a pattern that many more have followed in Germany, Russia, England, and America. With the propaganda of Zola and the Goncourts behind him, he opened the way for a new drama and a new style of acting.

Antoine was an amateur actor who kept himself alive through a clerk's job with the Paris Gas Company. In the spring of 1887 he gathered together a company of fellow amateurs, and gave a bill of one-act plays in a hall in Montmartre that seated 342 people. The Théâtre-libre moved twice, first to an eight-hundred seat house in the Latin Quarter, then to the Théâtre Menus-Plaisirs in the center of the city; but until Antoine's venture closed in 1894, it was an institution doggedly devoted to certain unique ideas and policies.

The Théâtre-libre was a private playhouse open only to subscribers. For a season and a half, there was a single performance of each bill; then at the Menus-Plaisirs there were two. Very rarely indeed Antoine offered a public performance to nonmembers. His theater was a showcase for playwrights who could get no production anywhere else. Many of the one-act plays were taken over as curtain-raisers in the regular playhouses. The playwrights who won success with full-length plays were free to offer their new work elsewhere. Antoine's job, as he saw it, was priming the pump, and he primed it well. The Théâtre-libre produced plays by fifty-one authors, forty-two of them under forty; among them were men who won notable success by the turn of the century. But of the 111 plays that Antoine produced, almost two thirds were short plays, for the one-act was a new and easier field for experiment.

Antoine wanted to make the Théâtre-libre a playhouse known for its broad and catholic repertory. In this he failed. He gave more than a dozen one-act plays in verse. He produced Hauptmann's *Hannele*, which mixed realism and poetry. Yet the Théâtre-libre was stamped in the public mind as a house of "naturalism." This was partly due to the fact that most of the new playwrights wrote in the realistic vein, and partly to the fact that the opening bill of the Théâtre-libre was carried to success by a short dramatization of one of Zola's stories. Furthermore, Ibsen's *Ghosts* and *The Wild Duck*, Strindberg's *Miss Julia*, and Hauptmann's *The Weavers* fitted best the acting and producing methods of Antoine.

REALISTIC TRIUMPH—FINANCIAL FAILURE

Though Antoine himself had a weak voice, he was unquestionably a fine actor. At the end of his first spring season, the state-endowed Odéon—which he was to direct twenty years later—tried to add him to its company. Antoine saw the Meiningen players in 1888 and adopted their way of handling crowds, but he had already developed an ensemble and had gone far beyond the Meiningen troupe or any other company in naturalness on the stage. He made his actors speak and move about as if the characters they played were actual human beings; greatly daring, he often had them speak lines with their backs to the audience. Antoine built his ensemble and achieved his reforms with a company that included at various times a traveling salesman, a bookbinder, a chemist, a wine merchant, an architect, a dressmaker, a manufacturer, and, of course, clerks. At the Menus-Plaisirs, he began to build realistic settings. He had never used "wood wings" and backdrops with stairs painted on them, but now he called for solid moldings, as well as doors and panels of wood instead of canvas. He borrowed or rented everyday furniture, and in one play he used as props real legs of lamb and carcasses of beef.

At the end of the season of 1889–90—when over twelve thousand articles had been written about the Théâtre-libre, and Antoine was in debt for the same number of francs—he drew up the first concrete, detailed plan and program for a truly modern playhouse and a repertory company; but no one came forward with the money to make it a reality. Without such a house and a paid company that could give many performances of a successful play, the Théâtre-libre was doomed to financial failure. Short tours to Belgium, Germany, England, and Italy brought no substantial profit. Other theaters lured away some of Antoine's best actors. Discouraged and owing 100,000 francs, in 1894 he turned over the Théâtre-libre to another director, who kept it going only through 1895 and 1896.

THE INFLUENCE OF ANTOINE

Besides giving distinguished foreign playwrights like Ibsen, Tolstoy, Strindberg, Björnson, and Hauptmann their first hearings in Paris, Antoine's theater did the same for Eugène Brieux and François de Curel. Brieux is known best as the writer of thesis-plays, dramas exposing social evils. In *Blanchette* he attacked discrimination against women in education, in *The Red Robe* he exposed legal chicanery, and in *Damaged Goods* he dealt with the menace of venereal disease. Today these plays seem a bit labored and doctrinaire, but he wrote two mordant comedies, *The Three Daughters of M. Dupont* and *Les Hannetons*. The same bill that introduced a second play by Brieux, the son of a carpenter, included the first production of a play by the son of a nobleman, François de Curel. A writer of uncompromising integrity, he submitted his first three plays to Antoine under pseudonyms. His second play at the Théâtre-libre, *Les Fossiles* (*The Fossils*), was a study of decadent aristocracy.

Another dramatist of distinction, Georges de Porto-Riche, turned definitely away from romantic historical drama when he saw

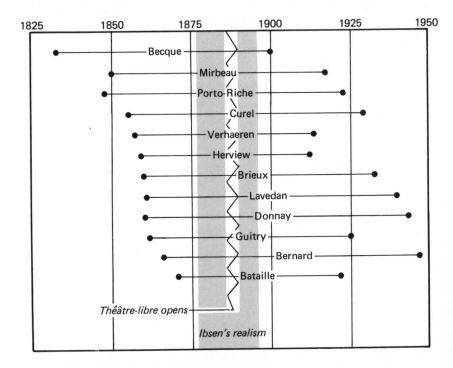

Figure 8.1   French Realism after Antoine

The first plays of Curel and Brieux were acted at the Théâtre-libre. There Porto-Riche turned away from historical drama and wrote a realistic one-acter, while Lavedan collaborated on a short play. All, including the Belgian Verhaeren, found other theaters receptive after Antoine had shown the way.

his realistic one-act play, *La Chance de Françoise*, produced at the Théâtre-libre in 1888. Three years later, he found himself completely in his comedy of married love *L'Amoureuse*.

Though Antoine's venture was a financial failure, it set a pattern of realistic drama that later playwrights followed even into the twentieth century. Among these were Henri Lavedan, who contributed only a short collaboration to the Théâtre-libre, but who went on to a series of sound dramas like *Le Prince d'Aurec*; Maurice Donnay with his *Amants (Lovers)* and *L'Age difficile (The Difficult Age)*; two moralizers, Paul Hervieu and Octave Mirbeau, the first best known in America for *Connais-toi (Know Thyself)*, and the second for *Les Affaires sont les affaires (Business is Business)*; and the sensitive Henri Bataille, author of *La Tendresse* and a dramatization of Tolstoy's *Resurrection*.

The Théâtre-libre accomplished four important things. It demonstrated how to produce realistic plays realistically, and it humanized the acting of poetic or romantic drama. It stimulated new playwrights; some wrote first for Antoine's venture, some only for the commercial theaters. Antoine himself went on to a distinguished career as the leading French director prior to World War I; in 1897, backed at last by stockholders, he made the Menus-Plaisirs into the Théâtre Antoine, and then he was called to head the Odéon from 1906 to 1914. More important still, the example of the Théâtre-libre created imitators in Paris itself and in Berlin and London. Even the "little theaters" of the United States with their amateur companies and their subscription memberships, as well as the Moscow Art Theater, owe something to Antoine.

A "FREE THEATER" FOR GERMANY

The effect of Antoine was greater, perhaps, on the German stage than on the French, for the German was in a far worse state. Though Prussia crushed France in 1871 and created the German Empire, French playwrights of the most conventional type dominated the Teutonic stage well into the nineties. To be sure, the Meiningen company, which was formed before the Prussian victory, produced no French trash, but the "Theater Duke" staged only one of Ibsen's plays besides *Ghosts* (his historical tragedy *The Pretend-*

ers) while the other court theaters and the playhouses under commercial management did nothing to open the way for realism.

Adolf L'Arronge, who made a fortune writing German farces, founded—in Berlin—the new Deutsches Theater in 1883 and attempted a few reforms. He boldly opposed the growing policy of long runs and kept to a changing repertory. He aimed at a high acting standard through a company headed by Ernst von Possart, Joseph Kainz, and Agnes Sorma. But the acting was not realistic, and the stars could not be molded into an ensemble. As for L'Arronge's repertory, he stuck largely to the Meiningen policy, *sans* Ibsen, of classic and historical drama.

The break came in 1889. In Berlin, the great journalist Maximilian Harden and eight friends chose a critic named Otto Brahm to direct a German version of the Théâtre-libre and to meet a serious and peculiar problem. Though theater monopoly had gradually disappeared in Germany between 1848 and 1870, police censorship as well as the mediocre taste of most playgoers barred the production of plays that dealt too frankly with sexual problems or the miseries of the common people. Following Antoine's policy, Brahm gave only private performances, which the police could not stop, and he drew upon a superior audience by selling tickets only to annual subscribers. Like Antoine, Brahm got his actors gratis, but he used professionals rather than amateurs. Instead of renting a small hall, he gave his performances at noon on Sundays in theaters that sympathetic managements let him have without charge. Again like Antoine, Brahm hoped that, when he had shown the merit of new plays, commercial managements would take them over or accept the later work of his writers.

THE FREIE BÜHNE'S SUCCESS ENDS ITS CAREER

Brahm began with *Ghosts*, which had been banned by the Berlin censor. Much more important, Brahm followed this in just a month with *Vor Sonnenaufgang* (*Before Sunrise*), the first play of a new writer, Gerhart Hauptmann, who was to lead the playwrights of Germany and excel most of them for more than a generation. In the spring of 1890, Brahm produced another new German drama, the naturalistic *Die Familie Selicke*, by Arno Holz and Johannes Schlaf.

Brahm also revived Anzengruber's *The Double Suicide* and staged translations of Tolstoy's *The Power of Darkness*, which Antoine had already produced, Zola's *Thérèse Raquin*, the Goncourts' *Henriette Maréchal*, Becque's *The Vultures*, and Strindberg's *The Father* and *Miss Julia*.

Just as Brahm had hoped, the example of the Freie Bühne improved the level of the commercial theater. It improved the level so much that within a couple of years there seemed to be no reason for Brahm to continue production. Occasionally, however, the Freie Bühne had to be reanimated. For instance, after L'Arronge had taken over *Lonely Lives* he refused Hauptmann's next play, *The Weavers*; so Brahm gathered his forces together again to produce it.

The rapid improvement of the Berlin stage is shown by two offshoots of Brahm's institution. During its second season, Bruno Wille organized in Berlin the Freie Volksbühne (Free People's Stage). This institution anticipated the Book-of-the-Month Club in another field. By paying for special performances of various plays by various commercial managements, it was able to sell tickets to its subscribers at lower than regular prices. Occasionally it made productions of its own, for example Ibsen's *The Pillars of Society*. As the level of the Berlin theater continued to rise, a new institution appeared called the New Free People's Stage. By 1914 it had 50,000 subscribers, and could build its own playhouse, the magnificent Volksbühne. During the 1920s the subscription list ran as high as 120,000.

BRAHM AN OUTSTANDING DIRECTOR

For the plays of the Freie Bühne, Brahm enlisted fine actors such as Joseph Kainz, Emanuel Reicher, and Agnes Sorma, and he fused them into a brilliant ensemble. In 1894, when L'Arronge retired from active management of the Deutsches Theater and entrusted the theater to Brahm, he had, besides these three, Else Lehmann, Max Reinhardt, Rudolf Rittner, and other excellent players. In 1905 Brahm moved to the Lessing Theater and enjoyed for a time the services of the distinguished Albert Bassermann, who had had his training with the Meiningen company.

As a critic, Brahm had been brilliant, incisive, and often bitter.

As a director, he was as uncompromising, but he was patient and selfless, calm and considerate. He excelled Antoine as a director of realistic plays, but unfortunately his range was not so wide. As his first production after he took over the Deutsches Theater, he tried to stage in the modern manner the classic *Kabale und Liebe* by Schiller. The result was a disaster. Though he once used or tried to use Gordon Craig, Brahm was never a contributor, like Reinhardt, to the fresh and imaginative ways of the twentieth-century theater. But Brahm made over the German theater, and he remained for twenty years a dominant figure on the realistic stage of Europe.

FROM HAUPTMANN TO WEDEKIND

Hauptmann turned from sculpture to playwrighting, and from 1889 almost until his death in 1946, his output was varied in kind and quality; but it always had some measure of distinction. He dealt with the personal tragedy of working class people in *Before Sunrise* and with their mass miseries in *The Weavers*. Of his peasant dramas, the best was *Rose Bernd*. He wrote plays in the vein of Ibsen, such as *Lonely Lives* and *Michael Kramer*, comedies such as *Der Biberpelz* (*The Beaver Coat*), and historic dramas such as *Florian Geyer*, dealing with the Peasant's War, and *Der Weisse Heiland* (*The White Redeemer*), about Cortes and the conquest of

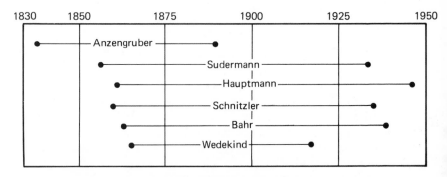

Figure 8.2   German Playwrights Born in the Nineteenth Century
The work of Anzengruber is almost unknown outside the teutonic stage. Sudermann now seems passé. Wedekind has not yet been successful in English.

Mexico. He also tried the poetic in *Hannele* and the symbolic in *Die Versunkene Glocke* (*The Sunken Bell*).

Other new German playwrights appeared in the early 1890s. Hermann Sudermann, best known for *Heimat*, which we call *Magda*, might have been a French practitioner of the well-made play. There was more stature to the comedies and dramas of Ludwig Fulda and Otto Erich Hartleben and to the tragedies of Max Halbe. The satirist Carl Sternheim introduced into his comedies the crisply "telegraphic" style that expressionistic writers later adopted.

Next to Hauptmann, the outstanding German who began to write for the stage in the last decade of the nineteenth century was Frank Wedekind. He was as obsessed as Strindberg with sexual tragedy. In 1890 with *Die junge Welt* (*The World of Youth*) and the next year with *Frühlings Erwachen* (*The Awakening of Spring*), Wedekind brought the "slice of life" technique to the problem of adolescents who are given no guidance as to sex. *Erdgeist* (*Earth Spirit*) of 1895 and *Die Büchse der Pandora* (*Pandora's Box*) of 1902 showed the same character, Lulu, instinctively and ruthlessly preying on men and meeting a horrible end. Wedekind's plays were both moral and morbid. They were naturalistic–realistic, and they also introduced some aspects of twentieth-century expressionism. The tragedy in *The Awakening of Spring* is as real as it is affecting, yet it ends bizarrely with one of the two boy heroes returning from the grave to urge suicide on the other, while "A Masked Man," symbolizing life, comes to persuade him not to kill himself.

SCHNITZLER AND THE AUSTRIANS

The tragedy and even morbidity that stamped the awakening drama in Germany is less apparent in the plays that came out of Austria at the same time. The greatest of her playwrights, Arthur Schnitzler, wrote comedies as well as dramas and tragedies. His first work for the theater, in 1893, was the group of gay, amatory one-act plays called *Anatol*. One of his finest tragedies, *Liebelei* (*Light o' Love*), came two years later and another, *Der Einsame Weg* (*The Lonely Way*), in 1904. Schnitzler had a fondness for the one-act play, wrote many, and often related them skillfully together—as with *Anatol*,

Reigen (Hands Around), and *Lebendige Stunden (Living Hours)*. He wrote one of his best, *Der grüne Kakadu (The Green Cockatoo)* in 1899. His strong attack on anti-Semitism, *Professor Bernhardi*, appeared in 1912.

After a fling at morbid drama in 1891, another Viennese, Hermann Bahr, turned toward comedy and won success in 1898 with *Josephine*, written around the young Napoleon. He is best known in America for the Belasco-Ditrichstein version of his amusing play, *The Concert*.

Though Hugo von Hofmannsthal wrote and adapted comedies, this Viennese poet was at his best in his tragedies in verse. He began these in the early nineties, but his finest is perhaps *Oedipus and the Sphinx* of 1906. From then onward he adapted many plays for Reinhardt—including *Jedermann*, from the medieval morality *Everyman*, and three from Calderón, *Dame Kobold*, *Der Turm*, and *Das grosse Welttheater*—and he wrote librettos for six of Richard Strauss's operas, including *Electra* and *Der Rosenkavalier*.

LONDON'S "INDEPENDENT THEATER"

A Dutchman brought the "Free Theater" idea to London. Like Brahm, J. T. Grein had been a dramatic critic. At twenty he wrote the introduction to a Dutch translation of Ibsen's *An Enemy of the People*. Two years later, he was the reviewer of an Amsterdam daily paper. When he was not yet thirty and had made London his home, he launched the Independent Theater Society in the spring of 1891. Grein himself and men like William Archer, translator of Ibsen, and George Moore, the novelist, hoped to discover and develop English playwrights. Grein began, of course, with *Ghosts*. Not content with hundreds of violent reviews and letters to the editor, he followed it up with Zola's *Thérèse Raquin*. Then he put on bills of short and full-length English plays that caused no great stir. At last, toward the end of 1892, the Independent Theater produced George Bernard Shaw's first play, *Widower's Houses*, thus doing the same service for the man who was to become England's leading playwright that the Freie Bühne had done for Hauptmann. Among Grein's later productions was Ibsen's *The Wild Duck*.

Though the plays of the Independent Theater Society—

produced at matinees with volunteer actors—were a heavy drain on Grein's income, this venture that ended in financial failure had a very considerable effect on the English stage. In 1899 came the Incorporated Stage Society, which for forty years gave outstanding Continental and English plays on Sunday nights with casts that included some of the best of London's actors. From the work of this society, the stimulus of Grein, and the great repute of Brahm and Antoine may be traced more successful undertakings of the greatest importance: the work of Granville-Barker, the Abbey Players, the Manchester Repertory Theater, and other ventures that we shall describe in due course.

IBSEN AND BJÖRNSON—GIANTS OF THE NORTH

As we have said, there were realistic playwrights—sound and effective ones—before there were theaters or audiences to welcome them. Only two, however, were writing steadily and abundantly before Antoine opened his Théâtre-libre. These were Henrik Ibsen and Björnstjerne Björnson, and they were born in remote and sparsely populated Norway.

Both Scandinavians began by writing historical and poetic plays that suited the taste of Norwegian audiences. Both men held posts, at various times during the 1860s and 1870s, in Norwegian theaters. Such modest success must have heartened them while they began to write a type of play not so readily accepted as the historical and romantic. Björnson—poet, novelist, and newspaper editor—turned to realism about five years before Ibsen wrote *The League of Youth*, and a decade before his next play in that genre, *The Pillars of Society*. Politically, both men were rebels; Björnson was a leader in the liberal party, while Ibsen was for a time a socialist. They both attacked the social evils of their day, but in different moods. For *A Bankruptcy*, built around a dishonest business man, and *A Gauntlet*, an attack on the "double standard" in sexual morals, Björnson found happy endings that Ibsen could never have conceived. While Ibsen placed a greater emphasis on psychological analysis and depth of character, his friend and rival wrote more superficially, though with a theatrical skill that won him a greater success at home than Ibsen enjoyed. The different outlook of the two men may have been somewhat due to the different circumstances of their youth. The happily optimistic Björnson was brought up by wealthy parents and lived in a lovely section of Norway. Ibsen's parents lost their fortune when he was eight; when he was fifteen, they apprenticed him to an apothecary in a grim provincial town.

Between 1855 and 1865 Björnson wrote a number of historical plays in verse, few of which were popular outside Scandinavia. During the same period Ibsen used the ballads and the sagas of old Norway as the material for a number of poetic plays such as *The Vikings at Helgeland* and *The Pretenders*. Toward the end of their work, both men emphasized spiritual rather than social values in their realistic plays. Björnson's *Beyond Human Power* (1881) is the outstanding play of his later period. From Ibsen's *The Master Builder* (1892) through *Little Eyolf* and his last drama, *When We Dead Awaken*, he injected more and more symbolism into his work.

FROM VERSE TO REALISM WITH IBSEN

When Ibsen first wrote of the contemporary scene in 1862, the poet in him forced the characters of *Love's Comedy* to speak in verse. Before he committed himself definitely to realistic prose in *The League of Youth*, he used poetic rhythms in two long plays dealing with his own times. (Like his later dramas, he wrote them in voluntary exile abroad.) *Brand*, of the middle sixties, is a somber all-or-nothing attack on compromise; it won no lasting popularity outside Scandinavia. *Peer Gynt*, which followed shortly after, is a colorful but rambling play which tells with considerable satire the story of a rascally country boy who becomes a millionaire and returns to face a peculiar and bizarre end. Between *The League of Youth*, which followed in 1869, and *The Pillars of Society*, the first of the realistic plays that occupied him for fifteen years, Ibsen wrote another historical drama in verse. This gigantic script, *Emperor and Galilean*, deals with the struggle between Christianity and paganism in the fourth century.

There is a dual greatness about Ibsen. One lies in his technique. The other is his ability to understand human beings and present them on the stage. Technically, he far outdistanced the men like Scribe and Sardou who had manufactured well-made plays. He threw away all their devious devices, their coincidences and startling denouements. He began his realistic plays just before the crisis in their stories, skillfully exposed the past, and used it to provide complications with ever-mounting suspense. His understanding of human character and his ability to make it come to life must be clear to anyone who has read *Ghosts, A Doll's House, The Wild Duck, Rosmersholm,* or *Hedda Gabler.* His gravest fault was to accept too literally at first the half-baked theories on heredity that had infected Zola and the naturalists, a fault shared by Hauptmann in his early plays. But Ibsen compensated for this by never clinging to the doctrinaire in other respects. His themes and his ideas grew from play to play. Even in his historical dramas there was character analysis. Philosophically as well as psychologically, his plays have a depth found in very few dramas before 1890.

STRINDBERG—GREATER THAN IBSEN?

Scandinavia contributed another giant to the modern theater. This was a Swede, August Strindberg. Like Ibsen and Björnson— though born a generation later—Strindberg began by writing historical plays, then took up realism, and finally turned to a form that might be called a symbolic interpretation of actuality and that was a forerunner of expressionism. He was even more versatile than Ibsen and Björnson; besides directing productions, managing two theaters, writing fifty plays, long and short, and theorizing radically on stage technique, he wrote novels, short stories, histories, and autobiographies that laid bare his inner life as if he were lying on a psychiatrist's couch.

In other respects Strindberg and the two Norwegians were worlds apart. Even in his realistic period—and much more so toward the end—he wrote with a far greater intensity and violence, and he analyzed and sublimated the materials of life as neither of his rivals ever did. His genius was tinged with madness. Some of the psychoses that are now familiar to so many laymen—from overcompensating arrogance, through mother-fixation, to persecution mania—are evident enough in the years that preceded and followed his nervous breakdown from 1895 to 1897.

Figure 8.3 The Intimate Theater of Stockholm
Twenty years after the founding of the Théâtre-libre, August Strindberg joined August Falk in the creation of another small experimental playhouse, the Intimate Theater of Stockholm, which opened in 1907. For this venture—at first devoted entirely to his works—Strindberg wrote *The Spook Sonata* and what he called "chamber plays." The interior of the theater, which seated only 125 spectators, is shown in the photograph.

Superficially, Strindberg is best known for his violent misogyny. From *The Father*—his first realistic play, written in 1887—through *Comrades, Creditors, The Stronger, Miss Julie*, and parts or all of many more dramas, Strindberg pictured women as preying on man and destroying him, usually in marriage and sometimes out of it. Into this theme he poured all the violence of his nature and all the vigor of his great art. After his mental illness and until his death from cancer in 1912, his plays ranged from a historical drama, *Gustavus Vasa*, through another sex struggle, *The Dance of Death*, and a symbolic religious drama, *Easter*, to a group of plays including *Toward Damascus, The Spook Sonata*, and *The Dream Play*, in which life is presented with a strange distortion that seems to be the basis and the root—even more than Wedekind's work—of German expressionism. This we will discuss in the next essay.

The work of this man who said he searched for God and found the devil won the warmest of praise from two later playwrights of outstanding position and a most significant comment from Ibsen. Sean O'Casey, author of *Juno and the Paycock*, wrote: "Strindberg, Strindberg, Strindberg, the greatest of them all! . . . Strindberg shakes flame from the living planets and the fixed stars. Ibsen can sit serenely in his Doll's House, while Strindberg is battling with heaven and hell." O'Neill called him "the precursor of all modernity in our present theater." And, commenting on Strindberg, Ibsen said to a visitor, "There is one who will be greater than I."

THE MOSCOW ART THEATER

Russia gave three great realists to the theater—Tolstoy, Chekhov, and Gorky. The work of all three is tied in closely with one of the finest institutions of modern theatrical history, the Moscow Art Theater. In 1891, when one of its two directors, Constantin Stanislavsky, was still an amateur, he produced Tolstoy's satirical comedy *The Fruits of Enlightenment*. Tolstoy's first outstanding play, the powerful peasant tragedy *The Power of Darkness*, was written just before Antoine opened the Théâtre-libre, and it had its world première there in 1888; but this drama was first staged in Russia by Stanislavsky only after the Moscow Art Theater was on its feet. By

Figure 8.4 The Moscow Art Theater Emblem

The sea gull, emblem of the Moscow Art Theater, was adopted by the company after Chekhov's play—the fourth to be offered by Stanislavsky and Nemirovich-Danchenko in 1898—revived an enterprise in danger of collapsing. The Moscow Art Theater soon became known as "the House of Chekhov."

successfully reviving Checkhov's *The Sea Gull*, after its failure at another house, the Moscow Art Theater dissuaded him from giving up playwriting. The success of Chekhov turned Gorky toward the stage, and the playhouse was able to present his powerful tragedy *The Lower Depths*.

More has probably been written about the Moscow Art Theater than about any modern playhouse. Constantin Stanislavsky was the son of rich parents who built him a log cabin theater on their country estate and another in their Moscow town house, where he acted with relatives and friends. In 1888 he helped to found the Society of Literature and Art, and in a few years—when he was hardly twenty-five—he began directing plays. We have heard how a man of similar interests, Vladimir Nemirovich-Danchenko, had been teaching acting at the Moscow Philharmonic Society, and how Stanislavsky and Danchenko met at a famous artists' restaurant and in fifteen hours of talk outlined the policy and the organization of the Moscow Art Theater. We know that the best of their student–actors and amateurs, together with certain professionals, were fused through long study and rehearsal—by what came to be called "the Stanislavsky method"—into a matchless ensemble. The purpose, as we have been so frequently told, was not to achieve the surface aspects of naturalism, but to capture and convey what Stanislavsky described as "the inner truth, the truth of feeling and experience."

The actors through whom the Moscow Art Theater created what might best be called a profound psychological realism came partly from the amateurs of Stanislavsky and Danchenko and partly from the profession. The best known and most adept—many of whom New York saw in 1922–23—were Olga Knipper, Ivan Moskvin, Vasili Kachalov, Maria Germanova, Leonid Leonidov, Alla Nazimova, Richard Boleslavsky, Leo Bulgakov, Akim Tamiroff, and Olga Baclanova. Among distinguished Russian actors who did not play in the Moscow Art Theater was Paul Orlenev; America saw him in *Ghosts* with Nazimova about 1905.

OTHERS BESIDES STANISLAVSKY

When any institution is so striking and so rich in detail as the Moscow Art Theater—and has lived in triumph for more than half a century—many aspects are underestimated or almost ignored. For

Meininger Tour of European Capitals	1874-1890
Théâtre-libre, Paris (Antoine)	1887-1894
Freie Büehne, Berlin (Brahm)	1889-1891
Neue Freie Volksbühne, Berlin	1890-
Independent Theater, London (Grein)	1891-1892
Elizabethan Stage Society (Poel)	1893-1905
Moscow Art Theater	1898-
Incorporated Stage Society, London	1899-1939

Figure 8.5   Influences on Modern Production

instance, hardly a writer mentions the fact that the wealth of the upper bourgeoisie made the theater possible, while Antoine, in Paris, pleaded vainly for money to build his ideal theater. Not only was Stanislavsky's family well supplied with worldly goods, but his pupils and Danchenko's, who were the nucleus of the company, came from the wealthier classes. More than that, a fabulous patron named Savva Morozov provided the funds for rebuilding a play-house and carrying the company and its repertory through the lean times before the plays of Chekhov brought fame and fortune.

There has never been enough credit given the predecessors of the Moscow Art Theater. The Maly Theater, the smaller of the two imperial playhouses, was the first to produce Gogol, Ostrovsky, and Ibsen in Russia. As far back as 1853, it threw away the French soubrette costume and coiffure of the maidservant and gave her a plain cotton frock and smooth hair. When the imperial monopoly of the theater ended in 1882, there appeared what were called "people's theaters." The manager of one of these—a man named Lentovsky—encouraged Tolstoy to write *The Power of Darkness*, though censorship balked its production till the theater of Stanis-lavsky and Danchenko waxed powerful. Lentovsky was the first Russian producer to take the direction of a play out of the haphazard hands of his cast; in addition, he introduced electric light to the Russian stage.

Because Danchenko was no actor—and perhaps because Stanislavsky centered attention upon himself with his fine book *My Life in Art*—Danchenko's share in the making of the Moscow Art Theater has been overshadowed by Stanislavsky's. It was Danchenko who called the meeting with Stanislavsky. By the initial agreement, Stanislavsky had absolute control of production—while, incidentally, he managed the business that his father had left him—and Danchenko was in charge of financial and "literary" matters. Literary matters, however, meant the choice of plays, and Danchenko was the one who lured Chekhov back to playwriting and made the fortune of the playhouse by reviving *The Sea Gull*. More than that, Danchenko—as novelist and playwright as well as teacher of acting—had the right to determine how each play was to be approached in order to bring out its meaning. Stanislavsky himself tells how his partner "hammered all the beauties of Chekhov into my head. He could talk of a play so well that one had to like it before he was through." Though under the basic agreement, Danchenko was not supposed to be concerned with the staging of plays, "two stage directors," wrote Stanislavsky, "sat at the director's table, Nemirovich-Danchenko and I." Later Danchenko had his own table, and created the Music Studio of the Moscow Art Theater, where *Lysistrata* became lyric, and *Carmen* took on the true qualities of drama.

CHEKHOV, GORKY, AND TOLSTOY

There was a curious paradox about the Moscow Art Theater. The founders said that, unlike the institutions springing up in France and Germany and England, it was to be an actor's theater, not a director's theater or a theater for playwrights. Yet, though Stanislavsky and his associates made over the art of acting in Russia, the theater also spawned directors of distinction—Stanislavsky himself, Danchenko, Meyerhold, Vakhtangov. Michael Chekhov, the playwright's nephew, even Balieff of the satiric Chauve-Souris. And just as definitely this was the playwright's theater.

After reviving *The Sea Gull* in 1898, it drew from Chekhov three more fine plays before his early death in 1904. Thus we owe to the Moscow Art Theater *Uncle Vanya*, *The Three Sisters*, and, above all, *The Cherry Orchard*. His last play is the finest demonstration of Chekhov's ability to build quietly into a simple plot—almost a formless structure—characters that are believable, poignant, touching, utterly human.

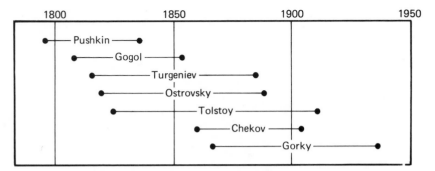

Figure 8.6 The Progress of Russian Realism

Though Pushkin wrote poetic and historical drama, his work was a commentary on his times. Gogol's comedies, bitterly observant, were swiftly followed by realistic dramas. Tolstoy finished no plays until 1886, when he wrote *The Power of Darkness*. Gorky, too, began late; his first play, *The Lower Depths*, came in 1902.

Gorky wrote plays from about 1902 to 1934. But only the second, *The Lower Depths*, and the next to last, *Yegor Bulychov*, are truly memorable. He drew the material for the first from the years he had had to spend in the flop houses of Russia with "creatures that had once been men." In *Yegor Bulichov* he saw tragedy from the other side; he showed us a rich merchant dying of cancer, surrounded by cruel, ignorant, corrupt, and contemptible friends, and dying disillusioned as the sound of the Bolshevik Revolution comes to his ears—"the burial service, singing me out of the world." When Gorky chose his nom de plume ("gorky" means "bitter") he chose well.

With or without Antoine or Brahm or Stanislavsky and Danchenko, Leo Tolstoy would have been a dramatist. And he would probably have written no fewer than the four plays that added stage repute to the author of the novel *War and Peace*. *The Power of Darkness* is a grim and horrifying tragedy of a debased peasantry. *The Fruits of Enlightenment* satirizes the country gentry. *Redemption*—as Arthur Hopkins called *The Living Corpse* when he produced it with John Barrymore—is a powerful and pitiful drama of a man who is forced by social circumstances to kill himself so that his wife may be happy with another man. In his last play, *The Light That Shines in Darkness*, Tolstoy left, with its last act unfinished,

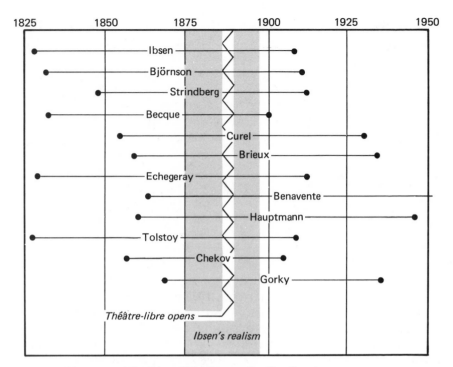

Figure 8.7　The Rise of Realism on the Continent
Omitting England, Ireland, and the United States, this chart shows the Norwegians Ibsen and Björnson as the forerunners of realism. The rest, including Tolstoy, turned to realism after Ibsen and Björnson had begun to write in that vein. The gray band indicates the years during which Ibsen concentrated all his power on the realistic medium.

an attempt to contrast the uselessness and the tragedy of a wealthy family and poverty-ridden peasants.

THE IRISH NATIONAL THEATER

Two women played a very important part in the creation of theater companies as well as in the promotion of the realistic drama in England and Ireland. To Lady Gregory and Miss A. E. F. Horniman the stage owes the so-called Irish Players at the Abbey Theater, Dublin, and to Miss Horniman the Manchester Repertory Company, whose pioneering led to other ventures in a number of British cities. Out of these theaters came playwrights of unusual quality.

The Dublin venture began as the Irish Literary Theater of 1899. It sprang partly from the Nationalist political movement and partly from the enthusiasm of the poet William Butler Yeats. He and Lady Gregory saw it, at first, as a vehicle for poetic drama. In the beginning, the players were English, and there were all too few Irish people who wanted to see their plays. Then, in 1901, some amateur actors of Dublin, the Fay brothers, joined Yeats, Lady Gregory, and their associates to form the Irish National Theater Company. The result was a performance of genuine native flavor. In 1903 the company appeared triumphantly in London. Miss Horniman—who had financed the first London production of Shaw's *Arms and the Man* almost ten years before—was so aroused by the Irish performances that she rebuilt the Abbey Theater for them, and supported the venture until 1910, when it was on its feet.

Under the direction of the Fays, the actors followed the realistic style that Antoine had set, and they played with simplicity and yet with both humor and power. New Irish writers turned to the stage because the Abbey was there to welcome them. Their work, from the plays of Synge to the plays of O'Casey, was rooted in the actualities of Irish life. Yeats continued loyal and indefatigable in the management of the company, but his poetic plays were few and they did not set the pattern. Paradoxically, the theater that was to be poetic turned to realism. Again paradoxically, this realism at its best rose to high beauty of expression because that was the nature of peasant speech. The theater had indeed, as Lady Gregory put it at the beginning, "a base of realism and an apex of beauty." America could recognize this even as early as 1911 when George C. Tyler brought over the company as the Irish Players.

IRELAND'S RICH DRAMA

Out of Dublin and also Belfast in Northern Ireland came a surprising number of native dramatists, writing both one-act and longer plays. Among the earliest, John Millington Synge, was easily the best. Yeats brought him from a Paris lodging to live with the Irish peasants and learn their tongue. The result, between 1903 and

Synge's too-early death in 1909, were six plays that combined truth of character with the beauty of Irish speech—and usually great humor. His second, *Riders to the Sea*, is still one of the finest one-act tragedies ever written in the speech of either Ireland or England. The peak of his work was the highly original and brilliant comedy *The Playboy of the Western World.*

Besides these and Yeats' fine *Cathleen ni Houlihan*, Ireland has given us—to name only a few plays—Lady Gregory's one-act comedies of folk life such as *Spreading the News* and *The Workhouse Ward*, as well as her patriotic drama *The Rising of the Moon*, and her tragedy *The Gaol Gate*, Lennox Robinson's delightful comedy *The White-Headed Boy*, St. John Ervine's *John Ferguson* and *Mixed Marriage*, Paul Vincent Carroll's subtle and significant *Shadow and Substance* and *The White Steed*, and Sean O'Casey's satirically bitter *Juno and the Paycock* and *The Plough and the Stars*. It is an output unequalled by modern English playwrights unless we include among them two Dublin-born men, Oscar Wilde and Bernard Shaw.

MISS HORNIMAN AND GRANVILLE-BARKER

With the Abbey Theater safely launched, Miss Horniman gave her native city, between 1908 and 1921, the Manchester Repertory Theater. It was distinguished by fine performances from new players, many of whom went on to success in London, and also by local plays. Half of the two hundred productions were of new material. Among these were Stanley Houghton's *Hindle Wakes*, Harold Brighouse's *Hobson's Choice*, and plays by St. John Hankin. Here Ervine's *Jane Clegg* had its first production, as well as John Masefield's fine play *The Tragedy of Nan*. Miss Horniman's pioneering work had its effect in London as well as in other British cities.

While Miss Horniman was supporting the Abbey Theater, H. Granville Barker—hyphenating himself later as Harley Granville-Barker—joined the manager John E. Vedrenne in repertory seasons in London from 1904 to 1907. A fine actor himself—as he had demonstrated in other performances besides Marchbanks in Shaw's *Candida* for the Incorporated Stage Society—he proved an able director and playwright. Besides Barker's dramas *The Voysey Inheritance, Waste,* and *The Madras House,* Vedrenne and he presented plays by Euripides, Maeterlinck, Schnitzler, and Hauptmann. They produced eleven plays by Shaw, five for the first time, and they brought out the first work of a new dramatist of distinction, John Galsworthy, who had made his reputation as a novelist. The Vedrenne-Barker seasons, through their high standards of plays and acting, had a greater influence on the British stage than Herbert Beerbohm Tree, George Alexander, Cyril Maude, and all the other actor–managers combined.

OSCAR WILDE AND BERNARD SHAW

Realism of a kind came to the British drama in the 1880s with Henry Arthur Jones and Arthur Wing Pinero. Both may have gained something from Ibsen but more from the well-made plays of France. Jones, the more conscientious writer, came close to something good in the middle nineties with his *Michael and His Lost Angel* and *The Liars.* Pinero waited until 1909 and 1910 to desert theatrical trash for *Mid-Channel* and *The Thunderbolt.* J. M. Barrie began successfully with comedy romance in the nineties, and produced some pleasant comedies ten years later in *The Admirable Crichton* and *What Every Woman Knows.* His fantasy *Peter Pan,* of 1904 was a foretaste of the somewhat more serious unreality of *A Kiss for Cinderella* and *Mary Rose.*

The 1890s offered to the English stage the first plays of Bernard Shaw—which it would not accept—and the four comedies that Oscar Wilde wrote before his disgrace and death. London adored the smartly cynical dialog of Wilde that reached its height in *The Importance of Being Earnest.* The fact that theatergoers of the nineties could also enjoy the artificial plotting of his *Lady Windermere's Fan, A Woman of No Importance,* and *An Ideal Husband* should account for the fact that the London stage had no use for Shaw's *Widower's Houses* or even *Arms and the Man.* It was Barker, with 701 performances of Shaw's plays in the years before the First World War, who saw Shaw through to victory in England. The comic genius that rose through *Candida, The Devil's Disciple,*

Caesar and Cleopatra, Man and Superman, Major Barbara, The Doctor's Dilemma, Androcles and the Lion, and *Pygmalion,* fell away pitiably after *St. Joan* of 1923. Yet—despite Galsworthy's fine social dramas such as *The Silver Box, Justice, The Skin Game, Loyalties,* and *Escape*—Shaw remained the greatest of modern English playwrights.

Somerset Maugham's best plays, *The Constant Wife* and *The Circle,* suffer by comparison with his own novel *Of Human Bondage,* let alone Shaw's work. From *The Vortex* to *Cavalcade* and *Design for Living,* Noel Coward is smart, witty, and at times moving, but he will be forgotten sooner than J. B. Priestley, Emlyn Williams, and Terence Rattigan with their few but deeply sincere plays.

REALISM LAGGARD IN AMERICAN DRAMA

The realistic playwright developed far later in the United States than in the Old World. Examples from the work of the better Europeans were scantily imported until after 1915. Pinero and Jones were popular because they were obvious; but Ibsen languished, and Shaw won meager attention only through three stars: Richard Mansfield in the nineties and Robert Loraine and Arnold Daly around 1905. Of Americans who began to write in the nineteenth century, Clyde Fitch was, except for a couple of plays, a maker of facile but shallow comedies, while Augustus Thomas turned from melodramas to turgid dramas about telepathy or the "double standard," such as *The Witching Hour* and *As a Man Thinks.* Only four writers of any merit appeared in America before 1915. Langdon Mitchell dramatized a few novels but wrote only one original play, a brilliant comedy of divorce, *The New York Idea,* which Mrs. Fiske produced with some success in 1906. In the same year came a rather powerful play by the poet William Vaughn Moody, *The Great Divide,* but his only other drama, *The Faith Healer,* proved less effective in the theater. Edward Sheldon wrote *Salvation Nell,* in which Mrs. Fiske starred, and *Romance,* which occupied Doris Keane for some five years. Elmer Rice—now known for his later plays *Street Scene* and *Counsellor-at-Law*—wrote his *On Trial* only a couple of seasons before that crucial year of 1915 when the Provincetown Players began to develop the talent of Eugene O'Neill.

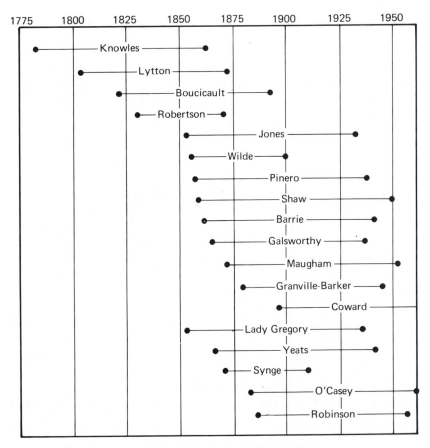

Figure 8.8 One Hundred fifty Years of British Drama
Reality did not invade the plays of London until Tom Robertson began to write comedies six years before his death. Nothing else of merit appeared before 1895. The Irish playwrights, grouped at the bottom of the chart, wrote mainly of and for their own people, but they wrote with outstanding distinction.

DAVID BELASCO AND ARTHUR HOPKINS

Realism in production came to the American stage through David Belasco. He had always been a pioneer of illusion through lighting, but it was not until after the turn of the century that he began to use solidly built box-sets. In 1909, for *The Easiest Way*, he literally

transferred to his stage wallpaper, doors, and furniture from a di-
lapidated rooming house. A few years later he reached the climax of
his realism by copying a corner of one of the Childs restaurants for
The Governor's Lady. His actors—good as were David Warfield,
Blanche Bates, Leo Ditrichstein, Holbrook Blinn, and George
Arliss—never matched the realism of the plays of Otto Brahm or the
Moscow Art Theater. Belasco had a theatrical instinct that forced
his actors beyond the realism of his sets.

A later director came nearer the ideal of Brahm. This was
Arthur Hopkins. In dramas by Ibsen, Tolstoy, Gorky, and O'Neill,
as in comedies by Philip Barry and in other plays, he used simplified
and suggestive backgrounds by America's best scene designer,
Robert Edmond Jones. In Hopkins' handling of his actors, he followed quite unconsciously Brahm's method. Movement and business
could be largely laid out by a stage manager; Hopkins concentrated
on content. To the actors he explained their parts, the quality of the
characters, the relation of one to the other. He never coached and
seldom interrupted a scene. He corrected an actor's performance
only after the rehearsal was over, in a quiet, intimate talk. Perhaps
he never brought out in his productions the ingenious intensities
that another outstanding director, Elia Kazan, achieved in *Death of
a Salesman* or *A Streetcar Named Desire*. Hopkins was content to
seek and find inner truth.

A number of the excellent directors that developed in the
twenties and almost all the actors that might have become legitimate players of distinction turned to Hollywood film production.
The New York stage was left to such fine players of the twenties as
Helen Hayes, Katharine Cornell, Alfred Lunt, and Lynn Fontanne
while the screen employed the magnetic personalities of John Barrymore, Charles Boyer, Katharine Hepburn, Edward G. Robinson,
Leslie Howard, James Cagney, and Fredric March, as well as many
vivid character actors.

THE PLAYWRIGHT'S THEATER

Until 1915, there was no theater so receptive to the new playwright
as Antoine's and Brahm's had been. Then came two. Both were
amateur, both were small, and both were started by the kind of
authors, painters, and actors who would have lived on the Left Bank

in Paris if they had not been living in the Greenwich Village of New York City.

The first, by about six months, was the Washington Square Players. Though it presented new plays by Zoë Akins and a few minor writers, the bulk of its bills were from established Europeans. A war casualty of 1917, it was resurrected two years later as the Theatre Guild. Again the emphasis was almost entirely on foreign playwrights until in its fourth season it found Arthur Richman's *Ambush*, in its fifth Elmer Rice's *The Adding Machine*, and in its seventh Sidney Howard's *They Knew What They Wanted* and John Howard Lawson's *Processional*.

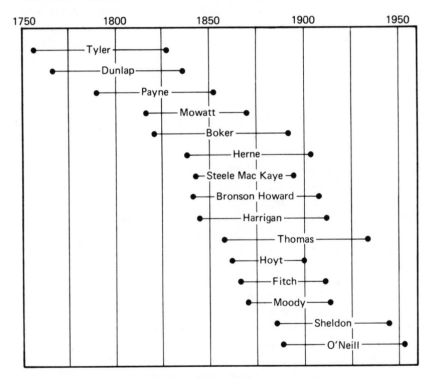

Figure 8.9 From the First American Playwright to O'Neill

After more than a century of slow development, the advent of William Vaughn Moody with *The Great Divide* in 1906, and Edward Sheldon with *Salvation Nell* in 1908, prepared the American stage for the significant drama that Eugene O'Neill and others were to provide from 1920 onward.

The Provincetown Players group was much more important to the development of American drama. It called itself the Playwright's Theater, and in its seven years it produced nothing but native plays. It began humbly enough in an artists' colony at the tip of Cape Cod, Massachusetts, during the summer of 1915. Its theater was still humble when the Provincetown Players moved to a stable in Greenwich Village. All of its new plays were not of lasting importance, though they included work by the novelists Theodore Dreiser and Susan Glaspell and by the poetess Edna St. Vincent Millay. The Provincetown's chief distinction was that it produced the first plays of Eugene O'Neill. If *Beyond the Horizon* and *Anna Christie* had not found Broadway sponsors, the Provincetown would have been ready to produce them. The spirit of the workers and the audience at the Provincetown gave O'Neill the stimulation and the confidence that he needed when he was beginning to write. Without the Playwright's Theater, his genius might never have found itself.

UNIVERSITY PLAYWRIGHTS

Even earlier than 1915, another force was beginning to create American playwrights, but the results were to be seen mainly in the twenties. This force was Professor George Pierce Baker. First at Radcliffe College and then at Harvard in 1906, Baker began to teach playwriting. He was not only an inspiring teacher, but among his early students he was lucky enough to have Edward Sheldon, whose *Salvation Nell* was successfully produced while he was still a student. Such publicity, plus Baker's own talents, brought to his classes unproduced playwrights like O'Neill, S. N. Behrman, Sidney Howard, Philip Barry, George Abbott, and Robert Sherwood. After studying with Baker, Frederick Koch began to cultivate the writing of folk drama in North Dakota and North Carolina; out of Koch's classes came another playwright, Paul Green.

The fame of Baker's work at Harvard caused other universities to develop theater studies much more extensive than Harvard permitted. Beginning with the Carnegie Institute of Technology in 1914 under Thomas Wood Stevens, many of the fifteen hundred colleges and universities offering theater arts programs in the 1970s had developed playwriting curriculums. The Eugene O'Neill Playwriting Center in Provincetown and the American Theater Association provided additional opportunities for many new university-trained playwrights.

THE NEW DRAMA OF THE 1920s

The effect of the Provincetown Players, the Washington Square Players-cum-Theatre Guild, and Professor Baker began to be felt sharply in the 1920s. Following O'Neill's *Beyond the Horizon* and *The Emperor Jones* of 1920 and 1921, there came a flood of new writers. Owen Davis turned from popular melodramas like *Nellie the Beautiful Cloak Model* to write the serious and mature plays *The Detour* and *Icebound*. During the twenties came more good drama of a realistic kind: Gilbert Emery's *The Hero*; Arthur Richman's *Ambush*; *Dulcy*, the first of George S. Kaufman's collaborations; George Kelly's *The Torchbearers* and *Craig's Wife*; Sidney Howard's *They Knew What They Wanted* and *The Silver Cord*; Philip Barry's *Holiday* and *Paris Bound*; Maxwell Anderson's and Laurence Stallings' *What Price Glory?*, Anderson's *Saturday's Children*; Lillian Hellman's *The Children's Hour*; Robert Sherwood's *Waterloo Bridge* and *The Road to Rome*; S. N. Behrman's *The Second Man*; John van Druten's *Young Woodley*; and Dorothy and Du Bose Heyward's *Porgy*.

To the later plays of importance by these writers—and to non-realistic dramas like O'Neill's many experiments, Anderson's poetic *Elizabeth the Queen* and *Winterset*, Marc Connelly's *The Green Pastures*, Howard's *Yellow Jack*, Rice's *The Adding Machine*, Clifford Odets' *Waiting for Lefty*, and Thornton Wilder's *Our Town* and *The Skin of Our Teeth*, as well as most of Miller's and Williams' plays—must be added Sidney Kingsley's *Men in White*, John Patrick's *The Hasty Heart*, Emmet Lavery's *The Magnificent Yankee*, Steinbeck's *Of Mice and Men*, and William Saroyan's *The Time of Your Life*.

REALISM IN SPAIN AND HUNGARY

As we have seen, sound realism came to France and Germany in the last decade of the nineteenth century. It won its place in England and Ireland around 1910 and in America only after 1920. On the

Continent, twentieth-century drama ran different courses in various countries.

Spain clung to realism from the early days of Echegaray till the destruction of the Loyalist republic—and the playwright García Lorca—in 1936. It was a realism touched at times with fantasy and lyricism. Jacinto Benavente ranged from his peasant tragedy *The Passion Flower* to his cynical comedy *The Bonds of Interest* with its use of *commedia dell'arte* characters. The Quintero brothers usually wrote lightly in the spirit of their one-act comedy *A Sunny Morning*, yet they touched a deeper note in the drama *Malvaloca*. In Gregorio Martinez Sierra's two plays *The Kingdom of God* and *Cradle Song*, he presented the life of a convent with delicate sympathy and deep feeling. In the few short years that the poet Federico García Lorca could give to the theater before he was shot by one of Franco's firing squads, he wrote with great and poetic power in *Blood Wedding* and *The House of Bernarda Alba* and with humor and fantastic imagination in lesser plays.

Hungary's playwrights, some of them remarkably successful in America, were varied in interests and styles. Alexander Brody handled social problems somewhat in the spirit of Brieux. Melchior Lengyel and Ernö Vajda were shallower, perhaps, but theatrically effective, as Broadway found in Lengyel's *Typhoon* and Vajda's *Fata Morgana*. Sigmund Moritz wrote mainly of small-town life, while Ferenc Molnár clung to the sophistication of his beloved Budapest. The most popular and brilliant of the Hungarians, Molnár

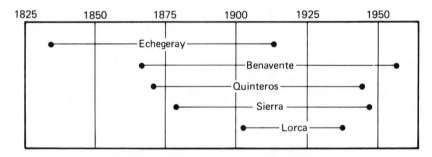

Figure 8.10   Spain's Modern Playwrights
Echegaray was rather a slow starter. He wrote his first plays in his forties. Within twenty years, Benavente was close upon the much older man.

ranged from the intricate comedy of *The Guardsman* and *The Play's the Thing* and the subtle drama of *The Swan* to the fantastic symbolism of *The Red Mill*. In between lay the fantasy of *The Phantom Rival* and the mingling of reality and other-worldliness in the deeply touching play *Liliom*.

IN FRANCE AND ITALY—POETIC DRAMA

In the early years of this century, poetic drama, romantic tragedy, and the subtle play of symbolic moods absorbed three outstanding playwrights: Edmond Rostand, Maurice Maeterlinck, and Gabriele d'Annunzio. Rostand's vastly popular *Cyrano de Bergerac*, Maeterlinck's fantasy *The Blue Bird* and his tenuous *Pelléas et Mélisande*, and d'Annunzio's *Francesca da Rimini* and *The Daughter of Jorio* are a few of the many plays that these poets wrote in rebellion against the rising power of the theater typified by Antoine.

Italy produced no realists of any merit after Guiseppe Giacosa with his *Falling Leaves* of 1900. France could point to little more than a few plays like Edouard Bourdet's *The Captive*, Sacha Guitry's *Pasteur* and Charles Vildrac's *S. S. Tenacity*. Realism faded out in Germany before the onslaught of expressionism toward the end of World War I. France found in Lenormand and Cocteau men to follow the German fashion, and in Giraudoux, Anouilh, and Sartre nonrealistic playwrights of a subtler and a more powerful kind.

The plays of Rostand, Maeterlinck, and d'Annunzio cried for a type of scenery and lighting that was to serve the expressionists and men like Sartre. It was also to serve, ironically enough, the Englishmen and Americans who still wrote in the realistic vein.

9: THE MODERN THEATER FROM STRINDBERG TO BRECHT

The nineteenth century gave to the stage the realistic play and its fourth wall. The twentieth century provided settings and lights that were far more beautiful and expressive than anything the theater had known before. The new stagecraft—as this movement came to be called—made over the production methods of the theater of the civilized world. Also, it enabled plays to be written in new ways. It made the realistic drama more illusive, but it also helped the writer to develop a very different technique.

ATTACKS ON PERSPECTIVE AND FOOTLIGHTS

Before 1905 in Europe and 1915 in America, the stage still made exteriors out of wings, borders, and painted drops; they were an unillusive sham compared with the solid and convincing box-sets that might be seen in the same production. The glare of footlights and border lights spoiled both kinds of settings. Zola, Antoine, and

Strindberg criticized the production methods of their day, but to little avail. Between 1895 and 1905 the writings and the sketches of two men—the Swiss Adolphe Appia and the Englishman Edward Gordon Craig—and six English productions by Craig set the basis for a complete revolution in the designing and lighting of scenery. The first battles of the revolution were won in Berlin by the Austrian-born director Max Reinhardt.

ADOLPHE APPIA—
PROPHET OF THE NEW STAGECRAFT

Critics had pointed out that the nineteenth-century type of scenery had been invented, some two hundred years earlier, for the production of opera. And it was for opera that Appia theorized and designed when he published *The Staging of Wagnerian Drama* in 1895 and *Music and Stage Production* four years later. Craig's first production, made in London in 1900, was also for an opera, Purcell's *Dido and Aeneas*, but his first book, *The Art of the Theatre*, published in 1905, and those that followed showed by their titles as well as their text and illustrations that his concern was with the drama. Appia too, turned away from opera and designed scenery for the works of Shakespeare, Goethe, Ibsen, and other playwrights.

Appia did not approach production as a painter. Indeed, in his first book there were no illustrations. Though he later drew and published brilliant designs, his value lay in the *theory* he put forth. His basic aim was to "strengthen the dramatic action." This was to be done not only through a three-dimensional setting with various levels for the actor to work upon, but quite as much through the lighting. Appia asked for "living light." He wanted the lighting on the stage to change with the passage of time; or to change in a way that threw the action of the play into sharper relief. "The mise-en-scène," he wrote, "is a picture composed in time."

In his writings Appia analyzed scene after scene from Wagner's music-dramas and showed how the effect of the setting, the moving actor, and the changing lights would follow and heighten the course of the action. For instance, in dealing with the third act of

Wagner's *Die Walküre* Appia did not provide merely one design, as most scenic artists do; he made seven drawings that traced the changing lights and the positions of the singers through the whole scene.

GORDON CRAIG'S CONTRIBUTION

By training, Craig was more a man of the theater than Appia. He practiced the art of acting before he practiced the art of design. If talents are inheritable, he drew the player's skill from his mother, Ellen Terry, and the designer's from his father, Edward Godwin, who was a painter and an architect and who did some scenery for the theater. Craig left the stage to think about the scenic problems of production. He returned in 1900 to mount *Dido and Aeneas*, and in the next few years he made almost a dozen productions. They caused no such stir, however, as his vividly written and richly illustrated book, *The Art of the Theatre*, and other volumes that followed.

Craig never exalted the artist above the theater. To him the stage was not a place that offered its backdrop as the hugest canvas any painter ever had. "The theater," he wrote, "should not be a place in which to exhibit scenery . . . it should be a place in which the entire beauty of life can be unfolded . . . the inner beauty and the meaning of life." If that is vague and even mystical, much of his theory and practice was intensely practical—as well as stimulating. Though most of his published designs were bigger than any proscenium arch could hold, they always had simplicity as well as grandeur. He knew the power of suggestion. He recognized, as Appia had done, that the stage must be three-dimensional. He forswore perspective unless at a great distance. He put into his designs no place "which could *not* be traveled into actually by the actors," unless so far away that no one could see figures and that "our imagination alone could people it."

TOWARD A NEW THEATER

Craig recognized that the theater is a synthesis of many arts and many skills. It is not merely the play or acting, scenery, lights, music, movement, or dance. The theater, he felt, was all or many of

Figure 9.1 Craig's Macbeth

Craig's drawings are as impossible to render completely in line sketches
as are Appia's. The sleepwalking scene from *Macbeth* conveys, however, the grandeur of his conceptions and the effectiveness with which
he organized forms, levels, and details to aid the dramatist. As Lady
Macbeth moves down the steps toward the audience she passes a
sculptured row of kings who have pursued their ambitions and gone
down to death. (Drawing by Gerda Becker With, after Craig, *Toward a
New Theatre.*)

Figure 9.2 Set Design for *The Pretenders*
Set design by Gordon Craig for Ibsen's *The Pretenders* at the Theatre Royale in Copenhagen, in 1926.

these things. From this thought, he moved on to the ideal conception that one man and one man alone must create all these things. Though this led him to ideas not so sound, we must recognize the immense effect that the man's brilliant writings and even more brilliant designs had on the new generation. We must turn to the passages in which he analyzed plays—*Macbeth*, for example—and drew forth, as Appia had done, the basis for imaginative and inspiring treatments.

Let us summarize the chief elements of the new stagecraft as established by Appia and Craig, and see what changes they led to in the physical side of production.

First comes simplification of means and effect: *A simple setting emphasizes the actor and therefore the play.* The complement to simplification is suggestion: *A single Gothic pillar can create in the imagination of the audience the physical reality and the spiritual force of the church that looms above Marguerite in* Faust. Finally, there is synthesis: *The production must be a clean and clear fusion of settings, costumes, movement, and perhaps music, so that the acting may present the play in its fullest effect.*

NEW EQUIPMENT FOR THE NEW STAGECRAFT

Giving up wings and drops in favor of three-dimensional structures meant that, whether the play was realistic or not, the settings were heavier than before. Quick changes of scene required new mechanisms in place of wings, grooves, chariots, or stage braces, and devices to supplement or supersede the lines and pulleys of flies and gridiron. There were three possibilities, and the burgeoning theater of Germany tried them all before the First World War. One was the revolving stage that Lautenschläger brought to Munich from Japan in 1896. Wheeled wagons carrying a whole set or a part of a set were invented by an American, Steele MacKaye, but were

Figure 9.3   Continental Post-war Designs

A design by Tobias Schiess for a projected Swiss production of Moliére's *Tartuffe*. Conditions since the war have compelled most artists in Germany to use the simplest of construction and materials. (From *Das Kunstwerk*, 1953.)

first employed effectively by Fritz Brand of Berlin about 1900. A third device was the elevator stage, which MacKaye had used in 1880. Between 1904 and 1913, the two court theaters in Dresden combined wagons and elevators.

MAX REINHARDT—THE PERFECT REVOLUTIONARY

If Steele MacKaye had lived in the time of Craig, the American playwright, director, manager, actor, designer, and inventor might have come close to Craig's ideal master of the theater. Instead we have Max Reinhardt. This revolutionary not only freed the world theater from nineteenth-century thraldom and made it over in the image—and, indeed, beyond the image—of Appia, but he also met the challenge of Craig as far as it could be met. He combined the widest possible range of theater talents.

For nine years Reinhardt was an actor in Brahm's company at the Deutsches Theater. Toward the end, he had permission to make experimental productions of his own at the Kleines Theater, and there he produced Strindberg's *There Are Crimes and Crimes*, Oscar Wilde's *Salome*, Wedekind's *Erdgeist*, and Gorky's *The Lower Depths*. On New Year's Day, 1903, he left Brahm, and within two months he opened the Neues Theater. There, early in 1905, Reinhardt made his first great directorial success with *A Midsummer Night's Dream*. It is not important that he placed his scenery on a revolving stage and chased his fairies and yokels through a moving and changing wood. In this production, and in every one that was not of necessity realistic, he threw out the dry conventions of the theatrical past, and he used one of a number of vivid and imaginative styles entirely fresh to the stage. Reinhardt's success was so electric that in 1905 L'Arronge selected him to direct the Deutsches Theater, which his old master Brahm had once managed.

REINHARDT'S WIDE-RANGING CAREER

Next to the Deutsches Theater, Reinhardt built a luxurious and intimate little theater called the Kammerspiele. There he made yet another new and very different success with Wedekind's *The Awa-*

Figure 9.4   Set for *The Miracle*

Max Reinhardt's most spectacular production opened in January 1911
at the Olympia Exhibition Hall in London. Subsequent performances
were given in Vienna, Berlin, and—much later—New York. The settings for the American production in 1924, shown in the illustration,
were designed by America's most gifted designer, Norman Bel Geddes,
for the Century Theater.

kening of Spring. From the opening of the Kammerspiele in 1906
until Reinhardt settled in America in 1938, his career was a fantastic
one. It included directing in Munich, Vienna, Salzburg, Paris, Venice, Stockholm, New York, Hollywood, and London. From the intimacy of the Kammerspiele, he plunged into a mass production of
Sophocles' *Oedipus Rex* in the huge Circus Schumann; then he converted the building into the Grosses Schauspielhaus, with a sky-
dome, a revolver, a deep forestage, and room for thirty-five
hundred spectators. He produced the pantomime *The Miracle* on a
similar scale in London, Vienna, Berlin, and New York. In
Salzburg, Austria, as the heart of the summer festival, he staged

Everyman in front of the cathedral, Calderón's *The Great World Theater* inside another church, and *Faust* in the old Imperial Riding School. He gave *The Merchant of Venice* across a canal in Venice, and *A Midsummer Night's Dream* out of doors at Berkeley, California, and in the Hollywood Bowl. Opera came under his hand: Strauss's *Der Rosenkavalier* in Dresden; Mozart in the Redoutensaal, the reconstructed ballroom of Maria Theresa's Viennese palace. He managed two more playhouses, the restored Theater in der Josefstadt in Vienna, and a new house, the Komödie, in Berlin, both for light comedy in the main. Meantime he toured his companies to Russia, Sweden, Switzerland, and America. Reinhardt built up an international repertory, a repertory that spread through all the German and Austrian theaters of his time. It was as varied as his styles of production, for it included, besides the dozen playwrights we have mentioned, Schiller, Shaw, Gozzi, Goldoni, Grillparzer, O'Neill, Büchner, Werfel, Kleist, Hasenclever, and Euripides. What he did to reanimate Shakespeare on the German stage is remarkable. Between 1905 and 1930, Reinhardt personally directed 136 plays for a total of 8,393 performances. Of this total, 2,531, or almost a third, were of plays by Shakespeare.

EXPRESSIONISM IN GERMANY

A new kind of play and a new kind of production followed or, in some cases, grew up side by side with Brahm and Reinhardt in Germany, the Moscow Art Theater in Russia, Antoine and the Théâtre-libre in France, and Grein and Barker in England. On the whole, the plays and the productions of Europe after the First World War veered away from the realistic concept. They followed paths that led to a greater and freer expressiveness, yet they sometimes ended in a blind alley of chaotic and ineffective theatricalism.

Expressionism came to the fore in the years of 1917 and 1918 when a disillusioned Germany realized that it was losing the war. Expressionism continued to feed, until about 1925, on the spiritual chaos of a broken nation. Yet the roots of expressionism lie farther back; there are strong hints of it in some of Wedekind's plays, and it is obvious in the later plays of Strindberg. Expressionism made its

Figure 9.5 Set for *Der Sohn*

While Meyerhold and Tairov were experimenting in Russia, German dramatists had begun to write plays that were expressionist in form, which demanded new styles of production. Written during or even before the First World War, most of these plays were denied public performance until after the German Revolution. Frankfurt-am-Main was an early center of expressionist productions. In 1918 Gustav Hartung produced in that city Fritz von Unruh's anti-war play, *Ein Geschlect*, with settings by Ludwig Babberger.

The chief impetus for expressionist drama came, however, from Walter Hasenclever's *Der Sohn*. Banned by the German government, as were a number of other expressionist plays, it was staged privately in Dresden in 1916. After its first production in Mannheim in 1918, *Der Sohn* swept the German theater and opened the way for other expressionist works. The design shown in the illustration was by Otto Reigbert from the Munich Kammerspiele production.

first important entry on the stage in 1916 with a private performance of *Der Sohn* (*The Son*), which Walter Hasenclever had written in 1912, but which was banned from public performance until 1918. Reinhardt, not very sympathetic to expressionism, produced one example privately, Reinhard Sorge's *Der Bettler* (*The Beggar*) in 1917.

EXPRESSIONISM IN PLAY AND PRODUCTION

In its materials, the expressionist play was a curious mixture of the abstract and the concrete. It tried to present subjective values, to see beyond and above reality to emotional truth. Yet it was also a drama of immediate revolt that often attacked war, the business world, or parental authority. Its construction was apt to be episodic, while the dialog ranged from the lyric to the telegraphic. Its characters were usually types instead of rounded human beings.

In production, expressionism went in for symbols rather than scenery. A Gothic arch made a cathedral. A snow-covered tree symbolized death. Stage design was flat, angular, distorted. Signs or numbers were projected on a setting to express a subjective idea. The stage became a phantasmagoria of startling and often incomprehensible effects.

Besides Sorge and Hasenclever, the most important writers in the new dramatic medium were: Georg Kaiser, with *From Morn to Midnight* and *Gas*; Ernst Toller, with *Masse-Mensch* (*Man and the Masses*), *Die Wandlung*, and *Die Machinestürmer* (*The Machine Wreckers*); and Fritz von Unruh, with *Ein Geschlecht* (*A Clan*). Two Czech writers of the twenties provided plays that were partly expressionist and partly more conventional. Karel Čapek, writing sometimes with his brother Josef, is remembered for his fantastic drama *R.U.R.* and his allegory *The Insect Comedy*, known in America as *The World We Live In*. Franz Werfel ranged from complete expressionism in *Spiegelmensch* (*The Mirror Man*) through his symbolic play *Bocksgesang* (*The Goat Song*) to his realistic drama of Mexican history *Juarez and Maximilian*. The German Bertolt Brecht, whose writing has lyric vitality, began in 1923 with his rather realistic *Trommeln in der Nacht* (*Drums in the Night*)

Figure 9.6 Jessner's Steps

Steps were a favorite production device of Leopold Jessner, a preeminent German director after the first World War. Sometimes they were used moderately, as in Emil Pirchan's settings for Wedekind's *Marquis von Keith* in 1920, where the dominant repetition is in the verticals. But in an earlier production of *Richard III*, Jessner had used the horizontal rhythms of his steps very effectively.

Jessner—a more conscientious student of Appia and Craig than was even Max Reinhardt—made over the former Prussian Royal Theater into the most challenging, modern, and famous theater in Germany.

and continued into the thirties with *Die Dreigroschenoper*, adapted from *The Beggar's Opera*, and with polemic pieces reminiscent of expressionism.

NEW RUSSIAN DIRECTORS AND DESIGNERS

It took no revolution to make the Russian theater more radical in production methods than any other in Europe. For a time the Soviet encouraged the wildest of experiments, then condemned them as "formalistic." In the 1920s the communist government encouraged—perhaps we should say, forced—playwrights to write propaganda plays.

Fine artists came into the Russian theater earlier than elsewhere, painters of the quality of Golovin, Roerich, Anisfeld, Benois, and Bakst. Most of them worked in opera—some before 1900—and for the ballet, painting brilliantly on huge backdrops and great wings. Very different kinds of artists, however, gave the Russian theater its particular flavor. There was the cubist Alexandra Exter, for example, employed by Alexander Taïrov in the intimate but very radical Kamerny Theater that he opened in 1914. In his *Salome*, on the brink of the Revolution, you could see a stage floor broken up into a maze of slanting levels and actors in stiffly formalized costumes like nothing in the history of man's clothing. Add cubist settings that anticipated German expressionism, and you were in a world of angular and splintered shapes and movements.

The Moscow Art Theater provided two of the most startling directors in Vsevolod Meyerhold and Eugene Vakhtangov. As early as 1905, Stanislavsky and Danchenko began to set up "studios" in which experiments could be carried on in methods far removed from the realism of their theater. Both Vakhtangov and Meyerhold worked in such studios. Michael Chekhov, nephew of the playwright, succeeded Vakhtangov when he died but left in 1927 to teach acting in America. Danchenko, as we have said, opened the Musical Studio about 1920.

Vakhtangov proved a director with both original ideas and a capacity for solid accomplishment. His *Macbeth* and *The Dybbuk*, which he directed for the Jewish group called the Habima, as well as

Turandot, which he did not live to see, all showed his devoted attempts to find new concepts of production, often grotesque, that fitted the plays he produced.

MEYERHOLD AND "THE THEATER THEATRICAL"

Meyerhold, the dominant director outside the Moscow Art Theater, began as one of its actors. He ended as a tragic sacrifice to communist policy toward the stage. His basic ideas were far removed from anything remotely approaching realism. Even more than Taïrov, Meyerhold stood for "the theater theatrical." He would have no "fourth wall." He wanted the audience to be eternally conscious that they were in a theater. To that end, he abolished the curtain, left auditorium lights blazing, and let the playgoers see the naked brick walls of the stage. He dressed his actors in overalls and trained them to run and leap over skeleton settings of wood, glass, and metal. In such a fashion—it was usually called constructivist because of his sets—Meyerhold produced plays like Belgium-born Fernand Crommelynck's *The Magnificent Cuckold* and in another radical style Gogol's *The Inspector General*. For a time, Meyerhold rode the wave of success. In 1937 the government began the building of a special kind of theater for him, a theater without a proscenium and with various new ways of relating audience to actors. Before it could be completed, Meyerhold fell under disfavor for what was called his "formalism"—a familiar charge during the time of the purges. He denied this publicly in a speech and called the state of the Russian theater "pitiful and terrifying." Meyerhold was arrested the next day, and was never heard from again.

There is one more director to consider, Nikolai Okhlopkov. Younger than the rest and innocent of any contacts with the Moscow Art Theater, he distinguished himself by creating the first professional "theater in the round," really a flexible playhouse. From 1932 to 1938—its success was not great—he staged Gorky's *Mother* and other plays with the actors in unexpected and intimate relations with their audiences. "On my stage," he said, "when the mother cries, a dozen people in the audience must want to leap up and wipe away her tears." Independently of the Russian developments, the theater in the round and a more flexible form developed in America after 1940.

THE FATE OF THE RUSSIAN PLAYWRIGHTS

Between the abortive rebellion of 1905 and the revolution of 1917, the baffled intelligentsia of Russia produced playwrights who were more extreme in expression than those of other European countries. Their work was far from satisfying or lasting. Michael Artsybashev dwelt hopelessly on sexual tragedy. Alexander Blok was extravagantly symbolic. Leonid Andreyev began with realism in *To the Stars* and satire in *The Sabine Women* and went over to allegory in *The Life of Man* and *King Hunger*. The one play from this period that has interested the audiences of other nations was his dramatic but perplexing tragedy *He Who Gets Slapped*. Nikolai Evreinov, director as well as playwright, dedicated himself to an eccentric vision of the theater. In his short "monodrama" of 1906, *The Theater of the Soul*, he divided his hero into three characters M1, M2, and M3, and presented his heroine as the different kind of woman each would see. After the materialistic revolution, he wrote in *The Chief Thing* a play that exalted the life of illusion.

The effect of the revolution on production and playwrights was profound. At first the government encouraged the theatrical "formalism" of Taïrov and Meyerhold largely because the regime of the Czar had been against it. Then communism turned thumbs down. The state, which looked on the theater as a weapon in its fight against capitalism, increased enormously the number of playhouses. In Moscow alone they grew from sixteen in 1914 to sixty in 1934. The new audiences may not have supported the aesthetically radical productions, but they thronged to the older plays that censorship had banned and to a wide range of drama from the rest of Europe and from America. They certainly delighted in the "socialist realism" of propaganda plays about the struggles and triumphs of revolutionaries and partisans, whether out of past history or from their own times. The Moscow Art Theater was preserved as an "academic" institution, a kind of museum of the best of the past. In time it began to produce some of the better propaganda plays. Among them should be mentioned *Days of the Turbins* and *Armored Train 14-69*. *Roar China!* and *Counterattack* were produced in New York, the first by the Theatre Guild.

JEWISH THEATERS IN RUSSIA

Facing the problem of the many racial elements of Russia, the Soviet encouraged two notable Jewish groups in Moscow. The first and the greatest was the Habima (a word meaning "stage") founded in 1917 by the brilliant Nahum Zemach with the help of the Moscow Art Theater. The Habima's outstanding production was Salomon Ansky's peasant play of demoniac possession *The Dybbuk*. Magnificently directed by Vakhtangov, it was the chief play in a repertory seen in New York in 1926–27. The Habima's permanent home is now in Tel Aviv. The State Jewish Theater, playing in Yiddish instead of the Hebrew of the Habima, had a fine director in Alexander Granovsky and produced in cleverly distorted settings a series of plays including Shakespeare's as well as works by Jewish writers like Sholem Aleichem and Isaac Peretz.

ROSTAND, MAETERLINCK, AND LUGNÉ-POË

Antoine and his realists were not the only significant figures on the Paris stage of the nineties. There was a romantic who turned to symbolism, and a symbolist who became romantic. These were Edmond Rostand and Maurice Maeterlinck. Each wrote a play of world-wide popularity.

Rostand had no ability new to the theater except the ability to write poetic drama that could be popular when the stage of Europe lay under the growing shadow of Ibsen. Rostand's first play, a short one called *Les Romanesques* (*The Romancers*), was an immediate success when the Comédie-Française produced it in 1894. Three years later came his *Cyrano de Bergerac*. The great actor Coquelin triumphed in this swashbuckling romance with a pleasantly tragic ending, and it was played by many other stars, including America's Richard Mansfield and Walter Hampden. After the sentimental *L'Aiglon*, which neither Sarah Bernhardt nor Maude Adams could save from failure, Rostand's lyric vigor returned in *Chantecler*, a play that made the birds of the barnyard symbols of man. He gave us both irony and tenderness in the play that he wrote just before he died at forty-nine, *The Last Night of Don Juan*.

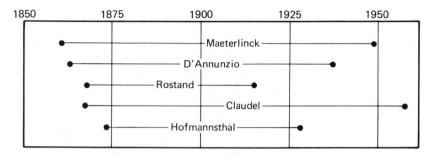

Figure 9.7 The Neo-romanticists

In the face of the realism of Ibsen and a score of other acclaimed playwrights, the men of this chart wrote almost nothing but poetic or imaginative drama. The first to attract attention was Maeterlinck with *Pelléas et Mélisande* in 1892. Rostand began with *Les Romanesques* in 1894.

Antoine, who tried vainly to make the Théâtre-libre a theater of poetry as well as realism, might have mounted *Les Romanesques* if Rostand's play had been offered to him. Antoine had no taste for Maeterlinck, however, and neither had the managers of the state and the commercial theaters. So the Belgian poet who wrote in rhythmed prose had to turn to another rebel theater. This was the Théâtre d'Art, founded in 1890 by the seventeen-year-old symbolist poet Paul Fort as an opening for plays by men called "symbolists" or "imagists." Here Maeterlinck's short plays *The Intruder* and *The Blind* were produced. Fort retired shortly to write poetry, and his collaborator, Lugné-Poë—who had worked under Antoine—turned the venture into the more celebrated Théâtre de l'Oeuvre, which he managed until 1929. He began with Maeterlinck's *Pelléas et Mélisande*, but he followed the eclectic pattern that Antoine had hoped to achieve. Among the plays he produced were Ibsen's *Rosmersholm* and *The Master Builder* and Tolstoy's *The Living Corpse*, as well as Hauptmann's *Hannele* and his symbolic drama *The Sunken Bell*, Wilde's *Salome*, a number of d'Annunzio's dramas, Crommelynck's *The Magnificent Cuckold, Shakuntala,* and *The Little Clay Cart, Peer Gynt,* and many poetic plays that are now forgotten. He staged Maeterlinck's romantic drama *Monna Vanna* in 1902, but he had to wait for the Moscow Art Theater to give the first performance of the playwright's symbolic fairy tale *The Blue Bird* in 1908. Lugné-Poë enjoyed the distinction of staging Paul Claudel's religious drama *L'Announce faite à Marie* (*The Tidings Brought to Mary*), thus launching on his theatrical career the man who in the fifties was the leading poetic playwright of France.

COPEAU—REMAKER OF THE PARIS STAGE

The greatest force in the French theater of the twentieth century was Jacques Copeau. His remarkable playhouse, the Théâtre du Vieux-Colombier, was the first to throw out the "fourth wall." His repertory was a fine mingling of the realistic and the poetic, of the classic and the modern drama. And from his company came three of France's leading directors and actors.

In 1913 Copeau turned from a brilliant career as a critic to create his Théâtre du Vieux-Colombier. During the First World War New York's wealthy patron of the stage Otto Kahn enabled Copeau to remake the Garrick Theater to suit his purposes. In 1922, Copeau was able to reopen the Vieux-Colombier in Paris and add some refinements to his stage. Whether in Paris or New York, Copeau and his company were dedicated to producing a wide range of drama with the greatest fidelity, simplicity, and clarity, and also to developing an ensemble of acting that departed from strict realism without indulging in theatrical display. Their artistic success was notable.

The theater that Copeau made over from a small hall had no obvious division between audience and actors, except that he did use a draw curtain during changes of setting or properties. Stage and auditorium were an organic whole, the walls of one merging with those of the other. There were no footlights between the spectators and a low forestage that led by three steps, at the sides and in the center, to the main platform. On and above this platform was a permanent structure that included an arch at the back and a stair at one side that led up to the arch and over it. On this stage of many levels Copeau placed screens or suggestions of realistic props and backings, and in the arch he set doors or windows. The lighting came from above and the sides; some sources were openly but gracefully displayed in the auditorium. The Vieux-Colombier was the first of many later attempts to break away from the theater of illusion dominated by the proscenium arch. It presented frankly to its audience the first "formal" stage.

NEW DIRECTORS, NEW PLAYHOUSES

When Copeau closed his theater he took with him to the countryside—as he had done before 1913—a group of young actors to study and practice their art. Under one of their number, Michel Saint-Denis, they later became the distinguished Compagnie des Quinze, which he took on tour before he began to work in England. In the early twenties two of Copeau's finest players, Louis Jouvet and Charles Dullin, left the Vieux-Colombier to act and direct with distinction elsewhere. Besides these men and Lugné-Poë, there were others who succeeded in bringing out new French playwrights: Jean-Louis Barrault, a brilliant actor and the producer of Claudel's *Le Livre de Christophe Colomb*; and Jean Vilar, who made a notable success of the management of the new Théâtre National Populaire.

Among the new playwrights whose plays these directors produced were: Jean Giraudoux, with *Siegfried, Amphitryon 38, The Mad Woman of Chaillot*, and *Ondine*; Romain Rolland, with his *The Game of Love and Death*; Jules Romains, with his satiric *Dr. Knock* and his *Donogoo* employing film effects; Jean Cocteau, with his *bizarreries* such as *Les Mariés de la Tour Eiffel, The Infernal Machine*, and *Orphée*; expressionistic Henri-René Lenormand, with *The Failures, Time Is a Dream*, and *Man and His Phantoms*; Jean-Paul Sartre, with *No Exit, The Flies*, and *The Respectful Prostitute*; and Jean Anouilh, with *The Waltz of the Toreadors, Time Remembered*, and *Ring Around the Moon*.

The total effect of the directors who came out of the theaters of Antoine and Copeau and of those who had their beginnings elsewhere was the making over of the Paris theater. Even the hide-bound Comédie-Française capitulated to the new playwrights; in 1936, it invited Copeau, Jouvet, Dullin, and Baty to direct plays, and in 1941 Copeau became its administrator. Beginning in 1945, the

French government organized four "centers" for the production and touring of plays in the provinces, while it maintained in Paris the Opéra, the Opéra-Comique, the Comédie-Française, and the Odéon, and added the Théâtre National Populaire.

ITALY ESCAPES FROM REALISM

Italy, like France, began the century with poetic drama. D'Annunzio's infatuation for the greatest of modern actresses, Eleonora Duse, may have increased his interest in the theater, but it did not

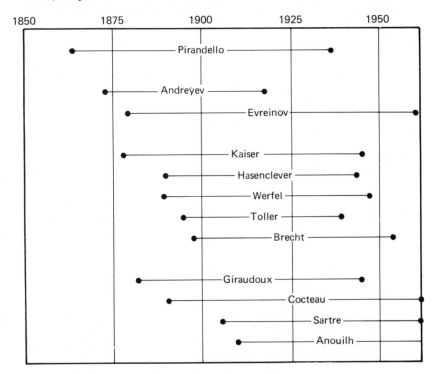

Figure 9.8 Modern Playwrights against Realism

The plays of these men are more "intellectual" than the work of neoromantic writers such as Maeterlinck and Rostand. All labored for a theater that abjured realism.

lift his poetic dramas much above the easy ideal of theatrical effectiveness. Duse played in *The Dead City* for many years and also in *La Gioconda*, which he wrote to exalt her beautiful hands. His best drama, however, *The Daughter of Jorio*, was played by another actress, Emma Gramatica.

The theater, even more than painting or the novel, is apt to lag behind life. In Italy we may have an exception. The end of the First World War, in which she lost a half-million men, left her in disillusioned chaos, a ready prey to the violence and corruption of Fascism. At such a time, writers might question the value of existence. Italy's outstanding dramatist, Pirandello, went further. He questioned its reality, and most playwrights followed him. The results were plays in which the values of life, as we have conceived them, are completely reversed. Nothing is objective; all is relative. Experience is useless. The sense of individual existence disappears, and psychic bewilderment and frustration take its place. To parody W. S. Gilbert, "Things are seldom what they seem; cream masquerades as skimmed milk," and usually it's sour.

Before the war, Pirandello wrote in *Sicilian Limes* a straightforward drama of unhappy reality. After the war, came *Six Characters in Search of an Author*, in which the inability of people to communicate with one another is complicated by a pretense that they are creatures in a play; *Right You Are If You Think You Are*, in which the psychic identities of a man's two wives and a mother-in-law are perversely confused; and *Henry IV*, which deals with the relativity of madness. At best, Pirandello anticipates in a minor way the French existentialists with faith in deeds as the only reality.

In *Madmen on the Mountain*, Alessandro de Stefani shows that only madmen are sane. Luigi Antonelli's *What You Don't Expect* shows a man mistaking a motion picture for reality and reality for a motion picture. The title of his *The Man Who Met Himself* is key enough to the play, and so is the title of Rosso di San Secondo's *What Passion, Ye Marionettes!* In Alberto Casella's *Death Takes a Holiday*, in which the Grim Reaper takes human shape, and no one dies while he is on earth, the heroine falls in love with him, knowing psychically who he is, and Death falls in love with life. In *The Mask and the Face* and other plays, Luigi Chiarelli followed the pattern of disillusionment with reality but treated the matter with comic cynicism.

BERTOLT BRECHT—MAN OF THE THEATER

Bertolt Brecht made his entrance into the German theater as an angry young man. Like Shakespeare, Molière, and G. B. Shaw, he was a man of the theater. He was a poet and *régisseur*, theorist and practitioner, who always listened to his public.

Lion Feuchtwanger, in one of the finest essays written on Brecht, recalled that the playwright questioned every member of an audience as to their impressions and used their reactions to develop new viewpoints of play and performance. As Feuchtwanger put it: "Brecht made every theatergoer with whom he talked his collaborator."

In *The Playwright's Song* Brecht set down, in that incomparably simple language that reminds one of the strength of Luther and Goethe, his credo:

> *I am a playwright. I show you*
> *what I have seen. In man's markets*
> *I have seen how man is bought and sold.*
> *That I show, I, the playwright.**

In his first plays, *Baal*, *Drums in the Night* (*Spartakus*), *Jungle of the Cities*, and *A Man's A Man*, he tried to effect change by shock. Brecht wanted to alter reality and thought this could be done through "Anger and Tenacity, Knowledge and Indignation." In his early writings, as well as in such master plays as *Saint Joan of the Stockyards*, *Galileo*, *Mother Courage*, and *The Caucasian Chalk Circle*, he anticipated themes of Beckett, Ionesco, and Albee, realizing the eternal loneliness of man and the impossibility of having human contact in a deserted, doomed world.

BRECHT, THE YEARS IN EXILE

Brecht's best plays were written and rewritten during the years of his exile that followed Hitler's rise to power in Germany in 1933. On February 28, 1933, the day after the Reichstag was burned, Brecht

---

*Bertolt Brecht, *The Playwright's Song*, translated by Darko Suvin, published in *Drama Review*, Volume Twelve, Number one (T37), Fall 1967, p. 61. Reprinted courtesy of *Drama Review*.

and his wife, Helene Weigel, escaped to Switzerland. For the next six years Brecht and his entourage lived in Denmark, where he wrote continuously. Finally he settled for the duration of World War II in Santa Monica, California, after fleeing from sanctuaries in Sweden and Finland. He was a fighter who enjoyed any challenge, a brilliant debater, and a fascinating conversationalist. A thorough study of Karl Marx influenced his work, but difficulties with Marxist authorities plagued Brecht for much of his life.

THE BERLINER ENSEMBLE

Following World War II Brecht returned to Germany and developed the Berliner Ensemble in East Berlin. The East German Government gave Brecht unlimited subsidy to work freely, and he succeeded, with his wife, in giving Europe its finest theater. Martin Esslin concluded his incisive "critical study of the man, his work, and his opinions"—*Brecht, A Choice of Evils*—with a lucid analysis of the playwright's life:

> *He wanted to be a writer for the common people, as easy to understand as fairground comics, but the simpler he tried to be, the more complex his work became . . .; he wanted to serve the cause of the revolution, but was regarded with suspicion by its recognized standard-bearers who reviled him as a formalist and banned him as a dangerous, defeatist influence; . . . he wanted to make his theater a laboratory of social change . . . and had to see it strengthen his public's faith in the enduring virtues of unchanging human nature; . . . he abhorred the very idea of beauty—and created beauty.**

Bertolt Brecht died in 1956, only fifty-eight years old. He lives as an influential, perhaps the most influential, playwright of our age.

---

*From *Brecht: The Man and His Work* by Martin Esslin (originally published in England as *Brecht: A Choice of Evils*). Copyright © 1959, 1960 by Martin Esslin. Used by permission of Doubleday & Company, Inc. and Eyre & Spottiswoode (Publishers) Ltd.

10: THE THEATER OF TODAY

ALFRED JARRY'S GRAND GUIGNOL

The beginnings of a modern, experimental theater of the *avant-garde* and of playwrights that encompass writers from Guillaume Apollinaire to Arthur Adamov can be traced to a single evening in Paris at the end of the nineteenth century. On December 11, 1896, at the Théâtre Nouveau, Jarry's *Ubu Roi* (*King Ubu*) created one of the most sustained theatrical riots of all time. Jarry flew in the face of conventional realistic and naturalistic practices of his day. Consciously theatrical in his approach to staging the play, Jarry wrote to Lugné-Poë, manager of the Théâtre Nouveau, three days before the production opened:

> *It would be interesting, I think, to be able to stage the play . . . in the following manner. A mask for the chief characters, Ubu . . . . A cardboard horse's head, which he would hang around his neck . . . . The adoption of a single set, or better yet, of a single backdrop . . . . A suitably costumed person*

> *would enter, as in puppet shows, to put up signs indicating the*
> *locations of the various scenes . . . . The elimination of*
> *crowds, which are a mistake on stage and hamper the mind.*
> *Thus, a single soldier in the review scene, a single soldier in the*
> *scuffle when Ubu says: "What a lot of people, what a retreat,"*
> *etc.**

In his letter, Jarry also recommended that the principal characters adopt "special voices" or "accents" for their roles and scorned verisimilitude and historically accurate costumes and settings.

Eyewitnesses to the remarkable production of Jarry's *Ubu Roi* were struck by the insistently anti-realistic qualities of the play, settings that displayed both outdoors and indoors simultaneously, apple trees and a fireplace, closed windows, and blue sky. Between scenes an old man tiptoed on stage and hung a placard indicating the next scene's location from a nail on the wall.

APOLLINAIRE—PROPHETIC VOICE OF MODERNISM

Jarry died in 1907 at the age of thirty-four; the author of three Ubu plays, the originator of the "science of pataphysics," and the subject of many legends. The next generation of writers in France looked to him as a leader, and none more so than Guillaume Apollinaire, who developed the theoretical and practical tenets of surrealism.

Apollinaire knew the value of Jarry's inspired contribution to the theater and penned a memorial tribute to his friend in 1907, remarking that Jarry, far from being a producer of lowly burlesque for the stage, was "the last of the sublime debauches." The first production of Apollinaire's *The Breasts of Teiresias* in 1917 took advantage of many of Jarry's stage innovations: A single character represented the "whole people of Zanzibar," and the use of a megaphone created staccato speech effects that gave the main characters a special voice or tone. But Apollinaire did not live long enough to see the results of his *drame surrealiste* become the basis for an entire literary/dramatic movement; war wounds suffered in 1917 ended his life a year later.

*Michael Benedikt, *Modern French Theater* (New York, E. P. Dutton, 1964), p. xi. Copyright © 1964 by Michael Benedikt and George Wellwarth. Reprinted by permission of Georges Borchardt, Inc.

THE DADA EXPERIMENT

Two years before Apollinaire's death, Tristan Tzara organized the anti-literary Dada movement in a small cabaret in Zurich, Switzerland. A number of refugees from various parts of Europe had gathered there to form a nonschool of the arts. They joined in common expression of a revulsion for the horrors of war and of a civilization that endured war. Dadaists derided every aspect of that civilization; family, loved ones, treasured objects, philosophies, theologies, nations.

The Dadaists chose the name for their movement at random from a French dictionary. *Dada* is a child's word for anything to do with horses. At the Cabaret Voltaire in Zurich, Tzara and his associates, Oscar Kokoschka, Max Ernst, and Richard Hülsenbeck staged Dada exhibitions. One such confrontation with established values, expressing Tzara's epigram "thought is made in the mouth," was described by Georges Hugnet:

> *On the stage keys and boxes were pounded to provide the music, until the infuriated public protested. . . . A voice, under a huge hat in the shape of a sugar loaf, recited poems by Hans Arp. Hülsenbeck screamed his poems louder and louder, while Tzara beat out the same rhythm* crescendo *on a big drum.* *

Tzara brought Dada to Paris in 1919, introducing to André Breton, Louis Aragon, and Philippe Soupault the Zurich perspective in nonart. Dada was an instant success, and many exhibitions followed Tzara's arrival. A Parisian journalist recorded the results of one such exhibit: A performer hid inside a wardrobe and insulted all the spectators, while André Breton sat on the stage chewing up matches. Other Dadaists, formally attired, with white gloves but without ties, paraded back and forth; a couple shook hands every two minutes, and others caterwauled on the stage. [Nadeau, p. 63].

The Dadaists were equally active in Germany. On one occasion they rented a glass cage large enough to hold a young girl. Access to the room that contained the glass cage was through a public urinal.

*Maurice Nadeau, *The History of Surrealism* (New York: Macmillan Publishing Co., Inc., 1965), p. 56. Translation: copyright © Macmillan Publishing Co., Inc. 1965. Reprinted by permission of Macmillan Publishing Co., Inc. and Georges Borchardt, Inc.

Spectators arriving in the room were confronted with the sight of a young girl, dressed as if attending her first communion, reciting obscene poetry in the center of the glass cage. The entire event created an infamous scandal, and the resulting controversy brought scores of converts to the Dadaist movement.

BEGINNINGS OF SURREALISM

Dadaism was not universally accepted even by the most *avant-garde* poets and writers of the period. Apollinaire had indicated in 1917 a new approach to drama in his anti-realistic *The Breasts of Tiresias*. The Foreword to the piece, subtitled *A Surrealist Drama*, stated:

> *The play must be an entire universe*
> *with its creator*
> *That is to say nature itself*
> *And not only*
> *Representative of a little part*
> *of what surrounds us or has already passed**

French writers André Breton and Francis Picabia quickly transferred their allegiances from Dadaism to Surrealism when it became clear that the principles of Dadaist exhibitions were hardly to be preferred to the dominant realistic art. Orthodoxy at either extreme was to be avoided, and by 1921 Breton and his followers had abandoned Tzara's group. That same year a mock trial was held for Maurice Barrès, an established writer who had once supported *avant-garde* principles. Barrès, who had needlessly left town during the trial, was accused of crimes against the "safety of the mind." He was found guilty of having betrayed Dadaist principles. In holding the trial Breton had attacked not only Barrès but Dadaism itself.

The final split between Dadaism and Surrealism occurred in 1922, when Breton convened a "Congress of the Modern Spirit." Tzara refused to attend. Supporters of Tzara and Breton were openly hostile to one another, and at the première of Tzara's *The*

*Excerpt from *The Breasts of Tiresias* by Guillaume Apollinaire, reprinted from Michael Benedikt, *Modern French Theater* (New York: E. P. Dutton, 1964). Copyright © 1964 by Michael Benedikt and George Wellwarth. Reprinted by permission of Georges Borchardt, Inc.

Gas Heart the two groups came to blows onstage. Paul Eluard and André Breton fought one another, the Dadaists physically abused Breton and Peret and broke the arm of Pièrre de Massot, a Surrealist. While a number of indignities and cuts were sustained by all participants, Paul Eluard was unfortunate enough to fall into the scenery and was ordered to pay 8,000 francs to the enraged theater owner. Surrealism emerged victorious. Subsequently, many Dadaists converted to Breton's Surrealist movement.

THE GOLDEN YEARS OF SURREALISM

By 1924 André Breton was the acknowledged leader of the Surrealist movement, which he had modelled after the research and writings of Sigmund Freud. Breton had met Freud briefly in 1921. Breton's first manifesto owed as much to his training as a psychiatric orderly in the French army, where he developed an interest in Freud's work, as it did to literary principles. Breton advocated automatic writing, a kind of internal psychic release of free-form thought processes. And he pointed to his own collaborative effort with Philippe Soupault, *Les Champs Magnetiques*, as an example for others to follow. But no one did. Breton's manifesto was more provocative than creative. Squabbles among the Surrealists were legendary. They acknowledged the superiority of dream images over "habitual" reality. They attempted to create their art uninhibited by the ego's logic and the superego's censorship. They saw dream images flow into the real in a variable dimension of time and space. They felt that even love must bloom unhindered by the espalier of life's demands. The Surrealists created for themselves a world in which it was impossible to live.

By 1929 Breton's Surrealist movement was politically polarized. In 1926 Philippe Soupault had been expelled from the movement for the heretical act of proclaiming the value of works of literature. In 1928 Roger Vitrac was also expelled. Robert Desnos gradually withdrew. Then, on June 7, 1928, Antonin Artaud opened his Théâtre Alfred Jarry with a production of Strindberg's *A Dream Play*. Breton and his friends attempted to storm the opening, as they had done six years earlier at Tzara's *Gas Heart*. This time the intruders were met by police, and the production went on as scheduled.

Breton's second manifesto had profound consequences for the movement. His focus on dream images and automatic writing shifted to social revolution. The Surrealist group that took Breton as its leader now advocated the Communist Party as its primary commitment, and by 1930 Surrealism's force was considerably diminished. Individual artists continued to champion the cause, as did Salvadore Dali in his paintings of the mid-1930s, "Soft Construction with Boiled Beans" (1936) and "Burning Giraffe" (1935). Dali's paintings featured the juxtaposition of familiar objects with bizarre dream-like landscapes, breaking the bonds of familiar reality. But Breton's belief that Western theater was far too decadent had a severely limiting effect on the creation of new dramatic works by Surrealist writers. The salad days of Surrealist drama passed almost before they began. Politics had spoiled the creative process.

GARCIA LORCA AND THE SPANISH DRAMA

The early years of the 1930s were fruitful ones for Spanish artists. Garcia Lorca, Salvadore Dali, and Luis Buñuel, the brilliant pioneer filmmaker, adapted some Surrealist principles for the Spanish theater. Garcia Lorca's best works appeared shortly before the outbreak of the Spanish Civil War—*Blood Wedding* (1933), *Yerma* (1934), and *The House of Bernarda Alba* (1936). They were the antithesis of the Don Juan legend of masculine supremacy. Lorca's plays depicted a society almost surrealistically lacking in vigor, in which women played the central roles.

ARTAUD AND THE THEATER OF CRUELTY

Antonin Artaud began a tormented life in the theater in 1920. His first job was acting for producer Lugné-Poë in Paris. Never more than a minor presence onstage, he worked backstage, designing sets in 1921 for Charles Dullin's production of Calderón's *Life Is a Dream*. That same year Artaud began to associate with the Surrealists. But his morbid fascination with his own deteriorating health soon caused him to reject Breton's orthodox dependence on

Sigmund Freud. Through Charles Dullin's acting–training Artaud developed an inclination toward asceticism and an interest in Eastern theater ritual that led him to quarrel with the Surrealists. In 1926 Artaud was expelled from the movement. A year later the Théâtre Alfred Jarry was formed, sponsored by Artaud, Roger Vitrac, and Robert Aron. A bill of programs, including *Burnt Belly* or *The Crazy Mother* (1927), Strindberg's *A Dream Play*, and a parody of Paul Claudel's *Break of Noon* (1929), was planned for the new enterprise, but the theater remained open for less than two seasons.

ARTAUD'S CONTRIBUTION TO THE THEATER

Artaud's lasting contribution was his theory of the theater of cruelty, a visceral drama of gesture and ritual, rather than one of the spoken word. Many events contributed to Artaud's eclectic development of a theory for the modern stage. An important event for Artaud was a performance of the Balinese Theater at the 1931 Colonial Exposition in Paris. The experience of watching the dancers profoundly influenced Artaud's thinking. Afterward he wrote a letter to Louis Jouvet announcing his intention of creating a theater of hieroglyphic-like gestures, symbolic of the workings of the unconscious. The purpose of his theatrical cruelty was to force spectators to project customary responses to stage events beyond their habitual expression. The theater Artaud envisioned resembled a nightmare come to life, a reflection of man's—and possibly Artaud's—sense of chaos within.

THE THEATER AND ITS DOUBLE

Artaud wrote his first play, *Jet of Blood*, in 1923. (It remained relatively unknown until Peter Brooke's production of it in 1963.) Artaud revealed his psychotic reaction to sex in general and to the "copulating couple" in particular in the concluding scene of *Jet of Blood*, when an army of scorpions escaped from under the Nurse's dress and swarmed over the Knight's sex, which swelled and burst. In 1926 Artaud completed a film scenario entitled *The Shell and the*

Clergyman. At the first screening of it in 1928 he was thrown out for violent behavior. Several years later he renounced film as a medium. He returned to the theater and devoted his energies to theoretical writings. In 1933 he began a series of essays that appeared in the 1938 publication of *The Theater and Its Double*, considered by many to be the most important work of its kind in modern drama. The previous year Artaud returned from the Aran Islands and was immediately committed to a mental institution, where he remained until the end of World War II. In 1948 he died of cancer, two decades before his work became a major influence in Western theater.

ARTAUD'S THEATER

Artaud's theater demanded a return to a psychic past of sympathetic magic; of the totemism of animals, stones, and objects; of everything that might determine, disclose, and direct the secret forces of the universe. To draw the hieroglyphs of his theater Artaud treated the great myths that told of superhuman passions. He was the first "environmental director," who advocated surrounding his spectators above and below. There were no sets for his productions, and costuming was designed to be timeless. His lighting concepts demanded instantaneous shifts in color to correspond with a language system described as "animated hieroglyphs and tonalities, yelps, and barks" in contrasting assonant and dissonant modes. Artaud believed the actor could find within himself a portion of the cosmos through the use of certain breathing techniques. He thought it possible to reach the vast energies of the unconscious through the passions loosed at moments of great crisis in the history of mankind, which could be constantly recreated in the theater.

In 1935 Artaud founded his Institute for a Theater of Cruelty in Paris. Its first production was to be his adaptation of Shelley's *The Cenci*. However, the production was not well received, and Artaud was bitterly disappointed with its abbreviated seventeen-day run. The ideas behind Artaud's Institute died with that venture, not to be reborn until the Royal Shakespeare's production of Peter Weiss' *Marat/Sade* in 1964 firmly established Artaud's reputation. French contemporaries of Artaud paid little attention to his theories. Theater owners and managers of Artaud's youth, such as Charles Dullin, Louis Jouvet, and Georges Pitoëff, concentrated on keeping their theaters open. But the next generation, led by Roger Blin and Jean-Louis Barrault, was strongly influenced by Artaud's concepts for the theater.

EDWARDIAN ENGLAND AND BEYOND— A POETIC DRAMA

At the beginning of the twentieth century England experienced a revival of poetic drama. The Pre-Raphaelites that gathered in the Celtic twilight of Dublin's Abbey Theater for the performance of plays of John Millington Synge, W. B. Yeats, and Lady Gregory influenced the development of native English dramatists. Playwrights like Thomas Hardy (*The Dynasts*, 1908), John Masefield (*The Tragedy of Nan*, 1909), and Lascelles Abercrombie (*The End of the World*, 1914) looked to Ireland for their inspiration. But the trend did not survive the war, and by the mid-thirties poetic drama was limited in its appeal and scope. Dorothy Sayers and Christopher Fry wrote a number of poetic dramas at that time, but probably the best known playwright in this genre was T. S. Eliot. His *Murder in the Cathedral*, which dealt with the assassination of Thomas à Beckett, Archbishop of Canterbury, in 1170 A.D. was representative of the best poetic drama of the period.

Other playwrights of the late 1920s and early 1930s were J. B. Priestly and James Birdie. Priestly had begun his career as a novelist. In 1931 he adapted *The Good Companions* as a stage piece and followed with *Dangerous Corner* in 1932. Sir Ralph Richardson made his first stage appearance in 1934 in Priestly's *Eden End*. Subsequent years saw numerous productions of his works, culminating with an adaptation of Iris Murdoch's *A Severed Head* in 1964. James Birdie, the pseudonym of the Scot, Osborne Henry Mavor, was noted for extravagant historical plots. *The Anatomist* in 1931 concerned a Scottish surgeon's dealings with two rather disreputable body snatchers. Birdie's greatest success came in *Storm in a Teacup*, in 1936. The decade from 1930 to 1940 was not notable for the performance of new works.

ENTER THE THEATRICAL BUSINESSMAN

If English plays of great quality were not forthcoming, English acting compensated for the lack. Entrepreneurs who had taken control of the American stage at the turn of the century began to dominate the English theater. With the rise of the businessman and the demise of the actor–manager, a trend that had begun in English theater with Thomas Betterton and David Garrick in the eighteenth century was reversed. New productions geared solely toward increasing box office receipts did little to enhance the quality of the English stage. But the best actors worked, and they were seen repeatedly in standard works that displayed their talents. A small number of independent London theaters, notably the Lyric, the Old Vic, and the Gate, and several provincial repertory houses, did manage to maintain an artistic integrity in their selection of new works by new playwrights.

THE INDEPENDENT THEATERS—
CONTINENTAL DRAMA IN ENGLAND

The demand for innovative stage techniques and for new playwrights came not from the established theaters of London's West End but from the small English art theaters. The Lyric Theater's revival of John Gay's *The Beggar's Opera* in 1920 brought simplified realism of theatrical settings to the English stage. The Gate Theater, created by Peter Godfrey, produced the best works and displayed the best techniques of the continent. Playwrights as diverse as Strindberg, Kaiser, Toller, Wedekind, Capek, Ibsen, Hauptmann, Rice, Pirandello, O'Neill, Cocteau, and others were regularly seen. But perhaps the most important theater of the time was the Old Vic, originally run by the temperence reformers Miss Cons and her niece, Miss Lilian Baylis. They were dedicated to bringing great works of art to the masses, and their production of *Troilus and Cressida* in 1923 made the Old Vic the first English theater to stage all of Shakespeare's works.

In the 1930s the Old Vic, under the leadership of Tyrone Guthrie, employed actors of the quality of John Gielgud, Dame Edith

Evans, Charles Laughton, and Flora Robson. Encouraged by Miss Baylis, Guthrie developed a repertory system for his company that equalled the best in England. Gielgud's *Hamlet* in 1934 was acclaimed by many as the most memorable production of the decade. Following the lead of the Lyric Theater, Gielgud stréssed simplified realism. His acting style stressed psychological motivations. In the late thirties the Old Vic was unofficially regarded as England's national theater.

Another innovation of the times was the London Theater School, begun in 1936 by Michel Saint-Denis. Out of Saint-Denis' training program came some of the best actors of the English stage for the next generation; Laurence Olivier, Ralph Richardson, Alec Guiness, Michael Redgrave, and Peggy Ashcroft. The London Theater School worked closely with the Old Vic to give London audiences the best productions of the period. But the repertory dwelt on the classics. With the exception of Noel Coward's witty comedies, *Private Lives, Tonight at 8:30,* and *Blithe Spirit,* plays of the period did not match its acting traditions.

SEAN O'CASEY—
AN IRISHMAN OF WORLD THEATER

The most important dramatist of the period was Sean O'Casey, an Irishman who was passionately committed in his early days to the Irish Republican movement. O'Casey's first play, *The Shadow of a Gunman,* was staged in 1923 at the Abbey Theater in Dublin. *Gunman* was followed by *Juno and the Paycock* a year later, which some considered his finest work. In 1926 *The Plough and the Stars* premiered at the Abbey Theater. The production ridiculed Irish patriots who advocated war and revolution. The controversy sparked by its opening night rivalled the Abbey Theater riots that greeted the "shifts" of Synge's *Playboy of the Western World* in 1907. Thereupon O'Casey left Ireland and settled in England. In 1928 he completed *The Silver Tassie,* but when the Abbey Theater refused to produce it, O'Casey severed all relations with his homeland. He continued to preach his unique brand of pacifism but developed expressionistic techniques that did not match the success of his earlier work.

AMERICAN THEATER INTO THE THIRTIES—
REBELLION AGAINST REALISM

Theaters in America were slow to emulate the advances of the Free Theaters of Europe because the businessmen that controlled major Broadway houses were reluctant to attempt anything that did not have a proven box office potential. The first organized attempt to bring art back into the theaters in America came with the New York Stage Society's invitation to Granville-Barker to bring two productions to New York in 1915. The French government subsidized Jacques Copeau's Vieux-Colombier troupe at the Garrick Theater in New York for two seasons beginning in 1917, and in 1923–24 the Moscow Art Theater performed in twelve American cities. During the visit Constantin Stanislavsky was encouraged to write a biography of his life and times.

"LITTLE THEATER" IN AMERICA

Copeau, Granville-Barker, and Stanislavsky set the tone for new theater in the major American cities. But without the encouragement of subscription theaters like the Provincetown Players, the Washington Square Players, Eva la Gallienne's Civic Repertory Theater, the Neighborhood Playhouse, and the Theater Guild, the new drama might have reached new American audiences more slowly. Much of the focus in little theater productions was on encouraging native playwrights, such as Eugene O'Neill or Elmer Rice or on producing experimental European playwrights, such as Shaw, Kaiser, Toller, Pirandello, Gorky, Ibsen, and Strindberg. But the most immediate change in American theater was the development of scenic designers trained in the techniques of the "new stagecraft," Lee Simonson, Robert Edmund Jones, and Norman Bel Geddes.

THE "NEW STAGECRAFT" IN AMERICA

In 1915 Robert Edmund Jones began to develop a native style when he designed sets for Granville-Barker's production of *The Man Who Married A Dumb Wife*. In 1924 Norman Bel Geddes, as gifted a designer as America has produced, designed sets for Max Reinhardt's *The Miracle*, which called for the transformation of the

Figure 10.1 Set Design for *The Man Who Married a Dumb Wife*
A signal event of 1915 was a double contribution from abroad. When
Harley Granville-Barker brought his English company and productions
to New York, he hired a young American designer who had spent some
time as an apprentice in Reinhardt's Berlin theaters. Robert Edmond
Jones won instant acclaim with his setting and costumes for this short
play by Anatole France.

Century Theater in New York into a gothic cathedral. Lee Simonson, the last of a trio of gifted first-generation American designers,
devoted most of his career to designing sets for the Washington
Square Players. In the 1930s Simonson designed Theater Guild
productions, including *Liliom*, *Peer Gynt*, and *Amphitryon 38*. In
later years new American designers emerged; Mordecai Gorelik,
Boris Aronson, Donald Oenslager, and Jo Mielziner. The latter two
were probably the most gifted of this generation.

THE GROUP THEATRE—HEIR TO STANISLAVSKY

In the 1930s, a period of social unrest and distrust of conventional
theater practices, two significant American theaters emerged—
the Group Theatre and the Federal Theater Project. Students

of Richard Boleslavsky's American Laboratory Theater, Stella Adler, Lee Strasberg, and Harold Clurman, founded the Group Theatre in 1931. Boleslavsky had modelled his training methods on those of Stanislavsky's Moscow Art Theater. The Group Theatre found support from members of the Theater Guild, its parental organization that supplied money and talent to the burgeoning collective, which also included Lee Strasberg, Cheryl Crawford, Elia Kazan, Franchot Tone, Morris Garnovsky, and J. Edward Bromberg. Productions were at first financially unsuccessful. But the Group Theatre discovered within its ranks a major talent in Clifford Odets. The Group also produced works of Irwin Shaw, Paul Green, and William Saroyen, as well as works of established playwrights such as Maxwell Anderson, George S. Kaufman, S. N. Behrman, Philip Barry, and Robert E. Sherwood. In 1937 internal dissension caused the resignation of all the directors. Other theaters born of political dissent and economic difficulties—the Theater Union, the Theater of Action, Labor Stage, Social Stage, Worker's Laboratory Theater, Theater Collective—all vanished in the turmoil of the period. The Group Theatre attempted to reorganize but unsuccessfully. In 1941 it ended.

THE FEDERAL THEATER PROJECT

The closest thing to a national theater that America has yet seen developed through the combined efforts of a triad of strong-willed individuals in the middle of the Depression: President Franklin D. Roosevelt, Harry Hopkins, and Hallie Flanagan. The Depression had deprived hundreds of thousands of workers of jobs, and theater craftsmen were no exception. Actor's Equity estimated that there were five thousand stage technicians without jobs in America. At first Hallie Flanagan refused an invitation to head the Federal Theater. She finally accepted in 1935. The Federal Theater was administered under Arthur Hopkin's Works Progress Administration with a budget of $10 million each year. Hallie Flanagan's organization supported twelve thousand theater workers in five regions of the country. A national theater, funded by the federal government and designed to be free of any censorship, was the promise Hopkins made to the country. It was one he could not keep.

THE LIVING NEWSPAPER

An innovation of the Federal Theater was the creation of the Living Newspaper in New York. The Living Newspaper was a dramatization of current events, in which actors presented published reports from newspapers, magazines, government periodicals, and other sources, which offered perspectives on an issue. Most living newspapers advocated social change. Arthur Arent edited two of the best productions, *Power* (1937) and *One Third of a Nation* (1938). The latter production looked at poverty in America, and it was produced and adapted in major cities throughout America. Other "newspapers" anticipated the documentary dramas of the 1960s: *Triple a Ploughed Under*, which dealt with farm problems, and *Spirochete*, a history of syphilis in the United States.

AN END TO THE DREAM OF A NATIONAL THEATER

Numerous productions of the Federal Theater prescribed radical social change. This provoked a negative response from Congress. Productions of black drama also posed problems far in advance of their time. Two pioneers in encouraging black actors, Orson Welles and John Houseman, produced a black *Macbeth* and *Dr. Faustus* under the auspices of the Works Progress Administration. But the WPA considered a production of *The Cradle Will Rock* too subversive to be sponsored. In 1937 Welles and Houseman left the Federal project and produced *Julius Caesar* at their newly created Mercury Theater. The production had the deliberate overtones of contemporary politics, disparaging those practiced by Hitler and Mussolini. The resulting furor reached Washington and the House Committee on Un-American Activities. Events of this magnitude both within and without the Federal Theater Project put an end to any professed neutrality on the part of the federal government. The project was labelled immoral and Communist-dominated. On June 30, 1939, the first national theater of the United States was ended by an act of Congress. But before the end an estimated thirty million spectators attended twelve hundred productions in the span of four short years.

EUGENE O'NEILL—DRAMATIC PIONEER

The escape of the American playwright from the bonds of strict realism came through a greater freedom in play construction and an exploration of the limits of the new stagecraft, rather than through poetic inspiration. In 1920 O'Neill demonstrated, with *The Emperor Jones*, a new element in American playwriting. A series of short scenes showed the black emperor regressing in a kind of panic delirium through the history of his race. This early attempt at Expressionism was followed the next year with *The Hairy Ape*, written in the style of German Expressionism.

Figure 10.2 Sketches for *Desire Under the Elms*
Among the plays that Robert Edmond Jones directed as well as designed was O'Neill's *Desire Under The Elms* in 1924. These are the playwright's sketches showing the house and the arrangement of the four rooms when the wall is removed.

During the next ten years O'Neill experimented with forms of nonrealistic theater. In one of his finest plays, *Desire Under the Elms*, he used a composite setting that juxtaposed the exterior and each of four rooms of a farmhouse. In later plays O'Neill dramatized the dual nature of personalities, alternating masks as well as faces for characters in *The Great God Brown* and playing two actors for each character in *Days Without End*. In his most symbolic play, *Lazarus Laughed*, all the characters wore masks. In *Strange Interlude* (and to a lesser extent in *The Great God Brown*) he used soliloquies to convey the inner thoughts his characters could not otherwise convey to the spectators. For *Mourning Becomes Electra* (like *Strange Interlude*, almost a trilogy in complexity), he met with remarkable success the severest problem he had ever set himself. Going to Aeschylus for the plot, he combined Clytemnestra's murder of her husband, the son's murder of his mother and her lover, and the atmosphere of the American Civil War all with certain Freudian concepts of the thirties. Some playgoers felt that the addition of the siblings' incestuous impulses at the end of the play marred the work. For some *Electra* replaced *Desire Under the Elms* as the writer's finest play.

In 1936 O'Neill was awarded the Nobel Prize in Literature. With the proceeds of the award he bought Tao House in Concord, California. Plays written at this time did not enjoy critical acclaim. *The Iceman Cometh* (1939) and *A Moon for the Misbegotten* (1943) were produced unsuccessfully after the war, and O'Neill's reputation appeared to have eclipsed. Palsy finally halted his work. O'Neill spent his last decade ignored by the theater. But in 1956, three years after his death, *The Iceman Cometh* was revived. That same year *Long Day's Journey into Night*, written in 1940, was produced posthumously at the Dramatiska Teatern in Stockholm, Sweden, the home of his idol, August Strindberg. Immediately the work was acclaimed the masterpiece of America's foremost dramatist of the century. The Tyrone family's hopeless quest recalled O'Neill's first great success at the Provincetown Theater forty years earlier, *Beyond The Horizon*. Robert and Andrew Mayo's search for an ideal by which to live (a quest O'Neill once described as man's relation to God), characterized all his best work.

As a realist O'Neill had shortcomings, particularly in his mastery of words. This may be why he experimented with so many devices to break the patterns of realism. Nevertheless, he went further than any other American dramatist in seeking and realizing deep and bitter psychological truths. O'Neill, more than any of his contemporaries, established American drama.

ENGLAND'S ANGRY YOUNG MEN

A number of English writers and directors from the 1930s continued to write good drama into the 1950s and beyond, such as Terence Rattigan (*French Without Tears*, 1936, *The Winslow Boy*, 1946, and *Separate Tables*, 1954). Peter Ustinov entertained with *The Love of Four Colonels* (1951) and *Romanoff and Juliet* (1956). Christopher Fry penned *A Phoenix Too Frequent* (1946) and *The Lady's Not for Burning* (1949). T. S. Eliot's best work was *The Cocktail Party* (1949). No date separates the new English theater from its traditional past as clearly as May 8, 1956, when John Osborne's *Look Back in Anger* premiered at London's Royal Court Theater. And no one captured the attention of the theater public as did Jimmy Porter in Osborne's poignant drama about a disaffected working class family. That same year Laurence Olivier, who together with Peter Hall had been instrumental in ridding the London theater of its star system, opened in Osborne's *The Entertainer*. The play dealt with the frustrated hopes of a class-conscious England, as seen by three generations of entertainers. No playwright of the old school had explored the cul-de-sacs of the English class structure or even recognized their existence.

With the public's acceptance of plays of social awareness, a flood of new playwrights appeared to take the place of the old. Soon George Devine's Royal Court Theater, begun with the intention of bringing new English plays and unfamiliar foreign plays to London audiences, had produced an entire generation of new playwrights. Among them were John Arden (*Live Like Pigs*, 1958, *Sergeant Musgrave's Dance*, 1959), Norman F. Simpson (*A Resounding Tinkle*, 1956), Brendan Behan (*The Hostage*, 1958), Shelagh Delaney (*A Taste of Honey*, 1958), and Arthur Wesker (*Chicken Soup with Barley*, 1958, and *Roots*, 1959). The works of these playwrights were produced either at Devine's Royal Court Theater or at Joan Littlewood's Theatre Workshop in London's East End.

THE RISE AND DECLINE
OF ANGRY YOUNG PLAYWRIGHTS

For some of the playwrights their first years of success brought fame and critical attention. But in most cases neither success nor fame lasted. Brendan Behan died in 1964. John Osborne's importance as a dramatist declined after his production of *Inadmissable Evidence* in 1965. John Arden did his best work in the last years of the fifties, and Shelagh Delaney's first work was her finest. One playwright was an exception. He was Harold Pinter, who followed his first success, *The Dumbwaiter*, with a full-length play, *The Birthday Party*, in 1958. Pinter had studied at the Royal Academy of Dramatic Art to be an actor. But his career on the stage, under the name of David Brown, was nothing compared to his success as a playwright. He proved to be particularly adept at reproducing the spontaneous irrelevancy of everyday speech patterns within situations that developed menacing qualities. His best plays possessed a kind of motiveless malignity that hovered over the stage. In *The Dumbwaiter* two hired killers waited in a dingy basement for their next victim. A dumbwaiter instructed the killers to bring an order of food: "Two braised steaks and chips. Two sago puddings. Two teas without sugar." The men improvised as best they could and were asked for more elaborate food stuffs. As Gus left for a glass of water the speaking tube beside the dumbwaiter gave Ben his final instructions: "Kill the next man who enters." A man entered, was shot, and turned out to be Gus, the intended next victim— apparently. In Pinter's subsequent works, *The Caretaker* (1960), *The Homecoming* (1965), *Old Times* (1971), he explored themes of estrangement and absurdity within a comic framework.

EXISTENTIALISM, ABSURDITY, AND BEYOND

Existentialism came to the theater long after it was developed as a philosophical proposition in the nineteenth century by Søren Kierkegaard. The holocaust of two successive World Wars caused men like Albert Camus and Jean-Paul Sartre to question the meaning of a world on the brink of existence. Camus, in 1942, published *The Myth of Sisyphus*, in which he described the sense of modern man as "absurd":

> *A world that can be explained by reasoning, however faulty, is a familiar world. But in a universe that is suddenly deprived of illusions and of light, man feels a stranger. His is an irremediable exile, because he is deprived of memories of a lost homeland as much as he lacks the hope of a promised land to come. This divorce between man and his life, the actor and his setting, truly constitutes the feeling of absurdity.* *

In order to exist authentically in an absurd condition man must be responsible for his own acts. Existence preceded essence. Man's actions, according to Camus and Sartre, determined his being.

THE INFLUENCE OF SARTRE AND CAMUS

Jean-Paul Sartre and Albert Camus brought existentialism to the world's attention. Sartre attempted to infuse his plays with his philosophical tenets; *The Flies* (1943), *No Exit* (1944), and *The Condemned of Altona* (1959). The works drew indifferent psychological portraits, which lacked the dramatic impact that should have issued from their heros' existential choices. Camus' plays achieved little more. Despite the best efforts of Jean-Louis Barrault, a production of Camus' *State of Siege* in 1948 was unsuccessful. The following year Camus completed *The Just Assassins*, a polemic on the nature of "positive action," based on an historical account of Russian terrorists' activities in 1905. Camus wrote no more plays. In 1957 he was awarded the Nobel Prize in Literature. Sartre and Camus quarrelled bitterly over the basis of existentialism. Today the philosophy of the absurd, which grew out of their joint endeavors, is more important than the plays of either one.

ROOTS OF THE THEATER OF THE ABSURD

The theory of absurdist drama had existed long before it found a spokesman in Camus. A Frenchman of letters, Auguste Hippolyte Taine, wrote in the nineteenth century that mental images linked to

*"Le Mythe de Sisyphe" from *The Theatre of the Absurd* by Martin Esslin. Copyright © 1961, 1968, 1969 by Martin Esslin. Used by permission of Doubleday & Company, Inc. and Methuen & Co Ltd.

exterior sensations to form concepts. In *A La Recherche du Temps Perdu*, Proust argued that external reality was merely the surface adornment to conceal the real. By 1930 a number of poets, including Hans Arp and Samuel Beckett, had signed the "Verticalist's Manifesto" published in Eugene Jolas' *Transition Magazine*, which declared:

> *Aesthetic will is not the first law. It is in the immediacy of the aesthetic revelation, in the alogical movement of the psyche, in the organic rhythm of the vision, that the creative act occurs.*

While Sartre and Camus expressed the idea of absurdity in terms of authentic acts, the absurdists went a step further and devalued even the acts. An inner direction, as described by the signatories of the Manifesto, could be seen in the early works of Samuel Beckett. In 1931 Beckett wrote *Proust*, his first extended piece of literary criticism, and exposed the dilemma of language as a vehicle of communication:

> *Either we speak and act for ourselves, in which case speech and action are distorted and emptied of their meaning by an intelligence that is not our own, or else we speak and act for others, in which case we speak and act a lie.**

Some of Beckett's contemporaries developed similar ideas nearly two decades before the first "absurdist drama" was acknowledged. In fact, the roots of absurdity can be traced back to classical literature and to the comedies of Aristophanes.

ABSURDIST DRAMA

Writers as diverse as Georg Büchner, Alfred Jarry, Anton Chekhov, Franz Kafka, Luigi Pirandello, Bertolt Brecht, and Antonin Artaud are arguably precursors of the mid-twentieth-century absurdists. No formal "school" existed for these playwrights, but their works shared common elements. Absurdist drama was

---

*Samuel Beckett, *Proust* (New York: Grove Press, Inc., 1957), p. 47. Reprinted courtesy of Grove Press, Inc.

typified by a concern for situation rather than for character or action. Plot was negligible, and characters' actions and language were indecipherable to the audiences. The structure was frequently circular, ending where it began, or demanding abbreviated repetitions. Most absurdist drama was chronologically unspecific, to accord with a freely flowing sense of time and space relationships. Apparently meaningless events took extraordinary significance in the development of the play, as gibberish was transformed into hieroglyphs, and conscious intentions into irrelevancy.

EUGENE IONESCO— PIONEER OF THE ABSURD

Barrault's adaptation of Franz Kafka's *The Trial* in 1947 preceded by several years the first productions of Rumanian-born Eugene Ionesco. *The Bald Soprano* appeared in 1950, followed by *The Lesson* (1951), and *The Chairs* (1952). His early plays, filled as they were with a babble of language, were the basis of Ionesco's later art. According to Ionesco language is nothing but "clichés, empty for-

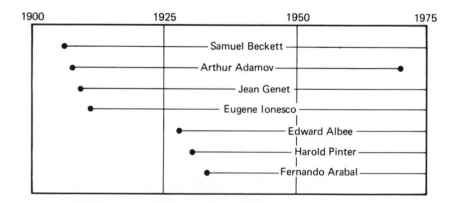

Figure 10.3   Playwrights of the Theatre of the Absurd

The most prominent of the post World War II anti-literary movements, writers as diverse as Jean Genet and Eugene Ionesco began to present concrete stage images of the absurdity of existence. The production of Beckett's *En Attendant Godot* at the Théâtre de Babylon on January 5, 1953, ran for over four-hundred performances and established the absurdist tradition at midcentury.

mulas, and slogans." Later he extrapolated his thesis in *Victims of Duty, Rhinoceros, Hunger,* and *Thirst.* In *Macbett,* a parody based on Shakespeare's play, Ionesco took the themes of power and corruption and modified them to his own purposes.

The major themes in Ionesco's works, of which *Macbett* was no exception, concerned the deadening nature of a materialistic society and the loneliness of man, irremediably isolated from his fellow beings. Unable to tolerate the pressures of conformity on individuals from any source, Ionesco opposed *agit-prop* drama in general and committed social action drama in particular. In 1970 he was elected to the French academy.

SAMUEL BECKETT AND THE IDEA OF WAITING

Samuel Beckett indicated his view of the world in a poem entitled "The Vulture" in 1935:

> *Dragging his hunger through the sky*
> *of my skull of sky and death*
> *Stooping to the prone who must*
> *soon take up their life and walk*
> *Mocked by a tissue that may not serve*
> *till hunger earth and sky be offal**

Beckett graduated from Trinity College, Dublin, and the École Normale Superieur, Paris. After an abbreviated career as a university lecturer he settled in France in 1937, already an established *literateur.* In 1928 he wrote the first essay in a publication that analyzed James Joyce's *Finnegan's Wake. Proust* appeared in 1931, and his first novel, *Murphy,* was published in 1938. In the 1940s he produced five more novels and two plays, and a number of shorter works. *Waiting for Godot* had been written in 1949, but Beckett had to wait four years, until Roger Blin agreed to direct the play. On January 5, 1953, *Godot* opened at the Théâtre Babylone in Paris. At first the mysterious play received mixed reaction, but soon it was recognized as a masterpiece of absurdist drama. Subsequently, the

---

*Samuel Beckett, *Poems in English* (New York: Grove Press, Inc., 1961), p. 21. Copyright © 1961 by Samuel Beckett. Reprinted by permission of Grove Press, Inc. and John Calder (Publishers) Ltd., London.

San Francisco Actor's Workshop produced *Godot* at San Quentin prison and focused international attention on the two tramps who wait and wait . . . for meaning in a world that never was.

SHORTER AND SHORTER WORKS

Beckett's stature as a dramatist grew in later years, and the length of his works decreased in almost direct proportion. It was as if he wished to put the impossible last word, and the last silence after the last word, onstage. *Endgame* premiered in 1957, *Krapp's Last Tape* in 1958, *Happy Days* in 1961, and *Not I* in 1972. Beckett's notion of stage time was almost Bergsonian: "the continuous creation of unforeseen novelty" which lay outside conventional time and space. Not only time but the very habits of being, speaking, seeing, and breathing seemed to be merely forms of a numbing process that separated man from his essential nature. In Beckett's plays, language seemed merely a game to pass the time. Hamm pointed out to Clove, in *Endgame*, the futility of words:

> *Babble, babble, words, like the solitary child who turns himself into children, two, three, so as to be together and whisper together in the dark . . . moment upon moment.* *

Beckett continued to write, more sparingly if possible, into the 1970s.

JEAN GENET AND
THE LIFE OF THE ABSURD

Playwrights of the theater of the absurd tried to restore a sensibility to a world encompassed by automatism. Their attempts resulted in works as diverse as Ionesco's *The Chairs*, Arthur Adamov's *La*

---

*Samuel Beckett, *Endgame* (New York: Grove Press, Inc., 1958), p. 70. Copyright © 1958 by Grove Press, Inc. Reprinted by permission of Grove Press, Inc. and Faber & Faber Ltd., London.

Parodie, and N. F. Simpson's *A Resounding Tinkle*. But no one since Alfred Jarry had lived by absurdist principles as did Jean Genet, "Saint Genet" according to Sartre, the arch criminal of French letters.

Harold Pinter's world revealed man fighting back against the darkness and the silence that threatened to engulf him; Beckett's world confronted man with the stark incomprehensibility of time and process; Arrabal's world found man reaching for an ironic extension of Friedrich Hebbel's "moral idea," which decreed that the order of things must be maintained at any cost. But Genet, born absurd, lived and wrote absurd.

Genet spent his early life in and out of prison, where he learned to write. His first play to be produced was *The Maids* in 1947. Two years later he finished *Deathwatch* and declared, in a moment of pique, that he would give up "the stupidity of actors and theater people." A few years later three more of his plays were produced: *The Balcony* (1956), *The Blacks* (1959), and *The Screens* (1961). In all his plays Genet explored the range of masks and appearances, creating an endless succession of images, a "hall of mirrors" that had no final reference point. Whereas Pirandello invested appearance with reality and declared it to be the best the world had to offer, Genet discounted appearance and celebrated evil as the only value. He stood outside order and applauded the chaos of nonorder, where every appearance had its counter-appearance. Genet's characters revealed an experience of being quite unlike Ionesco's desiccated automatons or Beckett's philosophical portraits.

THE THEATER
OF FACT

In the late twenties Erwin Piscator had begun, in Germany, a series of experiments in documentary drama that eventually found an audience in the 1960s—particularly in America. His early productions were far more artistic than the loosely assembled "living newspapers" of the Federal Theater Project. Fleeing the Nazi regime, Piscator returned to Germany in 1951. In the Freie Volksbühne in 1963 he produced Rolf Hochhuth's *The Deputy*, in which documentary evidence was used to indict Pope Pius XII for having failed to take a stand against the extermination of the Jews. Other documentary dramas on the same subject followed, notably Peter Weiss' *The Investigation*, which probed documents gathered from the Auschwitz concentration camp. Another German playwright, Heinar Kipphardt, examined the role of science in the atomic age in a production entitled *In the Matter of J. Robert Oppenheimer*.

Piscator died in 1966. Other playwrights continued to produce documentary drama: Hochhuth's *The Soldiers* (1967), Peter Weiss' *Vietnam Discourse* (1968), and *Trotsky in Exile* (1970). Donald Freed produced *Inquest* in 1970, which dealt with the trial of Ethel and Julius Rosenberg, the first American civilians to be executed for treason. Daniel Berrigan's *The Trial of the Catonsville Nine* appeared in 1971. The social unrest of the sixties, which had spread throughout Western Europe and America, fulminated the debate over the war in Vietnam and produced the central themes for documentary drama. Peter Brooke's Royal Shakespeare Company's *US* (1967), which looked at the whole question of Vietnam, was one of the best productions of the decade.

DIRECTORS INTO THE SIXTIES

In France the legacy of Jacques Copeau and his Théâtre du Vieux-Colombier was preserved by successive generations of theater directors. Disciplined men of the theater, Charles Dullin, Louis Jouvet, Michel Saint-Denis, Jean-Louis Barrault, and Jean Vilar, had led French theater until the outbreak of World War II. By the 1950s it was apparent that a new movement had begun, led by Ionesco and Beckett. In the later years of the decade the French government created a number of experimental theaters in Paris and the provinces. Some of France's best directors teamed with the new generation of writers for successful productions: Sylvain Dhomme, Roger Blin, George Vitaly, Jean-Marie Serreau, and Roger Plachon.

In England the Royal Shakespeare Company, under the leadership of Peter Hall, was largely responsible for the resurgence of

British drama in the 1960s. With a new charter from the British government, Hall's troupe expanded from an annual festival to a year-round company with a one season at Stratford-on-Avon and another at the Aldwych Theater in London. Peter Brooke, Michel Saint-Denis, and Charles Marowitz formed a core of dedicated directors that quickly made Hall's company the most experimental theater in England. A revitalized theater of cruelty appeared in the season of plays Brook and Marowitz produced in 1963 at the London Academy of Music and Dramatic Art (LAMDA).

Undoubtedly one of the best productions of the decade was Peter Brook's already mentioned *Marat/Sade* (1964). Peter Weiss' play, whose full title was *The Persecution and Assassination of Jean-Paul Marat as Performed by the Inmates of the Asylum of Charenton under the Direction of the Marquis de Sade*, had premiered at the Schiller Theater in West Berlin. The same year Brook opened his own production in London, incorporating many of Artaud's theater of cruelty techniques for that version. Brook's production techniques won instant acclaim in England and America.

Brook acknowledged a debt not only to Artaud but also to Brecht, for the innovative staging concepts he developed in *Marat/Sade*. In his book, *The Empty Space* (1968), Brook credited Brecht as the playwright without whose influence *Marat/Sade* would have been impossible. Brecht's alienation technique was most apparent in the last moments of the play: As inmates rioted within the asylum, a stage manageress suddenly walked onstage, blew a whistle, and the madness ended. *The Empty Space* summarized many of the British *avant-garde* directorial theories of the 1960s. Brook claimed there were four ways to fill the space of the stage: deadly theater of the past, holy theater of Artaud, rough theater of Brecht, and immediate theater of improvisation. His widely heralded production of Shakespeare's *A Midsummer Night's Dream*, with set designs by Sally Jacobs, opened in 1970. It toured the world and broke down decades of artfully stylized productions of the bard's work.

ENGLAND'S NATIONAL THEATER

Plans for a national theater for England were a hundred years in the making before the Barbazon Theater complex opened in 1976. A "Shakespeare Memorial Committee" was established in 1848 but its plans were never realized. Not until 1938, after William Archer's and Granville-Barker's 1904 scheme failed to find sponsors, did England finally get a site for its proposed theater in South Kensington. Immediately World War II interfered with the project. In 1949 the government passed a "National Theater Bill," and a cornerstone was laid on a new site on the south bank of the Thames. Sir Laurence Olivier was named director in 1962, and his Chichester Festival Theater formed the nucleus of the National Theater Company. They moved to the Old Vic, produced *Hamlet* in October of 1963, and remained there for thirteen years.

The Royal Shakespeare Company was a director's theater, so the National Theater focused on developing ensemble performers (like the Comédie Française) adept at diverse acting styles. Outstanding actors such as Paul Scofield, Albert Finney, Michael Redgrave, Maggie Smith, and Robert Stephens appeared in its productions. By 1970 the National Theater had achieved such an enviable production record that Laurence Olivier was knighted by Queen Elizabeth II. On October 25, 1976, the Barbazon Theater complex opened, built at a cost of 7.5 million. Poor health had forced Olivier to resign before the National Theater building opened, and Peter Hall was named the new director. The complex consisted of three theaters: the "experimental" Cottlesloe Theater, seating four hundred, the "traditional" Lyttelton Theater, seating eight hundred and ninety, and the "open stage" Olivier Theater, seating eleven hundred and sixty. Problems of creativity, style, and identity troubled the National Theater in the late 1970s, as the responsibility for administering a single complex in the interests of the nation proved difficult.

NEW PLAYS AND PLAYWRIGHTS IN ENGLAND

Nothing contributed more to a resurgence of English drama than the passage of the Theater Act of 1968. It reversed the effect of the English Licensing Act of 1737 that decreed that all plays produced in London had to be licensed by the Lord Chamberlain. To avoid the scrutiny of the official censor, nineteenth-century Free Theaters in England and on the continent had developed subscription houses. The English Theater Act transferred the responsibility of licensing theaters from the Lord Chamberlain's office to county governments. Almost immediately productions of *Hair* and *Oh! Calcutta!* appeared.

This new freedom encouraged a new generation of playwrights. Many of these writers had their first productions at the Royal Court Theater, under William Gaskell's direction. David Storey, Joe Orton, and Edward Bond formed a nucleus of promising new talent. Joe Orton wrote *Entertaining Mr. Sloane*, *Loot*, and *What the Butler Saw*. Peter Nichols produced *A Day in the Life of Joe Egg* and *National Health*. Edward Bond contributed an enigmatic *Saved*, and David Storey did *The Contractor* and *Home*. Robert Bolt wrote *A Man For All Seasons*. Peter Shaffer, who had written *Five Finger Exercise* and *The Royal Hunt of the Sun* years earlier, suddenly emerged with a brilliant new *Equus*.

Tom Stoppard's production of *Rosencrantz and Guildenstern Are Dead* at the 1967 Edinburgh Festival brought him instant fame. An enlarged version was taken to London and subsequently brought to New York, where it established Stoppard as a major talent. Later, *The Real Inspector Hound*, *Jumpers*, and *Dirty Linen* showed Stoppard's development from a Beckettian frame of reference to a post-absurdist analysis of language and game.

THE SOCIALIST REALISM EXPERIMENT

The repressive Stalinist regime's policies of the 1930s dominated the Russian theater through the 1960s and 1970s. Occasional lapses in control, when followers of Meyerhold's and Vakhtangov's nonrealistic methods found the freedom to stage productions, were brief. In the sixties the best directors working in a nonsocialist realist drama were Reuben Simonov, Alexei Popov, and Oleg Tabakov. But the general trend of Russian theater, typified by the Moscow Art Theater's approach, was to restrict any practice that smacked of "bourgeois revisionism."

THEATER IN AMERICA: THE BROADWAY ALTERNATIVE

A trend toward declining attendance in the fifties continued to plague Broadway productions in the sixties. Greatly increased costs and stagecraft union regulations contributed to the financial difficulties of New York theater. It became almost impossible to predict whether a show would succeed or fail. By the mid-sixties less than a dozen productions of seventy-five new shows each year succeeded. However, in 1965, two musicals, *Fiddler on the Roof* and *Hello, Dolly*, made millions for their sponsors. In the 1970s investors backed Broadway productions for tax write-offs; a promoter could summon backing for a show from businessmen who needed a loss for income tax purposes. When a show unexpectedly made money—as Tom O'Horgan's *Hair* did in 1968—the musical's backers greeted the success with applause and consternation.

One solution to the burgeoning costs of production in New York was the creation of an Off-Broadway theater. Actors' Equity defined it as staged in houses seating less than three hundred spectators outside the boundaries of the Times Square theater district. On April 24, 1952, Brooks Atkinson reviewed Jose Quintero's production of *Summer and Smoke*, starring Geraldine Page, at the Circle-in-the-Square Theater. Overnight the play became a sensation. Audiences began to attend other Off-Broadway houses, and actors saw the theaters as showcases for Broadway.

OFF-BROADWAY THEATER

The first great popular success of the Off-Broadway musical came with the revival of Brecht's *Threepenny Opera* at the Theater de Lys in 1954. After a short initial run, the production reopened in the same theater. That run lasted more than six years, with a top ticket price less than $5.

Taking its cue from the *Threepenny Opera*, Off-Broadway theater focused on topical reviews and polemical plays of both new American playwrights and continental dramatists. Mike Nichols, Elaine May, Barbara Harris, Alan Arkin, and others developed improvisational techniques in Chicago and San Francisco before taking them to New York. English reviews like *Beyond the Fringe* and *The Establishment* were hits in New York and contributed to the Off-Broadway spirit. New American playwrights Jack Richardson, Jack Gelber, Arthur Kopit, Murray Schisgal, and Edward Albee saw their plays produced. But by late 1959 the same problems that had beset Broadway theaters hit the Off-Broadway houses.

The "smash-hit-or-disaster" syndrome of Broadway reached Off-Broadway. The original purpose for developing Off-Broadway theater had been to produce the less commercial plays of well known playwrights, as well as works of new playwrights. But commercialism too often defeated creativity. There were some exceptions. Two of the more important artistic productions of the time were American premieres of Genet's works, *The Balcony*, at the Circle-in-the-Square in 1960 and *The Blacks*, at St. Mark's Playhouse in 1961. Beginning in 1959 plays of social protest were produced in Julian Beck's Living Theater: Jack Gelber (*The Connection*), Edward Albee (*Zoo Story*), and Jack Richardson (*The Prodigal*).

SOCIAL PROTEST AND
THE OFF OFF-BROADWAY THEATER

In the mid-fifties economic problems had led to the creation of Off-Broadway theater. The same economic problems, viewed by a generation of social protestors, led to the creation of Off Off-Broadway (sometimes referred to as OOB) theater in the mid-sixties. Off Off-Broadway sponsored a new group of playwrights, Sam Shepard, Paul Foster, Megan Terry, Leonard Malfi, Lanford Wilson, and Jean-Claude Van Itallie. A black playwrights' theater also arose, that would eventually find its place on Broadway.

Coffee houses, churches, lofts, and garages all served as "theaters" for early Off Off-Broadway plays. The first Off Off-Broadway productions took place in Joe Cino's Cafe Cino. Others followed, and OOB soon appeared in the Cafe Cino, Ellen Stewart's Cafe La Mama, Ralph Cooke's Theater Genesis at St. Mark's Church-in-the-Bouwerie, and Al Carmine's Judson's Poet Theater at Judson Memorial Church. Joseph Chaiken's Open Theater evolved from Julian Beck's Living Theater.

Edward Albee's plays typified the theater of social protest in the sixties. Born in 1928, he was adopted at an early age by the scion of the Keith-Albee Vaudeville chain. Struggling against his heritage of adopted wealth, Albee wrestled with his conscience, disowned his family, and finally wrote the *Zoo Story*—about a man who never had anything. Albee wrote in the tradition of the angry young man and insisted that his spectators take a stand against the self-satisfaction of middle America. In *Who's Afraid of Virginia Woolf* and *Tiny Alice* he stripped the principal characters of their illusions. In the latter play Julian, a lay brother of the church, found himself abandoned by all who should have aided him in his search for faith. In 1967 Albee won the Pulitzer Prize for *A Delicate Balance*.

NEW PLAYWRIGHTS FOR OLD THEATERS

Neil Simon had a more engaging outlook on life and a talent for writing consecutive successes for the Broadway stage. In the seven years between 1961 and 1968, Simon wrote eight Broadway hits as well as several screen plays. In 1966–67 four of his productions ran concurrently on Broadway. Beginning in 1970, with the *Prisoner of Second Avenue*, his comic vision developed a more sombre tone. In his screen plays, *Murder by Death* and *The Goodbye Girl*, he revealed in comical and farcical situations a deep tragic view of the world.

In 1959 Lorraine Hansberry's *A Raisin in the Sun* assured black theater a place on Broadway. The production received the New York Drama Critics' award for the best American play of the year. Before that moment, generations of black playwrights had tried in vain to reach a public, since Mr. Brown's African Theater had staged the first black drama on record, *The Drama of King Shotaway* in 1823. Through the nineteenth century, the minstrel theater provided the major showcase for black talent. But no dramas by, about, or for blacks appeared in the standard theaters until the 1970s. Broadway produced Willis Richardson's *The Chipwoman's Fortune* in 1923, Garland Anderson's *Appearances* in 1925, and Wallace Thurman's *Harlem* in 1929. But Broadway audiences were predominantly white. In the 1920s black audiences attended either the Lafayette Theater or the 63rd Street Theater in New York and the Pekin Theater in Chicago.

In the 1930s the Federal Theater Project had supported organizations devoted to the encouragement of black playwrights, the American Negro Theater, the Negro Playwrights' Company, the Harlem Showcase, and the Negro Drama Group. But with the advent of civil rights legislation in the 1950s, a new generation of black writers appeared. Prominent black playwrights of the fifties were

Alice Childress, William Brand, Ossie Davis, Lofton Mitchell, and Louis Peterson. Langston Hughes' play *Mulatto*, which had opened on Broadway in 1935, dealt with problems of miscegenation and with the futility of trusting white men. In 1964 Leroi Jones (Imamu Amuri Baraka) treated the same problems in *Dutchman*. Jones made the most forceful statement in the mid-sixties of the difficulties of being a black man in America.

PLAYWRIGHTS OF THE OFF OFF-BROADWAY THEATER

In 1960 the Off Off-Broadway theater presented the same benefits to its backers as the Off-Broadway house had in 1952. New playwrights, no censorship, no commercial pressures, free experimentation, low (sometimes nonexistent) budgets, were the ingredients of success. Along with the theaters came a number of experimental actors' workshops, principally Joseph Chaiken's Open Theater, Richard Schechner's Performance Group, and Andre Gregory's Manhattan Project. Among the best productions of the period was van Itallie's *America Hurrah*, which opened at the La Mama Theater on April 28, 1965. The Pocket Theater staged a production the following November, directed by Chaiken and performed by members of his Open Theater. Other important productions of the period were Paul Foster's *Balls* (1964), Sam Shepard's *Chicago* (1965), Lanford Wilson's *The Madness of Lady Bright* (1966), Megan Terry's *Calm Down Mother* (1966), and Frank O'Hara's *The General Returns from One Place to Another* (1966). The Open Theater's work with improvisational acting and writing techniques resulted in the creation of *The Serpent* by van Itallie. It premiered in Rome at the Teatro dell'Arte in May, 1968. Productions of *The Serpent* toured Western Europe, bringing a new awareness of what was novel and experimental in America.

TEATRO CAMPESINO AND THIRD WORLD ALLIANCES

Among the most promising indigenous theaters to emerge in the 1960s was the Teatro Campesino of Luis Valdes. It originated in San Juan Batista at the height of the 1965 California grape-pickers' strike. With it, the Farm-Workers' Union organizers created a living drama for the *gente*, the grape-pickers, to persuade them to join the strike for economic and human rights. By 1968 the Teatro Campesino had expanded its campaign to include resistence to the Vietnam War. The leaders of the theater continued to educate the poor, producing *actos* (one-act teaching plays) on such varied subjects as drugs, Chicano identity, and history. By 1970 the Teatro Campesino had expanded to become El Centro Campesino Cultural, with elaborate facilities for films, publications, and videotapes.

Most of the productions of the Teatro Campesino were improvised from the lives of the actors themselves. Valdes sought to create a theater that might serve as an instrument to develop a Chicano consciousness through ritual, music, and spiritual rebirth. Some groups like El Teatro Bilingue, worked with established scripts on more sophisticated levels and offered training for actors, writers, and stage technicians in Spanish drama.

In the 1970s pressures for similar achievements came from womens' rights groups. Plays by women, for women, and about women remained in vogue through the seventies. Among the more prominent groups were The New York Feminist Theater Troupe of Claudette Charbonneau, Sue Perlgut's It's All Right to Be a Woman Theater, and Roberta Sklar's Women's Limit and Womanrite Theater. The New York Feminist Theater adopted a conservative "complete script" approach to analyzing the sexist values of lower and middle America. Other women's companies worked from improvisational materials, seeking ways to break down the "housewife" stereotype of commercial theater. Frequently women's consciousness-raising discussions followed performances, during which spectators were encouraged to explore their own feelings.

VIETNAM AND BEYOND

The Vietnam War spawned a number of new-left theater troupes in the United States. Among the best was Peter Schumann's Bread and Puppet Theater. Schumann's company was created in imitation of a Sicilian puppet theater in New York's "Little Italy." Designed to appeal to "street people," the group quickly developed a rhetorical, new-left image. The main goal of the company was to evoke, via performance, a direct emotional response to problems of the day—

the Vietnam War, urban society, and social violence. Unlike most *agit-prop* groups, the Bread and Puppet Theater maintained its integrity, preferring to use their art to communicate with people. Julian Beck's Living Theater decided, on the contrary, that political activity was more important. The Living Theater spent the last year of the 1960s in Paris, where Beck divided his troupe into four cells: Paris, London, Berlin, and India. Beck went to Brazil, where he was imprisoned for political activity. The Living Theater returned in the 1970s to the Brooklyn Academy of Music.

With the end of the Vietnam War most new-left groups vanished. Other troupes, like the Mabou Mimes and the San Francisco Mime Troupe, found new directions.

THE LEGACY OF STANISLAVSKY

If new American playwrights and directors in the seventies seemed to evidence a dramatic renaissance, acting styles in the established theaters remained traditional. The legacy of Stanislavsky's method approach to acting, adopted by the Group Theater in the 1930s, remained a vital force into the decade. Supporters of Stanislavsky's early period renewed the debate with those who advocated "the method of physical action" from his later work. Lee Strasberg and John Houseman defended the early method approach, while Sonia Moore, Stella Adler, and Robert Lewis advocated the later, physical approach.

GROTOWSKI—MAN OF PAST AND FUTURE

A prominent acting theoretician of the 1960s and 1970s, whose work had world-wide influence, was Jerzy Grotowski. Born August 11, 1933, in Poland, Grotowski spent his early years in Krakow, where he trained as an actor in Stanislavsky's principles. During that time he visited Egypt, Paris, Moscow, and the Middle East on government grants. In 1955 he studied Sanskrit and Oriental philosophy in central Asia. He established himself at the 1966 Festival of Theaters in Paris with his production of Calderón's *The Constant Prince*. Grotowski appeared briefly in New York in 1969 and brought his troupe to the Brooklyn Academy of Music in 1972. A permanent research theater was set up for him at the University of Wroclaw, Poland, in 1975.

Grotowski's acting style was eclectic. Like Artaud he saw himself as a priest of the theater, who struggled to escape its facile interpretations. Like Brecht he sought a people's theater, a "poor theater," stripped of all illusions of the media age. Grotowski staged productions sparsely. He asked his actors to create their theater within themselves, to become, in his own word, "transluminous." Between 1961 and 1965 Grotowski staged *Cain, Shakuntula, Akropolis, Hamlet, Doctor Faustus*, and *The Constant Prince*. Later he abandoned texts for improvisational works that included spectators in the process of artistic creation.

WHITHER A UNIVERSITY THEATER?

One original American contribution to theater in this century was the development of dramatic studies and production techniques in the colleges and universities. Since Professor Baker's days at Harvard and Yale the university theater grew to such an extent that in the mid-1950s there were three hundred and twenty institutions at which students could study theater arts. By the late 1970s the American Theater Association listed over fifteen hundred directors or chairmen of theater programs in Canada and the United States, with an estimated 5,180 members.

Beyond building up a new audience of critical playgoers and training theater workers, the universities did much to fill the void left by the collapse of a national touring system. In 1978 the American Theater Association issued uniform standards for forty institutions offering higher degrees in theater arts. Central to the report was the concept of the producing theater as a laboratory for theater studies.

TOWARD A FEDERATION OF NATIONAL THEATERS

Regional theater revived after World War II under LORT, the League of Regional Theaters. In its first years there were as many failures as successes. Most institutions developed grass roots support and survived on subscription series, private and public gifts, state and local tax moneys, and perseverence. Among the best regional theaters were the Actors' Conservatory Theater (ACT) in San Francisco, the Guthrie Theater in Minneapolis, the Houston Alley Theater, the Ashland Shakespeare Festival, and the Canadian Stratford Shakespeare Festival. The Mark Taper Theater in Los Angeles, the Arena Stage in Washington, D.C., and the Long Wharf Theater in New Haven attested to the fact that in the late 1970s playwrights made more money from plays produced outside New York than within its precincts. Regional theaters' demands for new scripts was such that some companies had to share new productions, while other professional theater companies attached themselves to universities like Yale, Princeton, and Michigan.

The diversity and integrity of regional professional theaters (both profit and nonprofit) made it unlikely that any single theater would dominate. The idea was proposed that a number of centers could be created within regions of the country, where the finest professional actors, directors, scene designers, and theater technicians could develop playwrights and facilities for a National Federation of Theaters.

THE "FABULOUS INVALID"

Through a hundred centuries theater has never died. *The* theater—the theater of good plays and good performances—came and went, expired and was revived. Like its special god, Dionysus, its body was destroyed and its limbs scattered. But because of its divinity it will always be reborn. The history of the living stage proves the eternal vitality of the "fabulous invalid." There may well be among us a new Euripides, Shakespeare, Molière, Ibsen, or Brecht, to make the twenty-first century a new Golden Age of the Theater.

BIBLIOGRAPHY

The select list of paperbacks is mainly compiled from R.R. Bowker Company's *Paperback Books In Print* (1977), which should be consulted for additional titles.

CHAPTER 1: GREECE AND ROME

GOLDEN, LEON, trans., *Aristocle's Poetics*, Englewood Cliffs, N.J.: Prentice-Hall, Inc., 1968.

HAMILTON, EDITH, *The Greek Way to Western Civilization*, New American Library of World Literature, Inc., New York.

JONES, JOHN, *On Aristotle and Greek Tragedy*, Oxford: Oxford University Press, 1968.

KITTO, H.D., *Greek Tragedy*, 3rd ed. rev., New York: Doubleday & Company, Inc., 1966.

KOTT, JAN, *Eating of the Gods*, New York: Random House, Inc., 1974.

MCLEISH, KENNETH, *Greek Theater*, New York: Bantam Books, Inc., 1972.

CHAPTER 2: MIDDLE AGES

GASSNER, JOHN, *Medieval and Tudor Drama*, New York: Bantam Books, Inc., 1963.

KOLVE, V. A., *A Play Called Corpus Christi*, Stanford: Stanford University Press, 1966.

NELSON, ALAN H. and JEROME, TAYLOR, eds., *Essays Critical and Contextual*, Chicago: University of Chicago Press, 1972.

ROSE, MARTIAL, *The Wakefield Mystery Plays*, Garden City: Doubleday & Company, Inc. 1962, reprinted 1969.

SOUTHERN, RICHARD W., *The Making of the Middle Ages*, New Haven: Yale University Press, 1966.

CHAPTER 3: RENAISSANCE ITALY

BURCKHARDT, JAKOB, *The Civilization of the Renaissance in Italy*, New York: New American Library, 1950.

BURROUGHS, BETTY, *Vasari's Lives of the Artists*, New York: Simon and Schuster, Inc., 1967.

DUCHARTRE, PIERRE LOUIS, *The Italian Comedy*, New York: Dover Publications, Inc., 1966.

HERRICK, ROBERT, *Italian Comedy in the Renaissance*, New York: E.P. Dutton & Co., Inc., 1966.

SYPHER, WYLIE, *Four Stages of Renaissance Style*, New York: Doubleday & Company, Inc., 1955.

CHAPTER 4: SPAIN'S GOLDEN AGE

BENTLEY, ERIC, ed., *The Classic Theatre*, Vol. III, New York: Doubleday & Company, Inc., 1959.

RENNERT, HUGO, *The Spanish Stage in the Time of Lope De Vega*, New York: Dover Publications, Inc., 1963.

WILSON, MARGARET, *Spanish Drama of the Golden Age*, New York: Pergamon Press, Inc., 1969.

CHAPTER 5: ELIZABETHAN ENGLAND

CHUTE, MARCHETTE, *Shakespeare of London*, New York: E. P. Dutton & Co., Inc., 1956.

EVANS, G. BLAKEMORE, ed., *Shakespeare's Prompt-Books of the Seventeenth Century*, 5 vols. Charlottesville: University of Virginia Press, 1970.

HARRISON, GEORGE, *Elizabethan Plays And Players*, Ann Arbor: University of Michigan Press, 1956.

NAGLER, A. M., *Shakespeare's Stage*, New York: Dover Publications, Inc., 1977.

WILSON, JOHN D., *Life In Shakespeare's England*, Baltimore: Penguin Books, Inc., 1976.

CHAPTER 6: BAROQUE FRANCE

BARTHES, ROLAND, *On Racine*, New York: Hill & Wang Inc., 1964.

GILBERT, STUART, trans., Alexis De Tocqueville, *The Old Regime and the French Revolution*, New York: Doubleday & Company, Inc., 1958.

LEWIS, W. H., *The Splendid Century. Life in the France of Louis XIV*, New York: Doubleday & Company, Inc., 1957.

MOORE, W. G., *Molière. A New Criticism*, New York: Doubleday & Company, Inc., 1962.

CHAPTER 7: THE NINETEENTH CENTURY

BENTLEY, ERIC, *Bernard Shaw*, New York: W. W. Norton & Company, Inc., 1976.

DARWIN, CHARLES, *The Origin Of Species*, New York: W. W. Norton & Company, Inc., 1975.

LE GALLIENNE, EVA, *Mystic in the Theater: Eleonora Duse*, S. Carbondale: S. Illinois University Press, 1973.

MILLER, PERRY, *Life of the Mind in America from the Revolution to the Civil War*, New York: Harcourt, Brace Jovanovich, Inc., 1970.

MUELLER, CARL, *Büchner. Complete Plays and Prose*, New York: Hill & Wang Inc., 1963.

NAGLER, A. M., *A Source Book in Theatrical History*, New York: Dover Publications Inc., reprint 1977.

TAYLOR, JOHN, *The Rise and Fall of the Well-Made Play*, New York: Hill & Wang Inc., 1967.

CHAPTER 8: THE COMING OF REALISM

HEWITT, BARNARD, *History of the Theater: From 1800 to the Present*, New York: Random House, Inc., 1970.

CHAPTER 9: FROM STRINDBERG TO BRECHT

BENTLEY, ERIC, *Theater of War. Modern Drama From Ibsen To Brecht*, New York: The Viking Press, Inc., 1973.

BRECHT, BERTOLT, *Brecht on Theater*, New York: Hill & Wang Inc., 1964.

ESSLIN, MARTIN, *Brecht: A Collection of Critical Essays*, Englewood Cliffs, N.J.: Prentice-Hall, Inc., 1962.

SPRIGGE, ELIZABETH, trans., *Life of August Strindberg*, New York: Doubleday & Company, Inc., 1955.

VÖLKER, KLAUS, *Brecht Chronicle*, New York: Academic Press, Inc., 1975.

CHAPTER 10: THEATER OF TODAY

ARTAUD, ANTONIN, trans. M. C. Richards, *The Theater and Its Double*, New York: Grove Press, Inc., 1958.

BENEDIKT, MICHAEL and GEORGE WELLWARTH, eds., *Modern French Theater: The Avant-Garde, Dada, and Surrealism*, New York: E. P. Dutton & Co., Inc., 1964.

BENTLEY, ERIC, *The Theory of the Modern Stage*, New York: Penguin Books, Inc., 1976.

BRUSTEIN, ROBERT, *The Theater of Revolt*, Boston: Little, Brown & Company, Inc., 1964.

CLURMAN, HAROLD, *The Fervent Years: The Story of the Group Theater in The 1930's*, New York: Harcourt, Brace Jovanovich, Inc., 1957.

ESSLIN, MARTIN, *The Theater of the Absurd*, London: Doubleday & Company, Inc., 1968.

GROTOWSKI, JERZY, *Towards a Poor Theater*, New York: Simon & Schuster, Inc., 1968.

INNES, C. D., *Erwin Piscator's Political Theater*, New York: Columbia University Press, 1977.

MEYERHOLD, VSEVOLAD, ed. Edward Braun, *Meyerhold on Theater*, New York: Hill & Wang, Inc., 1969.

SOKEL, WALTER, *The Writer in Extremis*, New York: McGraw-Hill Book Co., 1964.

WELLWARTH, GEORGE, *German Drama Between the Wars*, New York: E. P. Dutton & Co., Inc., 1974.

INDEX

Abbey Theater, Dublin, 195, 204–5, 247, 249
Abbott, George, 212
Abercrombie, Lascelles, 247
Absurdist drama, 258–63
Actors:
  commedia dell'arte, 67–70; in Dark Ages, 29;
  Elizabethan, 103–4, 132–38; emergence of pro-
  fessional, 42–43; Greek, 5, 10–11; nineteenth
  century, 165–66, 169, 178–82; in passion plays,
  39; realism and, 187; Roman, 11; Spanish,
  88–89
Actors' Conservatory Theater (ACT), San
  Francisco, 275
Adamov, Arthur, 262
Adams, Maude, 231
Adding Machine, The (Rice), 211, 213
Adler, Stella, 252, 273
Admirable Crichton, The (Barrie), 207
Adrienne Lecouvreur (Scribe), 174
Aeneid, The (Virgil), 101
Aeschylus, 1, 6, 7, 10, 11, 20, 21, 23–25, 255
Affected Ladies, The (Molière), 152
Agamemnon (Aeschylus), 7, 11, 24
Aiglon, L' (Rostand), 231
Akins, Zoë, 211
Alarcón, Pedro Antonio de, 147
Albee, Edward, 237, 260, 268–70
Alchemist, The (Jonson), 108
Aleichem, Sholem, 231
Aleotti, Giambattista, 54
Alexander, George, 207
Alexandre le Grand (Racine), 148
Allegory, 99–100

Alleyn, Edward, 117, 119, 134, 137–38
Alley Theater, Houston, 275
All's Well That Ends Well (Shakespeare), 71
Amalarius, Bishop of Metz, 30
Ambush (Richman), 211, 213
America Hurrah (Van Itallie), 271
American Laboratory Theater, 252
American Negro Theater, 270
American theater, 208–13, 250–56, 267–73
American Theater Association, 212–13, 274
Aminta (Tasso), 63
Amoureuse, L' (Porto-Riche), 188, 189
Amphitruo (Plautus), 49, 51
Amphitryon (Molière), 155
Amphitryon 38 (Giraudoux), 234, 251
Anatol (Schnitzler), 193
Anatomist, The (Bridie), 247
Anaxagoras, 3
Anderson, Garland, 270
Anderson, Maxwell, 213, 252
Andreyev, Leonid, 230, 235
Androcles and the Lion (Shaw), 208
Andromaque (Racine), 148, 149
Anna Christie (O'Neill), 212, 213
Anne, Queen of James I, 130, 138–39, 140
Anouilh, Jean, 215, 234, 235
Ansky, Solomon, 231
Antoine, André, 179, 185–89, 195, 201, 216, 232
Antonelli, Luigi, 236
Antonio's Revenge (Marston), 107
Antony and Cleopatra (Shakespeare), 125
Anzengruber, Ludwig, 179, 192
Apollinaire, Guillaume, 240, 242

Apology for Actors (Thomas Heywood), 124–25
Appearances (Anderson), 270
Appia, Adolphe, 64, 217–18, 220
Apuleius, 9–10
Aragon, Louis, 241
Archarnians, The (Aristophanes), 21
Archer, Williams, 194, 266
Architettura (Serlio), 57–58
Arclight, 171
Arden, John, 256, 257
Arena Stage, Washington, 275
Arent, Arthur, 253
Arion, 5
Ariosto, Lodovico, 50, 55, 64, 65, 83
Aristophanes, 6, 10, 12, 21, 23, 25–26, 148, 259
Aristotle, 2–5, 20, 23, 46, 113, 146
Arkin, Alan, 268
Arliss, George, 210
Arms and the Man (Shaw), 205, 207
Arnold, Matthew, 172
Aron, Robert, 245
Aronson, Boris, 251
Arp, Hans, 259
Arrabal, Fernando, 260, 263
Artaud, Antonin, 243, 244–47, 259, 274
Art of the Theatre, The (Craig), 217, 218
Artsybashev, Michael, 230
As a Man Thinks (Thomas), 208
Ashcroft, Peggy, 249
Ashland Shakespeare Festival, Oregon, 275
Assomoir, L' (Zola), 177
Atellanae farces, 20
Athalie (Racine), 148
Athens, 3, 6–8
Augier, Émile, 176–77, 178
Austrian theater, 178–80, 193–94
Autores de comedias, 81
Autos sacramentales, 37–38, 74–79, 83
Avendaño, Francisco de, 94
Awakening of Spring, The (Wedekind), 193, 222–23

Baal (Brecht), 237
Babberger, Ludwig, 225
Baclanova, Olga, 200
Bacon, Francis, 139
Bahr, Hermann, 192, 194
Baker, George Pierce, 212
Bakst, Leon, 61, 228
Balcony, The (Genet), 263, 269
Bald Soprano, The (Ionesco), 260
Bale, John, 104
Balieff, Nikita, 202
Balls (Foster), 271
Balzac, Honoré de, 175, 178
Bancroft, Squire, 168, 171
Bankrupt, The (Ostrovsky), 175
Bankruptcy, A (Björnson), 195
Barbazon Theater complex, London, 265–66
Barber of Seville, The (Rossini), 69
Baroque theater (France), 141–59
  Comédie-Française, 157, 158–59; comedy-ballets, 154–55, 156; court theater, 144–45; machine plays, 147, 155; monopoly, 142–44, 158; playhouses, 157; playwrights, 145–57; scenery, 157–58
Barrault, Jean-Louis, 234, 247, 258, 260, 264
Barrès, Maurice, 242

Barrie, J. M., 207, 209
Barry, Philip, 212, 213, 252
Barrymore, John, 210
Bartholomew Fair (Jonson), 108
Bassermann, Albert, 180, 191
Bataille, Henri, 188, 189
Bates, Blanche, 210
Battle of Arminius, The (Kleist), 164
Baylis, Lilian, 248, 249
Beaumont, Francis, 106, 109
Beaver Coat, The (Hauptmann), 192
Beck, Julian, 269, 273
Beckett, Samuel, 237, 259–63
Becque, Henri, 177–78, 188, 204
Before Sunrise (Hauptmann), 190, 192
Beggar, The (Sorge), 226
Beggar's Opera, The (Gay), 248
Behan, Brendan, 256, 257
Behrman, S. N., 212, 213, 252
Belasco, David, 209–10
Bell Geddes, Norman, 223, 250, 251
Benavente, Jacinto, 204, 214
Berliner Ensemble, 238
Bernard, Jean Jacques, 188
Bernhardt, Sarah, 174, 179, 231
Berrigan, Daniel, 264
Betterton, Thomas, 248
Beyond Human Power (Björnson), 196
Beyond the Horizon (O'Neill), 212, 213, 255
Birdie, James, 247
Birthday Party, The (Pinter), 257
Björnson, Björnstjerne, 187, 195–97, 204
Blackfriars Theater, London, 119, 129
Black playwrights, 269, 270–71
Blacks, The (Genet), 263, 269
Blanchette (Brieux), 187
Blank verse, 101, 105
Blin, Roger, 247, 261, 264
Blinn, Holbrook, 210
Blithe Spirit (Coward), 249
Blok, Alexander, 230
Blood Wedding (Garcia Lorca), 214, 244
Blue Bird, The (Maeterlinck), 215, 233
Boccaccio, Giovanni, 45, 64
Boleslavsky, Richard, 200, 252
Bolt, Robert, 267
Bond, Edward, 267
Bondone, Giotto di, 28
Bonds of Interest, The (Benavente), 214
Bores, The (Molière), 155
Boucicault, Dion, 168, 171–72, 209
Bourdet, Edouard, 215
Bourgeois gentilhomme, Le (Molière), 155, 156
Box-sets, 168–69, 209, 216
Boyer, Charles, 210
Boy players, 102–3, 136–37
Brahm, Otto, 190–92, 195, 210, 222
Bramante, 57
Brand, Fritz, 222
Brand, William, 271
Brand (Ibsen), 196
Brazen Age, The (Thomas Heywood), 125
Bread and Puppet Theater, 272–73
Breasts of Teiresias, The (Apollinaire), 240, 242
Brecht, Bertolt, 226, 235, 237–38, 259, 265, 268, 274
Breton, André, 241–44
Bride of Messina, The (Schiller), 163
Brieux, Eugène, 187–88, 204
Brighouse, Harold, 206

Brody, Alexander, 214
Broken Pitcher, The (Kleist), 164
Bromberg, J. Edward, 252
Brook, Peter, 245, 264–65
Brunelleschi, Filippo, 57
Büchner, Georg, 174–76, 224, 259
Bulgakov, Leo, 200
Buñuel, Luis, 244
Buontalenti, Bernardo, 62
Burbage, Cuthbert, 117, 135
Burbage, James, 103–4, 112, 117–20, 127
Burbage, Richard, 104, 117, 134, 135, 137–38
Burckhardt, Jakob, 46
Business is Business (Mirbeau), 189

Caesar and Cleopatra (Shaw), 208
Cagney, James, 210
Cailleau, Hubert, 37–38
Calderona, La, 89
Calderón de la Barca, Pedro, 43, 75, 84, 91, 93, 150, 164, 194, 224, 273
Callot, Jacques, 70
Calm Down Mother (Terry), 271
Camerata of Florence, 63
Camille (Dumas fils), 175–77
Camus, Albert, 257–59
Candida (Shaw), 207
Candidat, Le (Flaubert), 177
Capek, Josef, 226
Capek, Karel, 226, 248
Captive, The (Bourdet), 215
Cardenio (Fletcher), 109
Caretaker, The (Pinter), 257
Carmine, Al, 269
Carnovsky, Morris, 252
Carroll, Paul Vincent, 206
Carros, 75–76
Carthagenian, The (Plautus), 51
Casella, Alberto, 236
Castle of Perseverance, The, 40
Castro, Guillén de, 93
Cathleen ni Houlihan (Yeats), 206
Caucasian Chalk Circle, The (Brecht), 237
Cavalcade (Coward), 208
Censorship, 117, 190
Cervantes, Miguel de, 77–78, 81–82, 84, 87, 90–91, 94, 150
Chaiken, Joseph, 269, 271
Chairs, The (Ionesco), 260, 262
Chambers, E. K., 34
Chance de Françoise, La (Porto-Riche), 188, 189
Chantecler (Rostand), 231
Chapman, George, 107, 108
Charbonneau, Claudette, 272
Charles I, King of England, 134, 138
Charles II, King of England, 127
Charles III, King of England, 79
Charles V, Holy Roman Emperor, 73
Charles VI, King of France, 43
Chekhov, Anton, 175, 199, 200, 202, 203, 259
Chekhov, Michael, 202, 228
Cherry Orchard, The (Chekhov), 202
Chester Cycle, 36
Chiarelli, Luigi, 236
Chief Thing, The (Evreinov), 230
Chicago (Shepard), 271
Chicken Soup with Barley (Wesker), 256
Children's Hour, The (Hellman), 213
Childress, Alice, 271

Chipwoman's Fortune, The (Richardson), 270
Chorus, 5, 10, 22–23, 114
Chronicle plays, 104, 107
Cid, Le (Corneille), 93, 147, 148, 149
Cinna (Corneille), 147
Circle, The (Maugham), 208
City Dionysia, 6–7
Civic Repertory Theater, 250
Clairon, Mlle. (Claire Léris), 166
Clan, A (Unruh), 226
Claudel, Paul, 232, 233
Clement V, Pope, 34
Clitandre (Corneille), 147
Clouds, The (Aristophanes), 12, 21, 26
Clurman, Harold, 252
Cockpit Theater, London, 119
Cocktail Party, The (Eliot), 256
Cocteau, Jean, 215, 234, 235, 248
Cogo, Nicollo del, 51
Cohen, Gustave, 38
Coleridge, Samuel Taylor, 165
Coliseo, Seville, 88
Colleen Bawn, The (Boucicault), 172
Comedias de santos, 79–83, 84, 93
Comédie-Française, 157, 158–59, 234, 235
Comédiens Ordinaires du Roi (Troupe Royale), 43, 144, 145, 158
Comedies and Proverbs (Musset), 165
Comedy-ballets, 154–55, 156
Comedy of Errors, The (Shakespeare), 71, 110, 113
Commedia all'improviso, 67
Commedia a soggetto, 67
Commedia dell'arte, 26, 67–71, 81, 84–85
Comrades (Strindberg), 198
Concert, The (Bahr), 194
Condell, Henry, 112, 137
Condemned of Altona, The (Sartre), 258
Confrérie de la Passion, 43, 141, 143–44
Connection, The (Gelber), 269
Connelly, Marc, 213
Cons, Miss, 248
Constant Prince, The (Calderón de la Barca), 273
Constant Wife, The (Maugham), 208
Conti, Prince de, 150, 151
Contractor, The (Storey), 267
Cooke, Ralph, 269
Copeau, Jacques, 233–34, 250, 264
Coquelin, Benoit Constant, 179, 231
Coriolanus (Shakespeare), 167
Corneille, Pierre, 43, 91, 93, 145, 146–51
Cornell, Katharine, 210
Corpus Christi festival, 34–36
Corral de la Pacheca, Madrid, 88
Corrales, 85–87, 89, 119
Costumes:
    Elizabethan, 131–32, 140; Greek, 12–13; nineteenth century, 166–67, 169; in Spain, 89
Council of Trent, 41–42
Counsellor-at-Law (Rice), 208
Court masques, 63
Coward, Noel, 208, 209, 249
Cradle Song (Martinez Sierra), 214
Craig, Edward Gordon, 64, 192, 217–20
Craig, Hardin, 34, 35
Craig's Wife (Kelly), 213
Crawford, Cheryl, 252
Creditors (Strindberg), 198
Crommelynck, Fernand, 229, 232

Cromwell, Oliver, 140
Cromwell (Hugo), 164
Cueva, Juan de la, 80, 81
Curel, François de, 187, 188
Curtain, The, 118, 119
Curtains, 61, 139, 170
Cycle plays, 28, 34–36, 39
Cyrano de Bergerac (Rostand), 215, 231

Dadaism, 241–43
Dafne, 63
Dali, Salvadore, 244
Daly, Arnold, 208
Damaged Goods (Brieux), 187–88
Damon and Pythias (Edwardes), 103
Dance of Death, The (Strindberg), 198
Dangerous Corner (Priestley), 247
D'Annunzio, Gabriele, 215, 232, 235–36
Dante Alighieri, 28, 45, 64
Danton's Death (Büchner), 174
Darwin, Charles, 173
Daudet, Alphonse, 177
Daughter of Jorio, The (D'Annunzio), 215, 236
D'Avenant, William, 106, 140
Davis, Ossie, 271
Davis, Owen, 213
Day in the Life of Joe Egg, A (Nichols), 267
Days Without End (O'Neill), 255
Dead City, The (D'Annunzio), 236
De Architectura (Vitruvius), 13, 52, 57
Death Takes a Holiday (Casella), 236
Deathwatch (Genet), 263
Deburau, 179
Decameron (Boccaccio), 28
Dekker, Thomas, 48, 106, 107
Delaney, Shelagh, 256, 257
Delicate Balance, A (Albee), 270
Demi-monde, Le (Dumas fils), 176
Dépit amoureux, Le (Molière), 151, 152
Deputy, The (Hochhuth), 264
Design for Living (Coward), 208
Desire Under The Elms (O'Neill), 254, 255
Desnos, Robert, 243
Detour, The (Davis), 213
Deutsches Theater, Berlin, 190, 222
Devil's Disciple, The (Shaw), 207
Devine, George, 256
Devrient, Ludwig, 180
Dhomme, Sylvain, 264
Diderot, Denis, 166
Difficult Age, The (Donnay), 189
Dionysus, 4–8, 41
Directors, 209–10, 264–65
Dirty Linen (Stoppard), 267
Dithyramb, 5
Ditrichstein, Leo, 210
Divine Comedy (Dante Alighieri), 28, 45
Divino Orfeo, El, 76
Docteur amoureux, Le (Molière), 152
Doctor Faustus (Marlowe), 105, 113, 125
Dr. Knock (Romains), 234
Doctor's Dilemma, The (Shaw), 209
Documentary drama, 263–64
Doll's House, A (Ibsen), 177, 197
Doña Diana (Calderón de la Barca), 93
Don Carlos (Schiller), 163
Don Fernando (Maugham), 92–93
Don Garcie (Molière), 155–56
Donnay, Maurice, 188, 189
Donogoo (Romains), 234

Don Quixote (Cervantes), 91
Double Suicide, The (Anzengruber), 179, 191
Dreaming Is Life (Grillparzer), 164
Dream Play (Strindberg), 198, 243, 245
Dreiser, Theodore, 212
Drums in the Night (Brecht), 226, 237
Duchess of Malfi, The (Webster), 107, 109, 127
Dulcy (Kaufman), 213
Dullin, Charles, 234, 244, 245, 247, 264
Dumas fils, 175–78
Dumas père, 164, 165
Dumbshows, 48, 101
Dumbwaiter, The (Pinter), 257
Dunlap, William, 211
Duse, Eleonora, 235–36
Dutchman (Jones), 271
Dybbuk, The (Ansky), 228, 231
Dynasts, The (Hardy), 247

Earth Spirit (Wedekind), 193
Easiest Way, The (Belasco), 209–10
Easter (Strindberg), 198
Eccyclema, 21, 22
Echegaray y Elzaguirre, José, 204, 214
Eden End (Priestley), 247
Edward I (Peele), 107
Edwardes, Richard, 103
Egloga de Fileno, Zambardo y Cardonio (Encina), 80
Egmont (Goethe), 163
Elevator stage, 222
Eliot, T. S., 247, 256
Elizabeth, Lady, 134
Elizabeth I, Queen of England, 63, 99, 101, 105, 116, 133, 138
Elizabethan Stage Society, 183, 201
Elizabethan theater, 42, 96–140
   actors, 103–4, 132–38; audiences, 126–27; censorship, 117; chronicle plays, 104, 107; costumes, 131–32, 140; court and, 101–3; economics of, 135; interludes, 99–100, 102; juvenile performances, 102–3, 129; language of, 100–101; masques, 138–40; monopoly, 117; playhouses, 116, 117–29, 183; playwrights, 105–15; private theaters, 127–29; repertory system, 132–33; scenery, 129–31, 139–40; at universities, 97, 99
Elizabeth the Queen (Anderson), 213
Eluard, Paul, 243
Emery, Gilbert, 213
Emperor and Galilean (Ibsen), 196
Emperor Jones, The (O'Neill), 213, 254
Empty Space, The (Brook), 265
Encina, Juan del, 80, 81
Endgame (Beckett), 262
End of the World, The (Abercrombie), 247
Endymion (Lyly), 103
English theater, 36, 37, 40, 42, 194–95, 206–8, 217–21, 247–49, 256–57, 259, 264–67 (*see also* Elizabethan theater)
Enough Stupidity in Every Wise Man (Ostrovsky), 175
Entertainer, The (Osborne), 256
Entertaining Mr. Sloane (Orton), 267
Entremeses, 78–79, 90, 91
Entries, 47–48
Epernon, Duc d', 150
Epicoene, or the Silent Woman (Jonson), 108
Epigenes, 5
Epilog, 114

Equus (Shaffer), 3, 267
Erdgeist (Wedekind), 222
Ernst, Max, 241
Ervine, St. John, 206
Escape (Galsworthy), 208
Esslin, Martin, 238
Este, Ercole d', Duke of Ferrara, 47, 49, 50, 51, 52, 61, 63, 66
Esther (Racine), 148
Etourdi, L (Molière), 151, 152
Eugene O'Neill Playwriting Center, Province-town, 212
Eumenides, The (Aeschylus), 7, 12
Euripides, 1, 6, 7, 11, 21, 23–25, 224
Evans, Edith, 248–49
Everyman, 40, 184, 194, 224
Every Man in His Humor (Jonson), 125
Evreinov, Nikolai, 230, 235
Existentialism, 257–58
Expressionism, 197, 199, 215, 224–27
Exter, Alexandra, 228

Fabula togata, 20
Failures, The (Lenormand), 234
Faithful Shepherd, The (Guarini), 63
Faith Healer, The (Sheldon), 208
Falk, August, 198
Falling Leaves (Giacosa), 215
Familie Selicke, Die (Holz and Schlaf), 190
Farce plays, 39–40
Farrant, Richard, 102, 129
Fata Morgana (Vajda), 214
Father, The (Strindberg), 191, 198
Faust (Goethe), 163, 224
Favola di Orfeo, La (Politian), 47
Fay brothers, 205
Fechter, Charles, 169–70
Federal Theater Project, 251–53, 270
Fédora (Sardou), 174
Festin de Pierre, Les (Molière), 154
Feuchtwanger, Lion, 237
Finney, Albert, 266
Fiske, Minnie Maddern, 208
Fitch, Clyde, 208, 211
Fitzgerald, Edward, 93
Five Finger Exercise (Shaffer), 267
Flanagan, Hallie, 252
Flaubert, Gustave, 177
Fletcher, John, 106, 109
Flies, The (Sartre), 234, 258
Florian Geyer (Hauptmann), 192
Fontanne, Lynn, 210
Fort, Paul, 232
Fortune Theater, London, 119, 123–25, 132, 140
Fossils, The (Curel), 188
Foster, Paul, 269, 271
Fouquet, Nicolas, 155
France, Anatole, 250, 251
Francesca da Rimini (D'Annunzio), 215
Francis I, King of France, 73
Freed, Donald, 264
Freie Bühne, Berlin, 190–91, 194, 201
Freie Volksbühne, Berlin, 191, 264
French theater, 37–38, 42–43, 175–78, 185–89, 215, 233–35, 240–44 (*see also* Baroque theater)
French Without Tears (Rattigan), 256
Freud, Sigmund, 243, 245
Frogs, The (Aristophanes), 26
From Morn to Midnight (Kaiser), 226

Fruits of Enlightenment, The (Tolstoy), 199, 203
Fry, Christopher, 64, 247, 256
Fulda, Ludwig, 193
Fulgens and Lucres, 99
Furtenbach, 58

Galileo (Brecht), 237
Galsworthy, John, 207, 208, 209
Gamblers, The (Gogol), 175
Game of Love and Death, The (Rolland), 234
Gammer Gurton's Needle, 100, 104
Ganassa, Alberto, 84, 88
Gaol Gate, The (Gregory), 206
Garcia Lorca, Federico, 214, 244
Garrick, David, 127, 248
Gas (Kaiser), 226
Gascoigne, George, 102
Gas Heart, The (Tzara), 242–43
Gaskell, William, 267
Gaslight, 170–71
Gate Theater, 248
Gauntlet, A (Björnson), 195
Gay, John, 248
Geistliche Spiele, 37
Gelber, Jack, 268, 269
General Returns from One Place to Another, The (O'Hara), 271
Genet, Jean, 260, 262–64, 269
Georges Dandin (Molière), 71, 156
Germanova, Maria, 200
German theater, 37, 161–64, 174–75, 189–93, 222–27, 241
Ghirlandajo, 57
Ghosts (Ibsen), 182, 186, 189, 190, 194, 197
Giacosa, Guiseppe, 215
Gielgud, John, 248, 249
Gioconda, La (D'Annunzio), 236
Giraudoux, Jean, 215, 234, 235
Glaspell, Susan, 212
Globe Theater, London, 112, 118, 119–20, 123, 127, 135, 136, 140
Goat Song, The (Werfel), 226
Godfrey, Peter, 248
Godwin, Edward, 218
Goethe, Johann Wolfgang von, 93, 162–63, 166, 168
Goetz von Berlichingen (Goethe), 162, 166
Gogol, Nikolai, 175, 201, 203, 229
Golden Ass, The (Apuleius), 9–10
Goldoni, Carlo, 71, 224
Goncourt, Edmond de, 173, 177, 178, 185, 191
Goncourt, Jules de, 173, 177, 185, 191
Gonzaga, Vespasiano, Duke of Mantua, 54
Goodbye Girl, The (Simon), 270
Good Companions, The (Priestley), 247
Gorboduc, or Ferrex and Porrex (Sackville and Norton), 100–101, 104, 114
Gorelik, Mordecai, 251
Gorky, Maxim, 199, 200, 203, 204, 222, 229, 250
Governor's Lady, The (Belasco), 210
Gozzi, Carlo, 71, 224
Gramatica, Emma, 236
Grand Guignol, 239–40
Granovsky, Alexander, 231
Granville-Barker, Harley, 195, 206–7, 250, 251, 266
Great Divide, The (Moody), 208, 211
Great God Brown, The (O'Neill), 255

Great World Theater, The (Calderón de la Barca), 93, 224
Greek theater, 1–27
  actors, 5, 10–11; chorus, 5, 10, 22–23; Dionysiac festivals, 6–8; dramatic origins, 5; forms of, 4; literary limitations, 22–23; masks and costumes, 11–13; playhouses, 2, 14–15; scenery, 20–22
Greek Way to Western Civiliaction, The (Hamilton), 25
Green, Paul, 212, 252
Green Cockatoo, The (Schnitzler), 194
Greene, Robert, 106, 107, 110
Green Pastures, The (Connelly), 213
Gregorian chant, 30, 31
Gregory, Andre, 271
Gregory, Lady Augusta, 204–6, 209, 247
Grein, J. T., 194–95
Griboyedov, Alexander, 175
Grillparzer, Franz, 93, 164, 165, 182, 224
Grotowski, Jerzy, 273–74
Group Theatre, 251–52, 273
Guardsman, The (Molnár), 215
Guarini, Battista, 63
Guénégaud Theater, Paris, 143, 157, 158
Guiness, Alec, 249
Guitry, Lucien, 179, 188
Guitry, Sacha, 179, 215
Gustavus Vasa (Strindberg), 198
Guthrie, Tyrone, 248, 249
Guthrie Theater, Minneapolis, 275
Gwyn, Nell, 127

Haase, Friedrich, 180
Habima, 228, 231
Hairy Ape, The (O'Neill), 254
Halbe, Max, 193
Halévy, Ludovic, 177
Hall, Peter, 256, 264–66
Halle, Adam de la, 39
Hamilton, Edith, 25
Hamlet (Shakespeare), 101, 103, 105, 107, 113, 114, 125, 127, 136, 183, 249
Hampden, Walter, 231
Hands Around (Schnitzler), 194
Hankin, St. John, 206
Hannele (Hauptmann), 186, 193, 232
Hannetons, Les (Brieux), 188
Hansberry, Lorraine, 270
Happy Days (Beckett), 262
Harden, Maximilian, 190
Hardison, O. B., 34
Hardy, Alexandre, 91, 143, 145–47, 150
Hardy, Thomas, 247
Harlem (Thurman), 270
Harlem Showcase, New York, 270
Harrigan, Edward, 211
Harris, Barbara, 268
Hartleben, Otto Erich, 193
Hartung, Gustav, 225
Hasenclever, Walter, 224–26, 235
Hasty Heart, The (Patrick), 213
Hathaway, Anne, 110
Hauptmann, Gerhart, 186, 187, 190–94, 204, 232, 248
Hayes, Helen, 210
Hebbel, Friedrich, 175, 176, 178, 263
Hedda Gabler (Ibsen), 197
Hegge Cycle, 36

Helen (Euripides), 25
Hellman, Lillian, 213
Heminge, John, 112, 137
Henriette Maréchal (Goncourt brothers), 177, 191
Henry IV (Pirandello), 236
Henry IV (Shakespeare), 169
Henry V (Shakespeare), 113, 114
Henry VI (Shakespeare), 104, 110
Henry VII, King of England, 42, 97, 99
Henry VIII, King of England, 97, 99, 138
Henry VIII (Shakespeare), 109, 169
Henslowe, Philip, 109, 110, 117–19, 121, 123, 131, 132, 134, 135, 138
Hepburn, Katharine, 210
Hernani (Hugo), 164
Herne, James A., 211
Hero, The (Emery), 213
Herodes und Mariamne (Hebbel), 175
Herodotus, 3
Hervieu, Paul, 189
He Who Gets Slapped (Andreyev), 230
Heyward, Dorothy, 213
Heyward, Du Bose, 213
Heywood, John, 39, 99, 104
Heywood, Thomas, 106, 107–8, 111, 124–25, 136, 137
Hindle Wakes (Houghton), 206
History of Spanish Literature (Ticknor), 76
Hobson's Choice (Brighouse), 206
Hochhuth, Rolf, 264
Hodges, C. Walter, 124
Hofmannsthal, Hugo von, 194, 232
Holiday (Barry), 213
Holz, Arno, 190
Home (Storey), 267
Homecoming, The (Pinter), 257
Honorable History of Friar Bacon and Friar Bungay, The (Greene), 107
Hope Theater, London, 118, 119, 121
Hôpital de la Trinité, Paris, 141–43
Hopkins, Arthur, 210
Hopkins, Harry, 252
Horace, 23, 113, 146
Horace (Corneille), 147
Horniman, A. E. F., 204–7
Hostage, The (Behan), 256
Hôtel de Bourgogne, Paris, 43, 141–43, 151, 153, 157, 158
Houghton, Stanley, 206
Houseman, John, 253, 273
House of Bernarda Alba, The (Garcia Lorca), 214, 244
Howard, Bronson, 211
Howard, Leslie, 210
Howard, Sidney, 211–13
Hoyt, Charles Hale, 211
Hroswitha, 49
Hughes, Langston, 271
Hugnet, Georges, 241
Hugo, Victor, 164–65
Hülsenbeck, Richard, 241
Humanism, 41, 46, 51, 99
Hungary, 214–15

Ibsen, Henrik, 172, 174, 176, 177, 185–87, 189, 191, 194–97, 199, 201, 232, 248, 250
Icebound (Davis), 213
Iceman Cometh, The (O'Neill), 255

Ideal Husband, An (Wilde), 207
Illegitimate Son, The (Dumas fils), 176
Illusion Comique, L' (Corneille), 147
Illustre Théâtre, Paris, 149, 151
Imaginary Invalid, The (Molière), 71, 149, 156
Immermann, Karl, 183
Importance of Being Earnest, The (Wilde), 207
Impromptu de Versailles, L' (Molière), 156
Inadmissible Evidence (Osborne), 257
Infernal Machine, The (Cocteau), 234
Incorporated Stage Society, London, 195, 201
Independent Theater Society, London, 194–95, 201
Innocent III, Pope, 41
Inquest (Freed), 264
Insect Comedy, The (Capek), 226
Inspector General, The (Gogol), 175, 229
Interludes, 37, 40, 99–100, 102
Intermezzi, 61–63
In the Matter of J. Robert Oppenheimer (Kipphardt), 264
Intimate Theater of Stockholm, 198
Introito, 80
Intruder, The (Maeterlinck), 232
Investigation, The (Weiss), 264
Ionesco, Eugene, 237, 260–64
Iphigenia (Goethe), 163
Ireland, 195, 204–6, 247, 249
Irish Literary Theater, 205
Irish National Theater Company, 205
Irish Players, 204–5
Irving, Henry, 61, 170, 171, 174, 182
Italian theater, 37, 42, 215, 235–36 (*see also* Renaissance theater)
It's All Right to Be a Woman Theater, 272

Jacobs, Sally, 265
James I, King of England, 63, 117, 134, 138
Janauschek, Fanny, 180
Jane Clegg (Ervine), 206
Jarry, Alfred, 239–40, 259, 262
Jessner, Leopold, 227
Jet of Blood (Artaud), 245
Jeu d'Adam (Play of Adam), 32–33
Jewish theaters, 231
Jocasta (Gascoigne), 102
Johan Johan (John Heywood), 39
John Ferguson (Ervine), 206
Jones, Henry Arthur, 207–9
Jones, Inigo, 63, 108, 130, 138–40
Jones, Leroi (Imamu Amuri Baraka), 271
Jones, Robert Edmond, 210, 250, 251, 254
Jonson, Ben, 48, 91, 103, 105, 106, 108–10, 125, 127, 137, 138, 140, 150
Josephine (Bahr), 194
Jouvet, Louis, 234, 245, 247, 264
Juan of Austria, Don, 89
Juarez and Maximilian (Werfel), 226
Judith (Hebbel), 175
Julius Caesar (Shakespeare), 105
Jumpers (Stoppard), 267
Jungle of the Cities (Brecht), 237
Juno and the Paycock (O'Casey), 206, 249
Justice (Galsworthy), 208
Justinian the Great, Emperor, 29
Juvenile performances, 102–3, 129

Kabale und Liebe (Schiller), 163, 192
Kachalov, Vasili, 200

Kafka, Franz, 259, 260
Kahn, Otto, 233
Kainz, Joseph, 180, 190, 191
Kaiser, Georg, 226, 235, 248, 250
Kamerny Theater, Russia, 228
Kammerspiele, Berlin, 222–23
Kazan, Elia, 210, 252
Kean, Charles, 169, 172, 180, 182
Kean, Edmund, 165, 166, 169
Keane, Doris, 208
Keats, John, 108
Kelly, George, 213
Kemble, Charles, 165, 167
Kemble, Fanny, 165
Kemble, John Philip, 165
Kempe, Will, 133, 137
Kernodle, George, 28, 40
Kierkegaard, Søren, 257
Kingdom of God, The (Martinez Sierra), 214
King Hunger (Andreyev), 230
King John (Shakespeare), 167, 169
King Lear (Shakespeare), 114
Kingsley, Sidney, 213
King Ubu (Jarry), 239–40
Kipphardt, Heinar, 264
Kiss for Cinderella, A (Barrie), 207
Kleist, Heinrich von, 164, 165, 224
Knight of the Burning Pestle, The (Beaumont), 109
Knipper, Olga, 200
Knowles, James Sheridan, 165, 209
Know Thyself (Hervieu), 189
Koch, Frederick, 212
Koch, Gottfried, 166
Kokoschka, Oscar, 241
Kolve, V. A., 34–35
Kopit, Arthur, 268
Kotzebue, August, 165
Krapp's Last Tape (Beckett), 262
Kyd, Thomas, 91, 103, 106–7, 132, 150
Kynge Johan (Bale), 104

Labiche, Eugène, 177
Labor Stage, 252
Lady's Not for Burning, The (Fry), 256
Lady Windermere's Fan (Wilde), 207
La Gallienne, Eva, 250
L'Arronge, Adolf, 190, 191, 222
Last Night of Don Juan, The (Rostand), 231
Laube, Heinrich, 180
Laughton, Charles, 249
Lavedan, Henri, 188, 189
Lavery, Emmet, 213
Lawson, John Howard, 211
Lazarus Laughed (O'Neill), 255
Lazzi, 68–69
League of Youth, The (Ibsen), 195, 196
Learned Ladies, The (Molière), 156
Le Brun, Charles, 155
Lehmann, Else, 191
Lengyel, Melchior, 214
Lenoir, Charles, 146–47
Lenormand, Henri-René, 215, 234
Leonardo da Vinci, 45, 48, 51, 57
Leonce and Lena (Büchner), 174
Leonidov, Leonid, 200
Lessing, Gotthold, 182
Lesson, The (Ionesco), 260
Let's Get Divorced! (Sardou), 174

Lewis, Robert, 273
Liars, The (Jones), 207
Libation Pourers, The (Aeschylus), 7
Life Is a Dream (Calderón de la Barca), 93, 164
Life of Man, The (Andreyev), 230
Lighting, 170–71, 201, 216, 217, 233, 246
Light o' Love (Schnitzler), 193
Light That Shines in Darkness, The (Tolstoy), 203–4
Liliom (Molnár), 215, 251
Limelight, 171
Little Eyolf (Ibsen), 196
Littlewood, Joan, 256
Liturgical drama, 30, 32, 40
Live Like Pigs (Arden), 256
Living Corpse, The (Tolstoy), 203, 232
Living Hours (Schnitzler), 194
Living Newspaper, 253
Living Theater, 269, 273
Loas, 80, 82, 90
London Assurance (Boucicault), 168, 172
London Theater School, 249
Lonely Lives (Hauptmann), 192
Long Day's Journey into Night (O'Neill), 255
Long Wharf Theater, New Haven, 275
Look Back in Anger (Osborne), 256
Loot (Orton), 267
Lope de Vega (*see* Vega, Lope de)
Loraine, Robert, 208
Lorenzaccio (Musset), 165
Louis XIII, King of France, 142, 144
Louis XIV, King of France, 142, 145, 147, 151–52, 154–56, 158–59
Love of Four Colonels, The (Ustinov), 256
Lovers (Donnay), 189
Love's Comedy (Ibsen), 196
Lower Depths, The (Gorky), 200, 203, 222
Loyalties (Galsworthy), 208
Ludi, 8
Ludus Coventriae, 36
Lugné-Poë, 232–34
Lully, Jean Baptiste, 158
Lunt, Alfred, 210
Lycurgus, 11, 15
Lyly, John, 103, 106
Lyric Theater, London, 248
Lytton, Edward George, 209

Mabou Mimes, 273
Macbeth (Shakespeare), 169, 219, 220, 228
Macbett (Ionesco), 261
Machiavelli, Niccolò, 65
Machine plays, 147, 155
Machine Wreckers, The (Troller), 226
MacKaye, Steele, 211, 221, 222
Macklin, Charles, 166
Macready, William Charles, 166, 167
Madame Bovary (Flaubert), 177
Madame Sans-Gêne (Sardou), 174
Madmen on the Mountain (Stefani), 236
Madness of Lady Bright, The (Wilson), 271
Madras House, The (Granville-Barker), 207
Madrid Steel (Vega), 92
Mad Woman of Chaillot, The (Giraudoux), 234
Maeterlinck, Maurice, 64, 165, 215, 231–33
Magda (Sudermann), 193
Magnificent Cuckold, The (Crommelynck), 229, 232
Magnificent Yankee (Lavery), 213

Maid of Orleans, The (Schiller), 163
Maids, The (Genet), 263
Maintenon, Mme. de, 148
Major Barbara (Shaw), 208
Malfi, Leonard, 269
Malvaloca (Quintero brothers), 214
Maly Theater, Russia, 201
Man and His Phantoms (Lenormand), 234
Man and Superman (Shaw), 208
Man and the Masses (Toller), 226
Manchester Repertory Theater, 195, 204, 206–7
Man For All Seasons, A (Bolt), 267
Manhattan Project, 271
Man's a Man, A (Brecht), 237
Mansfield, Richard, 208, 231
Mantegna, Andrea, 50–51, 57
Mantell, Robert, 136
Man Who Married a Dumb Wife, The (France), 250, 251
Man Who Met Himself, The (Antonelli), 236
Marat/Sade (Weiss), 246, 265
March, Fredric, 210
Mariage forcé, Le (Molière), 155
Maria Magdalena (Hebbel), 175, 176, 178
Mariés de la Tour Eiffel, Les (Cocteau), 234
Marketplace productions, 37
Mark Taper Theater, Los Angeles, 275
Marlowe, Christopher, 43, 91, 103–6, 113, 125, 134, 137, 150
Marowitz, Charles, 265
Marquis von Keith (Wedekind), 227
Marriage of Figaro, The (Mozart), 69
Marriage of Olympia, The (Augier), 176
Marston, John, 107
Martinez Sierra, Gregorio, 214
Marx, Karl, 238
Mary Rose (Barrie), 207
Masefield, John, 206, 247
Mask and the Face, The (Chiarelli), 236
Masks, 11–13, 70
Masques, 138–40
Massinger, Philip, 107, 109
Massot, Pierre de, 243
Master Builder, The (Ibsen), 196, 232
Mathews, Charles, 165, 172
Mathews, Charles James, 165
Matkowsky, Adalbert, 164
Matthison, Edith Wynne, 184
Maude, Cyril, 207
Maugham, Somerset, 92–93, 95, 208, 209
May, Elaine, 268
Mayor of Zalamea, The (Vega), 92, 93
Mazarin, Jules, 143, 145, 147, 157, 158
Measure for Measure (Shakespeare), 183
Mechane, 21, 22
Médée (Corneille), 147
Medieval theater, 28–43
  Corpus Christi festival, 34–36; cycle plays, 28, 34–36, 39; emergence of professional theater, 41–43; farce plays, 39–40; liturgical drama, 30, 32, 40; morality plays, 28, 37, 40, 99, 100; origin of, 28–29; passion plays, 37–39, 42; secular drama, beginnings of, 32–33; tropes, 30–32
Meilhac, Henri, 177
Meiningen players, 180–82, 189, 201
Mélite (Corneille), 147
Menander, 11, 23, 26
Men in White (Kingsley), 213
Menteur, Le (Corneille), 147, 149

Mercadet, the Jobber (Balzac), 175
Merchant of Venice, The (Shakespeare), 113, 224
Merry Wives of Windsor, The (Shakespeare), 117
Messalina, 121, 122
Meyerhold, Vsevolod, 202, 228–30, 267
Michael and His Lost Angel (Jones), 207
Michael Kramer (Hauptmann), 192
Michelangelo, 45, 57
Mid-Channel (Pinero), 207
Midsummer Night's Dream, A (Shakespeare), 105, 113, 222, 224, 265
Mielziner, Jo, 251
Millay, Edna St. Vincent, 212
Miller, Arthur, 213
Milton, John, 139
Miracle, The (pantomime), 223, 250–51
Miracle plays, 37
Miramé (Richelieu), 143, 144, 157
Mirbeau, Octave, 188, 189
Mirror Man, The (Werfel), 226
Misanthrope, The (Molière), 156
Miser, The (Molière), 69, 71, 156
Miss Julie (Strindberg), 186, 191, 198
Mitchell, Langdon, 208
Mitchell, Lofton, 271
Mitterwurzer, Friedrich, 180
Mixed Marriage (Ervine), 206
Modern theater, 216–75
    absurdist drama, 258–63; in America, 250–56, 267–73; documentary drama, 263–64; in England, 217–21, 247–49, 256–57, 259, 264–67; existentialism, 257–58; expressionism, 197, 199, 215, 224–27; in France, 233–35, 240–44, 257–59; in Germany, 222–27, 237–38, 241; in Ireland, 247, 249; in Italy, 235–36; in Russia, 228–30, 267; scenery, 217–23, 227; surrealism, 240, 242–44; symbolism, 231–33; theater of cruelty, 245–46, 265
Modjeska, Helena, 180
Molière, 43, 69, 71, 91, 92, 143, 145–52, 154–57, 182
Molina, Tirso de, 93, 94
Molnár, Ferenc, 214–15
Monna Vanna (Maeterlinck), 232
Monopoly, 117, 142–44, 158
Montdory, Guillaume, 143, 144, 146–47
Monteverdi, Claudio, 64
Month in the Country, A (Turgeniev), 175, 176
Moody, William Vaughn, 208, 211
Moon for the Misbegotten, A (O'Neill), 255
Moore, George, 194
Moore, Sonia, 273
Morality plays, 28, 37, 40, 99, 100
Moritz, Sigmund, 214
Morozov, Savva, 201
Mort de Pompée, Le (Corneille), 147
Moscow Art Theater, 180, 189, 199–202, 210, 230, 250, 252, 267
Moskvin, Ivan, 200
Mother (Gorky), 229
Mother Courage (Brecht), 237
Mounet-Sully, Jean, 179
Mourning Becomes Electra (O'Neill), 255
Mowatt, Anna Cora, 211
Mozart, Wolfgang Amadeus, 69
Much Ado About Nothing (Shakespeare), 113
Mulatto (Hughes), 271

Mummer's plays, 41
Munich Court Theater, 183
Murder by Death (Simon), 270
Murder in the Cathedral (Eliot), 247
Murdoch, Iris, 247
Murphy (Beckett), 261
Music, Elizabethan, 131–32
Music and Stage Production (Appia), 217
Musset, Alfred de, 165, 178
My Life in Art (Stanislavsky), 201
Mystery plays, 28, 37, 42–43, 47, 63, 73, 141
Myth of Sisyphus, The (Camus), 257–58

National Health (Nichols), 267
National Theater, London, 266
Naturalism, 172–73, 177–78
Nazimova, Alla, 200
Negro Drama Group, 270
Negro Playwrights' Company, 270
Neighborhood Playhouse, New York, 250
Nelson, Alan, 35, 36, 40
Nemirovich-Danchenko, Vladimir, 199–202, 228
Nestroy, Johann, 179
New Art of Writing Plays, The (Vega), 94–95
New Way to Pay Old Debts, A (Massinger), 109
New World Discovered by Columbus, The (Vega), 92
New York Feminist Theater Troupe, 272
New York Idea, The (Mitchell), 208
Nibelungen, Die (Hebbel), 175
Nichols, Mike, 268
Nichols, Peter, 267
Nicoll, Allardyce, 32, 67
Nicomède (Corneille), 151–52
Nineteenth century theater, 160–84
    actors, 165–66, 169, 179–82; costumes, 166–67, 169; lighting, 170–71; playhouses, 182–83; playwrights, 171–79; realism (*see* Realism); romanticism, 161–65; scenery, 168–70
No Exit (Sartre), 234, 258
Nombre de Jesús, El (Vega), 78
Norton, Thomas, 101
Not I (Beckett), 262
Nuit Vénitienne, La (Musset), 165

Oberammergau, Germany, 42
O'Casey, Sean, 199, 205, 206, 209, 249
Odets, Clifford, 213, 252
Oedipus and the Sphinx (Hofmannsthal), 194
Oedipus at Colonus (Sophocles), 11
Oedipus Rex (Sophocles), 3, 53–54, 223
Oenslager, Donald, 251
Off-Broadway theater, 268–69
Off Off-Broadway theater, 269, 271
Of Human Bondage (Maugham), 208
Of Mice and Men (Steinbeck), 213
O'Hara, Frank, 271
Okhlopkov, Nikolai, 229
Old Times (Pinter), 257
Old Vic, London, 248–49
Old Wives' Tale, The (Peele), 107
Olives, The (Rueda), 81
Olivier, Laurence, 249, 256, 266
Olympic Academy, 51
Ondine (Giraudoux), 234
One Does Not Trifle with Love (Musset), 165
O'Neill, Eugene, 64, 199, 208, 211–13, 224, 248, 250, 254–56
Onomastikon (Pollux), 13

On the Origin of the Species (Darwin), 173
On Trial (Rice), 208
Open Theater, 269, 271
Opera, 47, 62–64, 66
Oresteia (Aeschylus), 7
Orfeo (Politian), 63
Orlando Furioso (Ariosto), 55, 65
Orléans, Duc d', 151
Orlenev, Paul, 200
Orphée (Cocteau), 234
Orton, Joe, 267
Osborne, John, 256, 257
Ostrovsky, Alexander, 175, 201, 203
Our Town (Wilder), 213

Page, Geraldine, 268
Pageant wagons, 35–36, 75–76
Palais-Royal, Paris, 157, 158
Palladio, Andrea, 52–53
Palmer, John, 149
Pandora's Box (Wedekind), 193
Pandosto (Greene), 107
Pantomimes, 9, 69
Paris Bound (Barry), 213
Parodie, La (Adamov), 262
Pasos, 81, 90
Passion Flower, The (Benavente), 214
Passion plays, 37–39, 42
Pasteur (Sacha Guitry), 215
Pastoral plays, 47, 62–63
Patios, 85–87
Patrick, John, 213
Pavy, Salathiel, 137
Payne, John Howard, 211
Peele, George, 48, 107, 127
Peer Gynt (Ibsen), 196, 232, 251
Pelléas et Melisande (Maeterlinck), 215, 232
Penthesilea (Kleist), 164
Pepys, Samuel, 107, 136
Performance Group, 271
Periaktoi, 20, 22, 57, 58, 59, 139, 170
Pericles (Shakespeare), 111, 112
Perlgut, Sue, 272
Persians, The (Aeschylus), 25
Peruzzi, Baldassare, 57
Peter Pan (Barrie), 207
Peterson, Louis, 271
Petit-Bourbon, Paris, 143, 145, 152, 157
Petrarch, 45, 64
Phantom, The (Molnár), 215
Phèdre (Racine), 148
Phelps, Samuel, 166
Philaster (Beaumont and Fletcher), 109
Phlyakes, 20
Phoenician Women, The (Euripides), 11
Phoenix Theater, London, 119
Phoenix Too Frequent, A (Fry), 256
Physician in Spite of Himself, The (Molière), 92, 156
Philip II, King of Spain, 83, 84
Philip III, King of Spain, 83, 88
Philip IV, King of Spain, 83–84, 88, 89
Picabia, Francis, 242
Pièrre Pathelin, 39
Pigafetta, Filippo, 53–54
Pillars of Society, The (Ibsen), 191, 195, 196
Pinero, Arthur Wing, 207–9
Pinter, Harold, 257, 260, 262
Pirandello, Luigi, 235, 236, 248, 250, 259, 263

Pirchan, Emil, 227
Piscator, Erwin, 263–64
Pitoëff, Georges, 247
Pius II, Pope, 49
Pius XII, Pope, 264
Pixerécourt, René, 165
Plaideurs, Les (Racine), 148
Planché, J. R., 166–67
Plato, 3, 46
Plautus, 11, 26, 49–51, 61, 65, 113
Playboy of the Western World, The (Synge), 206, 249
Play Called the Four P's, The (John Heywood), 42, 99
Playhouses:
    Elizabethan, 116, 117–29; French baroque, 157; Greek, 2, 14–15; Hellenistic, 14–18; Italian Renaissance, 50, 52–57; nineteenth century, 182–83; Roman, 14, 18–20; Spanish, 85–88
Play of Robin and Marion, The, 39
Play of the Greenwood (Halle), 39
Play of the Lord's Prayer, The, 40
Play's the Thing, The (Molnár), 215
Playwright's Song, The (Brecht), 237
Playwright's Theater, 212
Plough and the Stars, The (O'Casey), 206, 249
Plutarch, 3
Poel, William, 183–84
Politian, 47, 63
Pollux, Julius, 2–3, 13, 14, 20, 21
Polyeucte (Corneille), 147
Pompey, 18
Pomponius Laetus, Julius, 52
Popov, Alexei, 267
Poquelin, Jean, 150
Porgy (Heyward and Heyward), 213
Porto-Riche, Georges de, 188–89
Possart, Ernst von, 180, 190
Power of Darkness, The (Tolstoy), 191, 199, 201, 203
Practica di fabricar scene e machine ne' teatri (Sabbatini), 59
Pretenders, The (Ibsen), 189–90, 196
Pride of Life, The, 40
Priestley, J. B., 208, 247
Prince d'Aurec, Le (Lavedan), 189
Prisoner of Second Avenue (Simon), 270
Private Lives (Coward), 249
Private theaters, Elizabethan, 127–29
Processional (Lawson), 211
Prodigal, The (Richardson), 269
Professor Bernhardi (Schnitzler), 194
Prolog, 80, 114
Proskenion, 16
Proteus (Aeschylus), 7
Proust, Marcel, 259
Proust (Beckett), 259, 261
Provincetown Players, 208, 212, 250, 255
Pushkin, Aleksander, 203
Pygmalion (Shaw), 208

Quintero, Joaquin Alvarez, 214
Quintero, José, 268
Quintero, Serafin Alvarez, 214

Rachel, Mlle., 179
Racine, Jean Baptiste, 43, 91, 145–50
Raimund, Ferdinand, 179
Raisin in the Sun, A (Hansberry), 270

Raked stages, 58, 59
Ralph Roister Doister (Udall), 100, 104
Rape of Lucrece, The (Shakespeare), 110
Raphael, 57
Rattigan, Terence, 208, 256
Real Inspector Hound, The (Stoppard), 267
Realism, 172–82, 185–215
    actors, 187; in America, 208–13; in Austria,
    193–94; in England, 194–95, 206–8; in France,
    185–89, 215; in Germany, 189–93; in Hungary,
    214–15; in Ireland, 204–6; in Italy, 215; in Rus-
    sia, 199–202; in Scandinavia, 195–99; in Spain,
    214
Redgrave, Michael, 249, 266
Red Mill, The (Molnár), 215
Red Robe, The (Brieux), 187
Reformation, 40, 41, 43
Regularis Concordia, 30, 31
Reicher, Emanuel, 191
Reigbert, Otto, 225
Reinhardt, Max, 64, 93, 174, 191, 192, 194, 217,
    250
Réjane, Gabrielle, 179
Renaissance, 28, 41, 43, 73, 96–97
Renaissance theater (Italian), 44–71, 97, 138
    academicians as producers, 51–52; *commedia
    dell'arte*, 67–71; entries, 47–48; *intermezzi*,
    61–63; link to medieval theater, 47; opera, 47,
    62–64, 66; pastorals, 62–63; playhouses, 50,
    52–57; Roman theater and, 49–50, 65; scenery,
    50–51, 57–62, 64
Repertory system, 132–33
Resounding Tinkle, A (Simpson), 256, 262
Respectful Prostitute, The (Sartre), 234
Revenge of Bussy D'Ambois, The (Chapman),
    107, 108
Revenge plays, 107, 113
Révolte, La (Villiers de L'Isle-Adam), 177
Rhesus, 23
Rhetoric, 43
Rhinoceros (Ionesco), 261
Riario, Cardinal, 50, 52
Rice, Elmer, 208, 211, 213, 248, 250
Richard II (Shakespeare), 169
Richard III (Shakespeare), 104, 107, 113, 124,
    227
Richardson, Jack, 268, 269
Richardson, Sir Ralph, 247, 249
Richardson, Willis, 270
Richelieu, Cardinal, 142, 144, 145, 157, 158
Richman, Arthur, 211, 213
Riders to the Sea (Synge), 206
Right You Are If You Think You Are (Piran-
    dello), 236
Ring Around the Moon (Anouilh), 234
Rising of the Moon, The (Gregory), 206
Ristori, Adelaide, 180
Rittner, Rudolf, 191
Road to Rome, The (Sherwood), 172, 213
Robbers, The (Schiller), 162, 163
Robertson, Tom, 168, 171, 209
Robespierre (Sardou), 174
Robinson, Edward G., 210
Robinson, Lennox, 206, 209
Robson, Flora, 249
Roqueries de Scapin, The (Molière), 71, 156
Rojas, Agustin de, 82
Rolland, Romain, 234
Romains, Jules, 234

Roman Academy, 51
Roman Actor, The (Massinger), 107
Roman Catholic church, 29, 41–42
Romance (Sheldon), 208
Romancers, The (Rostand), 231–32
Romanoff and Juliet (Ustinov), 256
Roman theater, 8–10, 11, 14, 18–21, 26, 27,
    49–50, 65
Romanticism, 161–65
Romeo and Juliet (Shakespeare), 105, 114, 124
Roosevelt, Franklin D., 252
Roots (Wesker), 256
Roscius, 8
Rose, Martial, 36
Rose Bernd (Hauptmann), 192
Rosencrantz and Guildenstern Are Dead (Stop-
    pard), 267
Rosenkavalier, Der (Strauss), 224
Rosmersholm (Ibsen), 197, 232
Rossini, Gioacchino, 69
Rostand, Edmond, 215, 231–32
Roxana, 121, 122
Royal Court Theater, London, 256, 267
Royal Hunt of the Sun, The (Shaffer), 267
Royal Shakespeare Company, 264–66
Rueda, Lope de, 81–82, 84, 91, 150
Rufián dichoso, El (Cervantes), 94
R. U. R. (Capek), 226
Rural Dionysia, 8
Rusian theater, 175, 180, 189, 199–202, 210,
    228–30, 250, 252, 267

Sabbatini, 58–59, 61, 70
Sabbioneta, Italy, 54–56
Sabine Women, The (Andreyev), 230
Sachs, Hans, 42
Sackville, Thomas, 101
Sacre rappresentaziones, 37, 47
Saint-Denis, Michel, 234, 265
St. Joan (Shaw), 208
Saint Joan of the Stockyards (Brecht), 237
Salisbury Court Theater, London, 119
Salle des Machines, Paris, 143, 145, 157
Salome (Wilde), 222, 232
Salvation Nell (Sheldon), 208, 211, 212
Salvini, Tommaso, 180
Sand, George, 165
San Francisco Mime Troupe, 273
San Secondo, Rosso di, 236
Sardou, Victorien, 172, 174, 177, 178
Saroyan, William, 213, 252
Sarto, Andrea del, 57
Sartre, Jean-Paul, 64, 215, 234, 235, 257–59, 262
Saturday's Children (Anderson), 213
Satyr plays, 4, 7
Saved (Bond), 267
Saxe-Meiningen, Duke of, 179, 180–82
Sayers, Dorothy, 247
Scamozzi, Vicenzo, 53, 54
Scenery, 59, 170, 233, 246, 250–51
    Elizabethan, 129–31, 139–40; entries, 48;
    French Baroque theater, 157–58; Greek,
    20–22; Hellenistic, 20, 21; Italian Renaissance
    theater, 50–51, 57–62, 64; nineteenth century,
    168–70; in Spain, 89–90; twentieth century,
    217–23, 227
Schechner, Richard, 271
Schiess, Tobias, 221
Schildkraut, Rudolph, 180

Schiller, Johann Friedrich, 162, 163–64, 182, 192, 224
Schinkel, Karl Friederich, 182
Schisgal, Murray, 268
Schlaf, Johannes, 190
Schnitzler, Arthur, 192–94
School for Husbands, The (Molière), 156
School for Wives, The (Molière), 154, 156
Schreyvogel, Josef, 169, 180
Schumann, Peter, 272
Scofield, Paul, 266
Scotti, Marchese di, 88
Scrap of Paper, A (Sardou), 174
Screens, The (Genet), 263
Scribe, Eugène, 172, 174, 177, 178, 197
Sea Gull, The (Chekhov), 199, 200, 209
Second Man, The (Behrman), 213
Second Shepherd's Play, The, 39
Semper, Gottfried, 183
Seneca, 26, 61, 65
Separate Tables (Rattigan), 256
Sergeant Musgrave's Dance (Arden), 256
Serlio, Sebastiano, 57–58, 61, 62, 70, 130, 139
Serpent, The (Van Itallie), 271
Serreau, Jean-Marie, 264
Severed Head, A (Murdoch), 247
Sforza, Francesco, 66
Shadow and Substance (Carroll), 206
Shadow of a Gunman, The (O'Casey), 249
Shaffer, Peter, 3, 267
Shakespeare, William, 42, 43, 64, 66, 69, 71, 91, 101, 103–15, 118, 124–26, 136, 137, 145, 146, 150, 166, 182–84, 224, 248, 265
Shaw, George Bernard, 64, 174, 184, 194, 206–9, 250, 252
Sheep Well, The (Vega), 92
Sheldon, Edward, 208
Shell and the Clergyman, The (Artaud), 245–46
Shelley, Percy Bysshe, 93
Shepard, Sam, 269, 271
Sherwood, Robert E., 172, 212, 213, 252
Shirley, James, 106
Shoemaker's Holiday, The (Dekker), 107
Shrovetide plays, 42
Sicilian Limes (Pirandello), 236
Siddons, Sarah, 165
Sidney, Sir Philip, 113–14, 126, 131
Siegfried (Giraudoux), 234
Silver Box, The (Galsworthy), 208
Silver Cord, The (Howard), 213
Silver Tassie, The (O'Casey), 249
Simon, Neil, 270
Simonov, Reuben, 267
Simonson, Lee, 38, 250, 251
Simpson, Norman F., 256, 262
Six Characters in Search of an Author (Pirandello), 236
Skene, 16
Skin Game, The (Galsworthy), 208
Skin of Our Teeth, The (Wilder), 213
Sklar, Roberta, 272
Sky borders, 59
Smith, Maggie, 266
Social Stage, 252
Soldiers, The (Hochhuth), 264
Son, The (Hasenclever), 225, 226
Son-in-Law of M. Poirier, The (Augier), 176
Sonnenthal, Adolph, 180

Sophocles, 1, 3, 6, 7, 10–11, 20, 23–25, 53–54, 223
Sorge, Reinhard, 226
Sorma, Agnes, 190, 191
Soties, 42
Soupault, Philippe, 241, 243
Spanish theater, 37, 42, 72–95
  actors, 88–89; *autos sacramentales*, 37–38, 74–79, 83; *carros*, 75–76; *comedias*, 79–83, 84, 93; *commedia dell'arte*, 84–85; costumes, 89; *entremeses*, 78–79, 90, 91; growth of national theater, 73–74; *loas*, 80, 82, 90; *pasos*, 81, 90 playhouses, 85–88; playwrights, 90–95; realism, 214; scenery, 89–90
Spanish Tragedy, The (Kyd), 103, 107
Spook Sonata, The (Strindberg), 198
Spreading the News (Gregory), 206
S.S. Tenacity (Vildrac), 215
Staging of Wagnerian Drama, The (Appia), 217
Stallings, Laurence, 213
Stanislavsky, Constantin, 180, 182, 199–203, 228, 250, 252, 273
State Jewish Theater, 231
State of Siege (Camus), 258
Stefani, Alessandro de, 236
Steinbeck, John, 213
Stephens, Robert, 266
Stepmother, The (Balzac), 175
Sternheim, Carl, 193
Stevens, Thomas Wood, 212
Stewart, Ellen, 269
Stoppard, Tom, 267
Storey, David, 267
Storm in a Teacup (Birdie), 247
Strange Interlude (O'Neill), 255
Strasberg, Lee, 252, 273
Stratford Shakespeare Festival, Canada, 275
Strauss, Richard, 194, 224
Street Scene (Rice), 208
Strindberg, August, 185–87, 191, 193, 197–99, 204, 216, 222, 224, 243, 245, 248, 250, 255
Stronger, The (Strindberg), 198
Sturm und Drang, 161
Sudermann, Hermann, 192, 193
Summer and Smoke (Williams), 268
Sunken Bell, The (Hauptmann), 193, 232
Sunny Morning, A (Quintero brothers), 214
Suppliants, The (Aeschylus), 10
Supposes, The (Gascoigne), 102
Suppositi, I (Ariosto), 55, 102
Surrealism, 240, 242–44
Surrey, Earl of, 101
Swan, The (Molnár), 215
Swan Theater, London, 121
Sword dance, 41
Symbolism, 165, 231–33
Synge, John Millington, 205–6, 209, 247

Tabakov, Oleg, 267
Tableaux vivants, 48
Taine, Auguste Hippolyte, 258
Taïrov, Alexander, 228
Tamburlaine (Marlowe), 103, 104, 113
Taming of the Shrew, The (Shakespeare), 71, 104–5, 183
Tamiroff, Akim, 200
Tarlton, Richard, 134, 137
Tartuffe (Molière), 71, 149, 154, 156
Tasso, Torquato, 63, 65

Taste of Honey, A (Delaney), 256
Teatro Campesino, 271–72
Teatro Farnese of Parma, 52, 54–57
Teatro Olimpico of Vicenza, 52–56
Telemachus, 29
Tempest, The (Shakespeare), 109
Tendresse, La (Bataille), 189
Terence, 11, 26, 49–50, 61, 65, 131
Terry, Ellen, 182, 218
Terry, Megan, 269, 271
Tertullian, 29
Tetralogy, 7
Theater, The London, 104, 116, 118, 119
Theater Act of 1968, 266
Theater and Its Double, The (Artaud), 246
Theater Collective, 252
Theater Guild, New York, 211, 250–52
Theater in the round, 36, 229
Theater of Action, 252
Theater of cruelty, 245–46, 265
Theater of the Absurd, 258–63
Theater of the Soul, The (Evreinov), 230
Theater Union, 252
Théâtre Alfred Jarry, Paris, 243, 245
Théâtre du Marais, Paris, 143–45, 147, 157
Théâtre du Vieux-Colombier, Paris, 233–34, 250, 264
Théâtre-libre, Paris, 179, 185–89, 201, 232
Thébaïde, La (Racine), 148
Theodora, Empress, 29
There Are Crimes and Crimes (Strindberg), 222
Thérèse Raquin (Zola), 177, 191, 194
Thespis, 5, 10, 11
They Knew What They Wanted (Howard), 211, 213
Thirst (Ionesco), 261
Thomas, Augustus, 208, 211
Three Daughters of M. Dupont, The (Brieux), 188
Three Musketeers, The (Dumas père), 164
Threepenny Opera (Brecht), 268
Three Sisters, The (Chekhov), 202
Thunderbolt, The (Pinero), 207
Thunderstorm, The (Turgeniev), 175
Thurman, Wallace, 270
Ticknor, George, 76
Tidings Brought to Mary, The (Claudel), 233
Tieck, Ludwig, 183
Time Is a Dream (Lenormand), 234
Time of Your Life, The (Saroyan), 213
Time Remembered (Anouilh), 234
Tiny Alice (Albee), 270
Tite et Bérénice (Corneille), 148
Titus Andronicus (Shakespeare), 107, 110, 113, 132
Toller, Ernst, 226, 235, 248, 250
Tolstoy, Leo, 187, 191, 199, 201, 203, 204, 232
Tone, Franchot, 252
Tonight at 8:30 (Coward), 249
Torchbearers, The (Kelly), 213
Torelli, Giacomo, 143, 145, 155
Torres Naharro, Bartolomé de, 80, 81
Torrismondo (Tasso), 65
Tosca, La (Sardou), 174
Tour de Nesle, La (Dumas père), 164
Toward Damascus (Strindberg), 198
Towneley Cycle, 36
Tragedy of Nan, The (Masefield), 206, 247

Tree, Herbert Beerbohm, 207
Trial, The (Kafka), 260
Trial of the Catonsville Nine, The (Berrigan), 264
Trilogy, 7
Triumph of Caesar, The (Mantegna), 50–51
Troilus and Cressida (Shakespeare), 248
Trojan Women, The (Euripides), 24
Tropes, 30–32
Trotsky in Exile (Weiss), 264
Turgeniev, Ivan, 175, 176, 203
Two Noble Kinsmen, The (Shakespeare and Fletcher), 109, 112
Tyler, Royall, 211
Typhoon (Lengyel), 214
Tzara, Tristan, 241–43

Uccello, Paolo, 47, 57
Udall, Nicholas, 100, 106
Uncle Vanya (Chekhov), 202
University theater, 97, 274, 275
Unruh, Fritz von, 225, 226
Urban IV, Pope, 34
US, 264
Ustinov, Peter, 256

Vajda, Ernö, 214
Vakhtangov, Eugene, 202, 228, 231, 267
Valdes, Luis, 271–72
Van Druten, John, 213
Van Itallie, Jean-Claude, 269, 271
Vedrenne, John E., 206–7
Vega, Lope de, 43, 66, 75, 78, 89–95, 145, 146, 150
Venus and Adonis (Shakespeare), 110
Verdad sospechosa, La (Alarcón), 147
Vergonzoso en Palacio, El (Molina), 94
Verhaeren, Émile, 188
Vestris, Lucia, 166, 167–68, 172
Vicente, Gil, 75, 80, 81
Victims of Duty (Ionesco), 260
Vienna Burgtheater, 180
Vietnam Discourse (Weiss), 264
Vignola, Giacomo da, 58
Vikings at Helgeland, The (Ibsen), 196
Vilar, Jean, 234, 264
Vildrac, Charles, 215
Villiers de L'Isle-Adam, Count Philippe de, 177, 178
Virgil, 45
Virués, Cristobal, 94
Vitaly, George, 264
Vitrac, Roger, 243, 245
Vitruvius, 2–3, 13–14, 20, 21, 44, 50, 52, 57, 61
Volpone (Jonson), 108
Voltaire, 161–62
Vortex, The (Coward), 208
Voysey Inheritance, The (Granville-Barker), 207
"Vulture, The" (Beckett), 261
Vultures, The (Becque), 178

Wagner, Richard, 179, 217
Waiting for Godot (Beckett), 260, 261–62
Waiting for Lefty (Odets), 213
Waltz of the Toreadors, The (Anouilh), 234
Warfield, David, 210
Washington Square Players, New York, 211, 250, 251

Wasps, The (Aristophanes), 148
Waste (Granville-Barker), 207
Waterloo Bridge (Sherwood), 213
Watteau, Jean Antoine, 70
Weavers, The (Hauptmann), 186, 191, 192
Webster, Ben, 183
Webster, John, 106, 107, 109, 137
Wedekind, Frank, 192, 193, 199, 222, 224, 227, 248
Weigel, Helen, 238
Weiss, Peter, 246, 264
Welles, Orson, 253
Werfel, Franz, 224, 226, 235
Wesker, Arthur, 256
What Every Woman Knows (Barrie), 207
What Passion, Ye Marionettes! (San Secondo), 236
What Price Glory? (Anderson and Stallings), 213
What the Butler Saw (Orton), 267
What You Don't Expect (Antonelli), 236
When We Dead Awaken (Ibsen), 196
Whitefriars Theater, London, 119
White-Headed Boy, The (Robinson), 206
White Redeemer, The (Hauptmann), 192
White Steed, The (Carroll), 206
Who's Afraid of Virginia Woolf (Albee), 270
Widower's Houses (Shaw), 194, 207
Wild Duck, The (Ibsen), 186, 194, 197
Wilde, Oscar, 207, 209, 222, 232
Wilder, Thornton, 213
Wilhelm Tell (Schiller), 163

Wille, Bruno, 191
Williams, Emlyn, 208
Williams, Tennessee, 213
Wilson, Lanford, 269, 271
Wilton, Marie, 168
Wings, 16, 57–61, 168, 182
Winslow Boy, The (Rattigan), 256
Winterset (Anderson), 213
Winter's Tale, The (Shakespeare), 107, 109, 169
Witching Hour, The (Thomas), 208
Woe from Wit (Griboyedov), 175
Woman Killed with Kindness, A (Thomas Heywood), 107–8
Woman of Arles, The (Daudet), 177
Woman of No Importance, A (Wilde), 207
Woman of Paris, The (Becque), 178
Woolf, Rosemary, 34
Worker's Laboratory Theater, 252
Workhouse Ward, The (Gregory), 206
World of Youth, The (Wedekind), 193
Woyzeck (Büchner), 175, 176

Yeats, William Butler, 205, 206, 209, 247
Yegor Bulychov (Gorky), 203
Yellow Jack (Howard), 213
Yerma (Garcia Lorca), 244
Young Woodley (Van Druten), 213

Zemach, Nahum, 231
Zola, Emile, 173, 175, 177, 178, 185, 191, 194, 197, 216
Zoo Story (Albee), 269